Allrightniks Row
"Haunch Paunch and Jowl"
The Making of a Professional Jew

MASTERWORKS OF MODERN JEWISH WRITING SERIES
EDITED BY JONATHAN D. SARNA

Academic Director of the Center for the Study of American Jewish Experience
Hebrew Union College—Jewish Institute of Religion

Allrightniks Row
"Haunch Paunch and Jowl"
The Making of a Professional Jew

BY SAMUEL ORNITZ

With a new introduction by
Gabriel Miller
Rutgers University

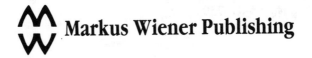 Markus Wiener Publishing

Hester Street, circa 1900
Museum of the City of New York

New York, circa 1900, unknown photographer
New York Public Library

CONTENTS

CONTENTS

CONTENTS

INTRODUCTION
BY GABRIEL MILLER

At the age of 32, having failed in the woolen business, Samuel Ornitz needed money to support a wife and two sons. Working eighteen hours a day for three months, he produced his first novel, *Haunch, Paunch and Jowl.* It is in many ways a compendium of his experiences and observations while growing up on New York's Lower East Side during the mass influx of East European Jews at the end of the nineteenth century.

The Lower East Side was the most densely populated section of New York city, claiming 522 inhabitants per acre. In *World of Our Fathers,* Irving Howe cites a report of the University Settlement Society stating that the density of the Tenth Ward was "greater than that of the worst sections of Bombay." Hester Street, near Ludlow, was one of its worst areas, called "the Pig Market." There, anything *except* a pig could be bought off pushcarts, while nearby newly arrived immigrants ("greenhorns") gathered nearby to wait for employers seeking cheap labor. Hester Street was also where Samuel Badisch Ornitz was born on November 15, 1890. His father was a small merchant, and the family lived in comparative luxury amidst the area's grim poverty. Ornitz attended the Henry Street School and went to *cheder* (Hebrew school) until he was 13 (Bar Mitzvah); he also spent two years at New York's City College.

Memories of growing up on the streets of the Lower East Side inform the atmosphere of *Haunch, Paunch and Jowl,* and much of the narrative's power derives from its naturalistic accumulation of detail. Ornitz was

ix

a gifted observer and listener, and his novel provides a remarkable record not only of the Lower East Side's squalor but also of its liveliness and of the variety of characters it embraced. In the depiction of the lives of the first generation of immigrants and their American-raised children, few novels can match it.

Equally important in the forming of Ornitz' world view were his experiences as a social worker. First as an assistant superintendent of the Society for the Prevention of Cruelty to Children in Brooklyn, then for five years as a representative of the New York Prison Association at the Tombs Prison, he learned about the city's criminal element and witnessed the behind-the-scenes administration of justice in the criminal courts. These jobs prompted his first published writing, an anonymous article in the *Review* (August, 1912), a monthly publication of the National Prisoner's Aid Association. Anonymity was probably an editorial ploy meant to strengthen the illusion that the essay, "What the 'Gun-Fighter' Thinks about It," was actually written by a gang member. Anticipating *Haunch, Paunch and Jowl*, the piece employs street dialect and displays a naturalistic bent. It realistically assesses the effect of the environment on character and the basically animalistic nature of man: "Every kid belongs to a gang, because every kid has got it in him to like the idea, and loves a fight." Other work experiences from this period also found their way into the novel. While going to school, Ornitz had "run copy" for news syndicates at the criminal courts, had driven a hansom cab, and had been a leader of boys' clubs—just like his protagonist.

At the end of Part III of *Haunch, Paunch and Jowl*,

the protagonist's Uncle Philip says to him, "You're nobody. You have no ancestors . . . I am going to be an ancestor myself . . . . Meyer, we've got nothing to look back to. It's up to us to be ancestors." Samuel Ornitz found himself in a similar position when in 1922 he set down to write. There was then no "American-Jewish novel" as it has come to be known, no sense of tradition, no real past on which to build. Only a few American-Jewish novels had appeared; the first notable one being Abraham Cahan's *Yekl: A Tale of the New York Ghetto* published in 1896. Cahan was one of the most influential Jews of his time, for, as founder and editor of *The Jewish Daily Forward*, he figured prominently in acculturating many Jews to the new land. *Yekl*, which was published at the encouragement of William Dean Howells, introduced what was to be Cahan's major fictional concern and a central theme of many early American Jewish novels: the spiritual dislocation caused by the Jewish immigrant's exposure to American life, resulting in feelings of loneliness and emptiness. Partly because of the poor sales of the book, Cahan then abandoned his novelistic career for twenty years, until he wrote what is generally considered the first important American-Jewish novel, *The Rise of David Levinsky* (1917). While other novels by Jews were published at about this time, such as Nathan Kussey's *The Abyss* (1916), which dealt with street life, and Elias Tobenkin's *Witte Arrives* (1916), which chronicled an immigrant's experience in the New World, these works yielded little of literary interest. Cahan excepted, Ornitz had no true literary ancestors.

Ornitz was, however, undoubtedly affected by

muckraking articles appearing in newspapers and magazines which exposed early twentieth-century readers to such phenomena as the ugliness of slum life as well as scenes of poverty and corruption. *McClure's Magazine*, a muckraking journal, originally published the sketches which formed the basis of *The Rise of David Levinsky*. Out of the muckrakers' interest in the ghetto also came Hutchins Hapgood's *The Spirit of the Ghetto* (1902) and Jacob Riis' *How the Other Half Lives*, published in the year of Ornitz' birth, 1890. The muckraking impulse is strong in *Haunch, Paunch and Jowl*, at times threatening to overwhelm the central story. Here as elsewhere, Ornitz never quite managed to curb his appetite for preaching, the novelist would occasionally yield to the reformer whose zeal had inspired his writing (in the first place).

Horace Liveright, Ornitz' publisher, contrived to give *Haunch, Paunch and Jowl* added interest by issuing it anonymously and representing it as the actual memoirs of a judge who had died five years earlier. Press releases claimed that Ornitz had prepared the manuscript because of his knowledge of "all the facts and characters involved," and the book was even subtitled an "anonymous autobiography." To some extent, Liveright was probably trying to protect himself from an expected storm of protest. A number of publishers had gone so far as to turn the book down for fear of insulting Jewish readers. One told Ornitz, "The Jews will boycott you, they will force us to suppress the book, they will say it is anti-semitic, and that our company is anti-semitic."

Some reviewers, however, were not fooled. Leo Markun in *The New York Tribune* wrote:

> ... this is a hoax. Not exactly. If the man
> called here Judge Meyer Hirsch didn't write
> these confessions, he stands nevertheless
> revealed in them. The book is the work of a
> poet, with the poet's gift of sympathy and
> understanding. The judge couldn't have told
> the true story even had he desired: Rousseaus
> aren't born every minute ...

Indeed, the narrative does display the discipline and imagination indicative of a gifted novelist, as Ornitz consciously drew on established fictional forms. *Haunch,
Paunch and Jowl* is a kind of *bildungsroman*, focusing
on rogue hero, Meyer Hirsch, a boy of Orthodox Jewish
upbringing whose rebellion against his heritage leads
to a picaresque tour of the larger world. The novel is nar-
rated by Meyer, who promises to "tell everything," and
he does, thereby ruthlessly exposing his own amoral ambitions. He begins with his childhood in the East Side
ghetto and concludes with his rise to the position of
Justice of the Superior Criminal Court of New York. It
is the narrative of a man who does not think in terms
of good and evil, but nurtures an all-consuming desire
to succeed at whatever cost.

Ornitz breaks with one dominant feature of the early American-Jewish novel, for unlike the David Levinsky of Cahan's novel, Meyer Hirsch has no roots in the
shtetl world of Eastern Europe. Ornitz does not directly consider the Old World experience, although the
psyches of some of his characters are rooted there. His
is a novel that takes place wholly in America, and it is
the reality of America that Meyer has to come to grips
with at an early age. Accordingly, the experiences of the
fathers receive scant attention, as Ornitz focuses instead

upon the son's need to escape both the Old World ethos of his parents and the *cheder* which he attends until he is 13. In *Haunch, Paunch and Jowl,* Meyer's father, who never adjusts to America, is a figure of such slight importance in his son's life that his death is referred to only as an afterthought, a mere detail that Meyer feels obliged to report after the fact to give a sense of completeness to the story he is telling. As such there is no conflict between father and son, for the father and his values have no control over the son whatsoever. Meyer's conflicts are rather over the problem of how to emerge from the ghetto and "make it" in America. This is the first important American-Jewish novel to focus wholly on America with a central character who suffers not the spiritual dislocations of Cahan's David Levinsky, but rather the typical dislocations of a child of immigrants, eager above all to be an American story of success.

The characteristic flavor of the novel is that of naturalism, a dominant strain in American fiction in the early part of the twentieth century. From the first page of the novel Meyer observes that the strongest survive, equated in a typical naturalist image with the survival proclivities of a goat:

> A goat manages to get along where any other creature would perish. Stubble, twigs, anything is food and nourishment for him. He is a sidestepper, can walk a narrow ledge or fence, if need be. He is for himself; unfeeling and befriends no one.

Meyer is affectionately referred to by his mother as *ziegelle,* the Yiddish word for goat. His first memories are of his own goat-like existence foraging through the rubble of street-gang life and gang warfare. The Ludlow

Street gang soon becomes the most important influence in his life: "When I became a Ludlow streeter I swept away the last rag of swaddling clothes and life became real." It is significant that the novel begins with images of life on the street, for to Ornitz this *is* America: the battle of the strong against the weak, Jewish gangs against Irish gangs. No room here for romantic idealism.

Turn-of-the-century America presented Jewish immigrants with undreamed-of possibilities. Dealing with this sudden freedom, however, often proved traumatic. Rabbinical and communal institutions no longer carried the weight of cultural identity: the slum, the city, and the workplace all made it increasingly difficult to maintain Old World values intact. David Blaustein, a Jewish community worker on the East Side, observed that the struggle for survival became more severe in America than in the Old World. There the Jews suffered collectively, here they suffered as individuals.

Individualism pervades the world of *Haunch, Paunch and Jowl*; Meyer absorbs it very early. The notion of communal values has all but disappeared. Jewish gang members extort money from Jewish shopkeepers. In America the naturalistic law of the jungle prevails:

> It did not take them long to see that the straight and narrow path was long and tortuous and ended in a blind alley. There was nothing in the conspicuous examples of American life to inspire anything else. Politics stank of corruption and chicanery. Big business set even a worse example . . . . The order of the day was – PLAY THE GAME AS YOU SEE IT PLAYED . . . . It was a sordid

generation creeping out of the mud into the murk.

This attitude is seconded by Meyer's Uncle Philip, introduced early in the novel as an intellectual and Talmudist who is constantly observing and ruminating about the social milieu of the Lower East Side. After attending a meeting of Leftists, Philip rejects their theories on improving the lot of the worker and devises his own theory. Concluding that the road to success is paved with the sweat of immigrant labor, he resolves to exploit it and thus out-manipulate the hated German-Jewish bosses by dealing directly with non-unionized immigrant labor. He urges Meyer to take full advantage of the freedom America offers by exploiting everyone else. Meyer's work ethic may be derived from the struggle of growing up on the street, but Philip's represents a deliberate choice, a wholly analytical process of self-determination. He carries out his ambitions with talmudic logic.

Both men achieve the success they so fiercely seek. Philip becomes one of the wealthiest and most powerful garment manufacturers in New York, even breaking into the hated German-Jews' social circle by marrying the homely daughter of one prominent family. Philip despises his wife and marries her only for social position, for his single-minded attitude has effectively sapped him of all emotion except hate and revenge. At last, ravaged by stomach cancer, a result of his neglectful eating habits while pursuing success, he dies unrepentant, proud that he has lived and succeeded by life's competitive rules.

Meyer too achieves considerable success in pursuing

his own goals, yet despite his unethical conduct he remains a more sympathetic character than his uncle. Having intellectualized all feeling from his life, Philip suffers from Hawthorne's hardness of the heart; Meyer, on the other hand, is a man of passion. He enjoys a varied love life, and eventually marries Gretl, an illiterate woman initially introduced into his home as a maid but thereafter promoted to the status of mistress. Never having planned to marry her, Meyer is at length forced to do so when she refuses to be bought off by Philip. But their marriage at the end of the novel, even if it ruins Meyer's political ambitions, leaves him content. He has Gretl, now renamed Gertrude, deemed a more suitable name of an Americanized wife, and he has a judgeship. He lives in *Allrightniks Row.*

Meyer's other love is Esther, an idealistic woman who dedicates herself to social change and who eventually marries a wealthy sociologist. She seems to represent Meyer's spiritual side, or at least his potential for a nobler standard of behavior. His rejection of her early on is symbolic: ". . . I try to reason with her not as a goddess but as a human being. I think idealism is the refuge of the incompetent." Esther disappears as a character midway through the novel; apparently she can function only as an abstraction. Similarly, her male counterpart, Dave, a childhood friend of Meyer and a poet, dies of tuberculosis shortly after marrying. In the world of *Haunch, Paunch and Jowl* the ideal cannot survive, but must die or disappear before an overwhelming reality. When Meyer learns of Esther's marriage late in the novel, he becomes depressed, gets drunk and ends up in a whorehouse; afterwards Esther is all but forgotten.

The narrative closes as Meyer, who has become very fat (hence the nickname that supplies the novel's title), is called away by his wife from a fantasy about his new mistress to come to a dinner of *Gedamfte brust und patate latkes* (potted breast and potato pancakes). Concluding thus on juxtaposed images of fleshly appetites, the novel provides final testimony to the true power of the real and the carnal – the unspiritual nature of life.

Meyer Hirsch is an unique protagonist in early American-Jewish fiction. Unlike Yekl and David Levinsky, or Sara in Anzia Yezierska's *The Bread Givers* (1925), all of whom come to regret rejecting the values of the Old World in favor of success in the New, Meyer remains unrepentant to the end. He enjoys his success, money, and position, rarely recalling the past or analyzing himself – a damning portrait of a man who has swallowed America whole without pausing to consider the consequences of his actions. He is meant to serve as an example to Jews of what could befall them if they fail to integrate into the promise of America the better parts of their cultural heritage.

Meyer Hirsch is certainly one of Ornitz' greatest fictional creations. A representative figure, the sinister American Jewish hero, he takes his place beside the more lonely and tragic David Levinsky: these two emerge as the most important character portraits of first-generation American-Jewish writers. *Haunch, Paunch and Jowl*, however, possesses other strengths as well, for it recreates a vanished world. In his novel, Ornitz presents the Lower East Side in all its variety, from the religious life of the *cheder* and synagogue, to the whorehouses on Allen Street, to the claustrophobic environment of the tenements. There are the flavors of cabaret and saloon life and of Tammany Hall politics, and vivid portraits of consumptive needle workers as well as labor leaders and reformers. Under Ornitz' pen the ghetto comes alive as it does in few other works, as he manages to compress forty years of history into a short novel that comprises an entire social panorama. Reflecting the turbulence of the twenties, it yet anticipates in tone and narrative some aspects of the "tough guy" writers of the thirties.

Haunch, Paunch and Jowl attracted a great deal of contemporary attention. Newspaper accounts chronicle sermons by rabbis who damned it as "lecherous and degrading." One such denunciation, by Rabbi Dr. Samuel Schulman, drew a response from Ornitz in the *Jewish Tribune:*

> . . . most gratifying to me was the spontaneous testimony of non-Jewish men and women, who spoke, expressing surprise that the Jews themselves, were reading race consciousness into the book, while, they, the non-Jews, read it as a book of general or universal significance, in which they found sympathy, beauty, truth and understanding. One speaker, sounding the true keynote, resented the fact that *Haunch, Paunch and Jowl* was regarded in any way other than a book of Americans by an American . . . Their answer explains why Dr. Schulman now finds himself on the defensive; he has written the hurt and harm into my book.

On the other hand, many Jews and Jewish organizations praised the novel, and it was serialized in two working-class papers, the pro-Communist *Morning Freiheit* in America and, years later, in the *Rote Fahne* in Germany. It was also later dramatized on stage by the working-class theatre, the Artef.

Haunch, Paunch and Jowl was Ornitz' only commercial success. At the time of its publication Ornitz told an interviewer that he was working on a book about Jewish women in America, but that work was never completed. He did publish two other books in the twenties, however: the first, *Round the World with Jocko the Great* (1925), was a children's book; the second, *A Yankee Passional* (1927), a novel which contains his finest writing, is all but forgotten today. Like *Haunch, Paunch and Jowl* it reflects a reformist intent, this time focused on the Catholic Church, but this novel is more ambitious, encompassing a larger period of time and a variety of locales and themes. *A Yankee Passional* did not sell well despite good reviews, and in 1928 at the encouragement of Herman Mankiewicz, Ornitz put aside another project, *Power and Peace*, to go to Hollywood. His first project there was a film called *The Case of Lena Smith*—it is now lost—made with Josef von Sternberg; its story was derived from a case Ornitz had handled while with the Prison Association.

Ornitz disliked Hollywood and left it several times before settling there permanently. Prompted to more direct involvement in social causes by the onset of the Depression and the rise of Fascism in Europe, he gave up writing fiction entirely; later he remarked, "To write novels seemed as puerile as they were profitless." Instead, while continuing to write films in order to support himself and his family, he devoted most of his time to studying Fascism and speaking against it, and he helped to organize the Hollywood Anti-Nazi League. As a screenwriter he was thus undistinguished, for he cared little about the craft and devoted little mental energy to its advancement. As a fighter for social causes, however, he made his mark. He worked to free the Scottsboro Boys and in 1931, with Theodore Dreiser, John Dos Passos and others, he went to help starving coal miners and to investigate labor conditions in Kentucky. From this experience came a short play, *In New Kentucky*, published in *New Masses* in 1934.

After World War II, Ornitz became embroiled in another struggle – against the forces of repression in the film industry. Although he had not worked in films for three years, when the House Un-American Activities Committee's investigations into Communist infiltration in the film industry began, he felt compelled to join those writers, producers, and directors who challenged Congress' right to ask questions about individuals' political affiliations. He became one of the group later known as the Hollywood Ten, which stood on the First Amendment and challenged the Committee's very right to exist. He later wrote about his decision:

> I felt I had to make a conscientious stand on the right to silence. After all, this right was the very soul of what I was writing. During the Nazi extermination, this right meant survival for Jewish babies whom Christians were sheltering more with their silence than with their care; even nuns in orphan asylums avowed this right to silence and thus saved Jewish children. The first Christians worshipped in secret on catacombs. The right to silence sav-

ed them from the Roman Security Police who wanted to arrest them on the charge of atheism because they denied Rome's numerous gods in acknowledging only One.

Called before HUAC, Ornitz refused to say whether he was a member of the Communist party or a member of the Screenwriters' Guild, explaining that it involved "a serious question of conscience for me." He was not allowed to read his prepared statement accusing John E. Rankin, a leading member of the committee, of being an "outstanding anti-Semite" and one who "revels in this fact." He would have gone on to say, "It may be redundant to repeat that anti-Semitism and anti-Communism were the number one poison weapon used by Hitler – but still terribly relevant, lest we forget."

Denied the opportunity to speak his piece and convicted for his refusal to cooperate, Ornitz was sentenced to a year in prison at Springfield, Missouri. There he completed a novel begun earlier in 1940s; it was published in 1951 as *The Bride of the Sabbath*. In certain respects a companion piece to *Haunch, Paunch and Jowl*, it is a more searching and detailed study of the physical and psychological struggles of first- and second-generation Jews in America, and its protagonist is an idealist. An explanatory note for the book's dust jacket explains its purpose:

Now I will tell you for whom I wrote this book – for the several million Americans who are bewildered by their peculiar isolation who must want to know how they got that way and their own contribution to it. I want them to understand why they are isolated in uniqueness as a result of trying to be more American

then the Americans . . . .
Bride of the Sabbath was a commercial failure, leading Ornitz to put aside a sequel he was writing in order to concentrate on a book about homosexuality in prisons, a condition that had much disturbed him during his nine-month incarceration. Neither project was completed when Ornitz died of a cerebral hemorrhage in 1957 at the age of 66.

Samuel Ornitz's three novels display a degree of intelligence and talent that might have made him an important writer. But for him life meant more than art. His novels, even his masterwork *Haunch, Paunch and Jowl*, lack the finesse and discipline of great literature, for Ornitz was always impatient to move on to some new project or social cause. His output was small but it provides a moving, compelling and insightful record of an important period of our times. It also stands as emphatic testimony to a man who, unlike Meyer Hirsch, never stopped believing in ideals or in the human capacity to achieve them.

FIRST PERIOD

All men . . . who have done anything of excellence . . . ought . . . to describe their life with their own hand.
                              BENVENUTO CELLINI.

HAUNCH PAUNCH AND JOWL

FIRST PERIOD

I

I begin my history. I want to tell everything. Everything: so that even if I tell pathological lies the truth will shine out like grains of gold in the upturned muck. . . . I grope for first definite memories.

Early childhood is a mist world: fantastic and fearful, glamorous and grotesque. One is not really born into life until one breaks through this fine-webbed cocoon of vagueness. . . . I am nine; that stands out fully and firmly blocked. . . . Ramshackle New York during the sprawling awkward age of its growth. . . . A keen December evening. Gas lamps burning orange beacons upon the blue sea of a wintry night. I am returning from *cheder* (Hebrew School).

I close the door behind me. The kerosene lamp with its sooty chimney and ragged wick smokes more than ever. It stands high on a shelf and its uncertain light makes a foggy etching of our kitchen . . . blurred charcoal figures of mother and father and Uncle Philip seated close by the cook-stove drinking tea . . . and of the furnishings, exaggerated silhouettes.

Throwing my books on a chair I snatch up the huge slab of bread and the apple mother laid out for me and without a word start for the street. I am in a hurry to join the Ludlow Street Gang. Just yesterday

I was admitted to its glorious ranks as the fourteenth
leader. I was not Leader the Fourteenth, but of the
whole gang fourteenth in prowess and importance.
However, I had only thirteen superiors. Being the
lowest step in the ladder I was most frequently trod
upon; but it was sweet suffering, the travail of a
hero. . . . When I became a Ludlow Streeter I swept
away the last rag of swaddling clothes and life became
real. . . . So I hurry away, silently, detachedly, as
a man of importance. . . . But Uncle Philip's voice
halts me. Meanwhile, I am busy munching the apple.
Here is Uncle Philip lecturing like a Rabbi on a fast
day. He intimidates: not he, but his way of speaking
Yiddish. It is not just Yiddish—guttural, jargonish,
haphazard; but an arresting, rhythmical, logical language. . . . Yiddish, the lingo of greenhorns, was held
in contempt by the Ludlow Streeters who felt mightily
their Americanism. Yet even the gang fought shy of
making fun of the green Uncle Philip for he had a
way of accompanying his Yiddish with gestures that
left smarting memories.

"*Nu, yeshiva bochar* (seminary student), what
says one? So, like a wanton puff,—in and out. A grab
and gone. *Fertig!* (Done). And now what of your
social duties, your filial respects! What are you aim-
ing to be? A man for men? Or a drayman, companion
of horses? Really, what says one?"

"*Tahke*, what says one?" interrupts kindly, chiding
mamma.

My mouth is chockful of bread and apple and I
nearly choke with indignation when she calls me by my
hateful love name—"*Ziegelle*" (little goat).

Papa looks on in his brooding way, hunched in his

[14]

chair, as always too tired and spent to talk. His eyes
light gratefully on the young and vigorous Philip,
family mentor, whom he idealizes and loves so
much . . . just as though he were not his brother-in-
law. Philip, he says, is his star of hope showing the
way out of the wilderness—the sweatshop.

"Remember," quoth Philip in his best manner of
Talmudical harangue, "gone are the diaper days. This
day you are nine." . . . Follows a solemn pause. . . .
"Tomorrow begins your tenth year——"

"The tenth year. Long years to you, *Ziegelle.*"

Ziegelle! ziegelle! Eternally, the little goat. The
curse of my life. The Ludlow Streeters know me by
no other name. They greet me with "maa, maa" and
tug my chin as though pulling a beard. . . . A love
name indeed! Other children did not have to put up
with an insulting diminutive, *a la Russe.* They were
called, say *poppale* (little father) or *zadelle* (little
grandfather), or *hertzalle* (little heart), but I, only
I was marked for scorn as the little goat. Wherefore?

Philip rose and placed his glass on the table. We
did not boast saucers at that time. With a gallant bow
he took mother's glass. Father continues to gnaw a
lump of sugar and draw tea from his glass with a com-
placent hiss. . . . As Philip moves between the lamp
and the table shadows dance on the wall, shadows that
take the shape of goats cavorting at my discomfiture.
And I want to throw things at them.

"Meyer," says Philip, raising an impressive finger,
"remember that learning without breeding is like a
kugel (pudding) without *gribbenes* (rendered chicken
fat). It is food without flavor: so with a man, a fellow
without favor."

"Gee," I plead in English, "I ain't got time for everything."

A quick reproving gesture menaces me to silence.

"Speak to me *momme loschen* (mother tongue) not that nasty gibberish of the streets."

Again he humiliates me—he—the greenhorn. He knows I am not speaking genteel American.

I make a plea . . . in Yiddish . . . and because my phrasing is facile, mother smiles proudly and even Uncle Philip's stern demeanor softens.

"All day I have been in English school, and then in *cheder* all evening, and I want to play with the boys a little bit. And it was hard in *cheder* today, for I had to read a page of *Targum* and *Rashi* without even one mistake."

Mother beams. . . . "*Nicht schlecht* (not bad), *nu* what say you, Philip? And only nine."

"But your studies are not done," says Philip. "A lesson in manners is never out of place. Remember, Meyer, no matter how wealthy, no matter how learned, you will be as nothing if not a gentleman." The last word he enunciates sharply in English.

"What is that—that a gentleman?" I ask.

"A gentleman. Ah! A gentleman—hem—is a person whom you cannot exactly describe—hum—but whom you know to be a gentleman the second you set eyes on him." . . . He looks at me steadily, expectantly, but my face is blank with ignorance.

"Then, Uncle Philip, I won't know what it is a—gentleman—till I see one."

"Not until then, Meyer."

"All right," I offer conciliatingly, "I will be on

the watch out for one." . . . But Philip seems disappointed.

"So, Meyer," he muses, "so, you can read the old French-Hebrew text of *Rashi* and *Aramic Targum,* the dialect that Christ spoke, but you know not a gentleman—so."

"Christ spoke it," I whisper in a cautious echo, reluctant to utter the forbidden name.

Mother flutters in alarm. Father stirs uneasily.

"Brother," she says, "mention not the unspeakable one."

"Bah, unmentionable, why, why keep the boy ignorant——"

"I am not ignorant, Uncle Philip, although you can't expect me to know a gentleman when I never even saw one."

"And then," demands Philip with apparent displeasure, "am I not a gentleman?"

"No, you are my Uncle Philip."

"So it is," mutters Philip, "because I am your uncle."

He takes a small notebook from his pocket and holding it up says, "Observe, Meyer, this booklet, it is entirely given over to your affairs." He turns to the first leaf and reads, "Notes upon the education of my nephew, Meyer Hirsch." Then, using his knee as a rest, writes and reads aloud at the same time. "Item one: Family Pride."

II

The gang is at the corner huddled about a wood fire in a grocer's milk can with large holes cut out for vents. It is a compact circle seated shoulder to shoulder on assorted boxes. I long, passionately, to be part of it and hear the grave and grim pow-wow of the chieftains, and share the pungent promise of potatoes baking in the embers. . . . I hover, hopefully, and scrape my feet, and place a suppliant hand on the shoulder of the humblest of the gathering, the thirteenth leader, but he puts it off with a quick shrug . . . a terrible feeling of being left out in the cold . . . and I become angry, and a daring idea is born. . . . I pull Hymie, the twelfth leader, from his place. . . . Words are not needed; the challenge speaks volumes. . . . A scrap! Partisan cries—"Give it to him, Hymie"; "Use your left"; "Come on, nannie-goat, butt him in the *kischkes* (guts)." . . . The surprise attack gives me an edge on him, and soon Hymie is persuaded to relinquish his place at the fire and the twelfth leadership. And the thirteenth leader by inaction and silence abdicates his right. Thus I dispose of two enemies by first vanquishing the stronger. . . . My first victory . . . my first seat at the fire . . . and I tingle with joy. . . . And then came the potatoes. What if they were charred. A feast of feasts. . . . I thrill to the talk of war, war on the nearest clan, the Essex Street Guerrillas. . . . Says Boolkie, in manner and tone cryptic, as fitting a first leader, "Don't take none of their guff. We'll give them what for any time they wants it." . . . The fire is now a mellow glow of embers. . . . A sud-

[18]

den alarm! A lookout shrilly warns: "A *shammos!* A *shammos!*" (Synagogue beadle. In the secret lingo of the gang *shammos* was the warning that a policeman was coming). Whereupon, the indomitable clan of Ludlow Streeters scatters in all directions.

I fly to the cellar of our house, where works and lives Berel, a fixer of harness. Berel smiles at my headlong, breathless entry. He sits before his bench mending reins. Lutz, the *shicker goy* (drunken Gentile), seated on a box, is laboriously sewing up a rent in his pants. He is the local *Shabbos* (Sabbath) fire lighter and lodges with Berel. These two and Yoshke the *Golitzianer* (Galician), a peddler, sleep in this small cellar workroom. Yoshke is already asleep on a couch with a sagging belly. Lutz beds on the floor and Berel boasts a cot.

I like Berel. He doesn't talk to me: he talks with me. He is a teller of tales, tales of the forests and fields of his sunny and verdant Bessarabia. And he is a wit, but always kindly. For instance, as now, he never neglects to greet me as a grown-up, not ironically, but caressingly, "What make you, (How are you) *Reb* (Mr.) Meyer?"

"Ollaright, a pretty thanks to you for asking, *Reb* Berel."

"Is it from a bear you are running, or has your shadow tripped you in the dark alley?"

"Oh, no, I have not a fear of such things. I just escaped from a policeman." I confide proudly.

He whistles and smacks his lips in awesome tribute to my daredeviltry. "Sit you down here, sit on this saddle, my adventurous friend, you must be tired."

I watch Berel sewing thongs of leather. . . . "Those

[19]

reins you are fixing, I guess must be for a little pony."

"No, Meyer, they are for a goat."

A goat, . . . the very mention of my bearded nemesis is enough to spoil this glorious night.

"I guess you know all about horses, don't you, Berel?"

"Yes, something."

"Do you know all about goats, too?"

"Yes, when I was a boy I used to take care of herds of goats."

"Then tell me, Berel, be so good, what's the matter nobody likes a goat and everybody makes fun of them."

"First place, nothing bothers a goat and that makes people angry. A goat manages to get along where any other creature would perish. Stubble, twigs, anything is food and nourishment for him. He is a sidestepper, can walk a narrow ledge or a fence, if need be. He is for himself; unfeeling, and befriends no one. An unlikable, ugly thing with a most unreasonable smell. And I have noticed that a goat is the only thing ridicule can't kill."

Surely a pleasing portrait of my namesake, and it made me despondent. . . . Lutz, done with his stitching, stares vacantly at the lamp. Berel is busy with an awl. Suddenly, Yoshke shrieks in his sleep, one word piteous, imploring, "*Mommale*" (little mother).

Berel putters away and Lutz stares, unblinkingly, and the silence is of a tomb.

"*Mommale, mommale,*" hums Berel under his breath, "*scheine mommale,*" in the minor tones of a *Yom Kippur* chant. (Little mother, little mother, lovely little mother).

I watch Yoshke in shocked surprise: here is a bearded man crying in his sleep for his mother.

"Poor Yoshke," says Berel with a sigh. "Yoshke was hurt today, Yoshke who is as gentle as a lamb. . . . A policeman felled him to the ground."

"A policeman! Yes? What for?"

"Yoshke had no more than taken his place with his pushcart on Hester Street when the policeman came around to collect the graft, a quarter a day from each peddler. Yoshke begged the policeman to wait a little while until he could get money from customers, explaining that he had spent his last cent on a stock of potatoes. The policeman's answer was to club him to the gutter."

Yoshke stirred fitfully.

"He's got no one, Yoshke, and he's as gentle as a lamb, and I'm thinking it's not a world for lambs." . . .

And he smiled at me, sadly, sagely, "I think, Meyer, I think a goat has a got a better chance in this world."

III

Uncle Philip is asleep on the sofa in the kitchen and mother dozes by the stove against my return.

"So late, Meyer, so late and tomorrow you must be up early for school."

"Aw, it ain't so late," I remark with the diffidence of a twelfth leader.

In the smoky glow of the expiring lamp, mother's beckoning arms become monstrous shadows on the whitewashed walls. I watch the shadows, wondering if they will turn into goats. . . . Mother whispers, "Come to me, child, mine, come now and sit here," drawing me to her lap, which act I resist as offensive to a person of my years and station. I pull away, reminding mamma, sharply, "Say, I ain't a baby no more." . . . Ridiculous. . . . What would Boolkie think of such a performance? His twelfth leader—a lap baby. . . . Mother smiles . . . a coughlike sob in her voice . . . and tears glisten on her fine long lashes. *"Mein ben yochid* (my only son), always, you will be my baby, always." . . . I am drawn tenderly to her bosom and her face nestles on my head. . . . I am annoyed: mother's hair tickles my forehead. . . . *"Mein teir ziegelle* (my beloved little goat)." . . . I become rigid with resentment.

"Mamma, I don't want you to call me *ziegelle* no more. I've got a regular name, haven't I?"

"Don't you like your pet name?"

"No. Everybody makes fun of me. Don't call me that any more."

[22]

"Only tonight, this night only," she whispers soothingly, "I will call you *ziegelle*: this night of your birth and nevermore." And she cries, which amazes me; embraces me, and bespatters my face with kisses. Quite a fuss over nothing, I think, and a nice climax to a heroic evening.

"Oh, *mein teir* (my darling), you should not dislike the goat—a goat saved your life."

"Saved my life?"

"You may say it, *mein hertz* (my heart) saved your life! A goat was your wet nurse."

What a scandal. . . . The gang must never know. . . . And I swear mother to secrecy. But I beg for the story.

"But ten days before you were born, papa was called to the military . . . to serve the Tsar . . . and he made up his mind to run away to America, and I would not let father go alone. . . . Three days out from Hamburg . . . in the bowels of a sailing vessel . . . while it seemed we were tumbling into a pit in the deep . . . you were born. . . . Worry and seasickness and fright. . . . I had no milk for my baby . . . and there was no milk on board. And we wept over you as for the dead and lighted candles as for the dead. . . . Until there happened a miracle. . . . A miracle. . . . The seamen's pet, a she-goat with udders plump with milk, escaped from her quarters and came wandering in the steerage. . . . And the she-goat suckled my baby and he lived to see the promised land. . . . And so here you are, *mein ziegelle*. . . ."

And mother gathered me to her bosom in a transport of joy and gently rocked me to sleep, singing, tremu-

lously, a lullaby, a lullaby oft sung but now crooned for
the last time—

> *"Unter der viegelle*
> *Shtait ein weisse ziegelle,*
> *Ooh, ooh, ooh,——"*
> (Under the little crib stands a little white kid.)

SECOND PERIOD

Neither to him nor his brothers or sisters was religion real.

HENRY ADAMS

SECOND PERIOD

I

Three years . . . bad times . . . hunger years. . . .
Yet the great rush continues like a stampede. Droves
of hungry and hounded and despairing people from
Eastern and Southern Europe crowd into a new Ghetto
of tenements and sweatshops.

Every little home is congested with its quota of
boarders, the men who left wives and children behind
to seek their fortune in the Land of Gold.

Grocers, butchers, peddlers and buttonhole-makers
turn bankers and steamship ticket agents overnight.
Everybody is saving to buy a *shif carte* (ship ticket)
for wife or child or brother or sweetheart.

And all these newcomers, men, women, boys and
girls are immediately drafted into the needle industries
to become, as Uncle Philip says, slaves to the German
Jews, masters of the wearing apparel enterprises.

Night after night Philip is engrossed in his books,
passionate as a lover, untiring as an alchemist seeking,
seeking the secret of—gold. And every day, as our
poverty deepens, he swears that soon, soon, to be sure,
he will deliver us from bondage; that he is on the verge
of discovering the secret of the German Jews' riches.
And, to me it has now become as unlikely and chimeri-
cal as the daily legend I con in *cheder*—the imminent
delivery of Israel from exile and his return to the Land
of Milk and Honey. . . . Mother, I daresay, discour-
aged by the utter lack of *tisch gelt* (table money),

[27]

is openly dubious, but father's hope does not wane.
There is nothing else left, he says, but to hope. He is
a broken man, silent and withdrawn from the world,
and apparently life is sustained in him by the oxygen
of Philip's airy promises.

There is little work. Labor is too plentiful. The
manufacturers know it and squeeze the contractors,
who in turn squeeze that dry thing, a day's wage. And
labor knows only one thing—one must live, and accepts
anything. But Philip is always busy . . . libraries,
lectures, exploring the city, listening to every kind of
person. . . . When there is work in the clothing
factory, the short seasonal, body-destroying rush, he
sits at his sewing machine, alongside of father, twelve
hours, fourteen hours, and thinks nothing of a twenty-
hour stint. . . . But always returning hungrily to his
books . . . books that make him despair and cry out in
anguish. I have seen him clutch volumes to his breast
and groan: "Oh, how ignorant I am. . . . " A madness is over him: a madness of envy and lust . . . and
how he hates the German Jews, they who look down
upon Russian Jews as an animal, apart; they who are
proud, powerful and rich. . . . And daily Philip warns
me . . . "Meyer, Meyer, remember a laborer is lost,
a dog. Never be a laborer. Let others labor for you—
there's the trick—that's brain work, that's cleverness——" . . . And father repeats solemnly as though
pointing to himself as a horrible example: "Don't be
a workman—anything else—but don't be a dog of a
workman. . . . " But mother is wishing me an evil
fate. Just because I am doing well in *cheder* she has
a fervent ambition in my behalf—wants me to be a
Rabbi. But, thank goodness, Philip laughs at the

idea. . . . Father and Philip are operators and father
has a distinct curvature after years of bending over a
sewing machine, guiding seams in poor light, but Philip
holds himself erect, declaring that he will not bend his
back to man, let alone a machine. . . . He growls and
curses at the meanness of our living:—two little dark
rooms in a rear house, smelly kerosene lamps, water
from the yard pump and toilets in the backyard . . .
no better than roaches . . . worrying over the slender
wherewithal, sleeping on a verminous couch . . . not
even enough crockery or eating things. Two'soup plates
must do for the four of us. Mother has it that respec-
tability requires that the family must eat together. So
mother and father eat out of one plate and Philip and
I share the other. Mother is always slower than father,
a little trick on her part so that father may get a little
more of the stew. But Philip and I have regulated
our spoon operations to ensure equal division. . . .
"Meyer," he says, "you have the appetite of a bear
but I have the eye of a hawk. Don't cheat."

II

It is a good thing I don't have to rely upon the home supply to satisfy my hunger or it would not be satisfied. During these days of unemployment our dining is almost an empty form. But the gang knows how to supplement the scanty home provender. Wares on pushcarts, stands, and in shops yield to nimble fingers, and magically disappear in capacious pockets. . . . Chunks of black bread, potatoes, smoked fish, fruit in season, and a variety of other eatables diversify the day's forage. . . . I am the cover guy. In other words, I distract the owner and screen the thief. My ways are modest, my talk quiet, respectful, aye, pious, and thus I beguile the storekeeper whilst my accomplice lifts and loads. . . . Even in the beginning, when I started to play the game of life, I found it was better and safer to use my wits and let the other fellow do the manual or risky share of the job—the dirty work.

We boys lived several kinds of lives, traveling from planet to planet. First there was the queer relationship of American street gamins to our old-world parents. Indeed, an ocean separated us. And distance does not encourage confidings and communings, but creates misunderstanding and leads to contempt and intolerance. Many of us were transient, impatient aliens in our parents' homes. Then there was that strict, rarefied public school world. The manners and clothes, speech and point of view of our teachers extorted our respect and reflected upon the shabbiness, foreignness and crudities of our folks and homes.

HAUNCH PAUNCH AND JOWL

Again, there was the harsh and cruel *cheder* life with its atmosphere of superstition, dread and punishment. And then came our street existence, our sweet, lawless, personal, high-colored life, our vent to the disciplines, crampings and confinements of our other worlds.

In our *cheder* on Thursday mornings we boys got a foretaste of the Day of Judgment. On hot summer days Hymie Rubin and Sam Rakowsky, who did not take readily to the intricacies of ancient tongues, came to *cheder* dressed in overcoats, and storm hats with earlaps. Archie Wotin, known in later gang history as Archie the Cannon, arrived with the seat of his knickerbockers lined with tin sheeting and his stockings stuffed with excelsior. Their outer works were prepared for hostilities.

Woe unto the lad who made more than three mistakes in translating the weekly portion of the Law! A sewing machine strap, lively and venomous as an infuriated snake, fell mercilessly over the offending boy, awrithe in the righteous grasp of *Melamud* (teacher) Mordecai. . . . Earlaps, overcoats, tin sheeting and excelsior were hardly enough. The well-oiled thong's sting was true and terrible. . . . It was not that *Melamud* Mordecai was brutal but that parents and pupils were pitiless. A *melamud* who spared the strap was soon mad and ruined. Parents, paying him the princely retainer of one dollar a month per child, required him to be their rigorous disciplinary officer. And, as always, cruelty begets cruelty. The boys lost no chance to plague, pester and persecute the *melamud*. The unfortunate pedagogue, old and resourceless, could rely only upon his strap, while his ingenious charges, in retaliation, devised many forms of torture.

[31]

HAUNCH PAUNCH AND JOWL

I think the Creator fashioned Mordecai to amuse his pupils. His stature and design were the funniest in the world. I never saw such bowlegs as he had: he seemed to walk on his ankles with much swaying and rolling, and because of this deformity he was no taller than a child. His long white beard was all out of proportion to his height. He looked like a comical dwarf or gnome shown in our school story books. And his face was an old parchment with thousands of marks, the wrinkle-records of his trials, and his eyes were like inky smudges on the parchment. . . . To us there was nothing funnier than the picture of old Mordecai, the hobbling, swaying dwarf, pursuing an agile boy who leaps under and over benches. The strap smites the bench or boy and our laughter roars out as raucous applause. . . . And this woebegone, misshapen creature has a wife—*die Rebbitzan* (the title given to a *melamud's,* or Rabbi's, wife), a frail, timorous figure in colorless calico. No matter how much we torment her husband, she never fails to call us *kinderlach teire* (little children, dears) and give us her blessings, coming and going. . . . A pious woman, her head is never uncovered. A black *sheitel* (wig) or a black lace headdress, makes of her bloodless, shrunken face a bleached death mask. She stands, a picture of sorrow and humility, her head nodding and body rocking as though in prayer before the last Temple Wall in Jerusalem. . . . The *melamud* never looks at his wife, not so much as a sidelong glance does he bestow, nor does he ever speak to her, directly. He speaks to her in generalities addressed to no one in particular. A devout pair, devoted, perhaps, who knows? but obeying fan-

[32]

tastically the rabbinical dictum that a pure, pious man shall not look upon any woman—not even his wife.

The Grodno Synagogue, named after the Russ-Lithuanian city from which its members emigrated, was over Witkinsky's livery stable on Hester Street. It was not a pretentious place: pine benches with blotchy coats of paint, a central service platform balustraded, and a *torah* cabinet (the ornate sanctum of the hand-inscribed scrolls of the Law) between the windows of the East Wall—the point nearest Palestine. The walls were decorated with crude legends of the zodiac. In the rear, facing the backyard, was a small section partitioned off for the women's devotions, and in this cubby hole of a place *Melamud* Mordecai held his school. . . . Seated at the head of a long pine table, Mordecai assigns us to our places, the wicked signaled out for honorary positions nearest himself, within convenient reach of his weapon of offense, the long oil-slimy sewing machine strap.

On this hot summer day we were nearly suffocated by the incense of smoldering candle wicks and ripe manure. The place abounded in cheap *yahrzeit* (death anniversary) candles and lamps and the backyard was heaped with manure. The pupils, of all ages and degrees, are gathered around the table. The tots, no more than four or five years old, drone and buzz, interminably, *aleph, beth, gimel* (a, b, c) backwards and forwards, break ranks and reassemble the scattered alphabet under the *melamud's* little pointer. Meanwhile, the advanced scholars attest devotion to their studies by rehearsing their tasks in the loudest possible sing-song. . . . Soon the minor pupils are dismissed. In the classroom they are like titmice, barely audible and awe-stricken, but no sooner do they get out on the staircase than they begin to squeal and scamper. The *melamud* rushes out and they retreat, before his brandished strap to take up a hooting and howling on the dung-piles in the backyard. . . . And then we are taken over the hurdles and hazards set up by Rashi, that Middle Age scholar and wine merchant, whose interpretations of the Bible are written in Hebrew entwined with Old French.

III

At last we are free. It is the riot of a jail delivery. And now for the real business of life. We follow a prearranged roundabout way back to Ludlow Street. We dare not pass Essex Street. Civil war has begun— over differences never quite specified or identified—between the two principal Jewish gangs, the Ludlow Streeters and the Essex Guerrillas. The first battle is expected tonight. We hurry—hot for the adventure. Nearing home, we see a glow in the sky—promise of a big fire. Hastening, hilarious lads join us. The clan is gathering. A great bonfire burns in the cobbled square at Ludlow and Canal Streets. And boys are careening in all directions, their forms seeming to leap skyward with the flames. Barrels, boxes, plundered wooden signs, canvas signs, cellar doors, chicken coops, a broken pushcart, lumber, abandoned mattresses and couches, paint cans, beer kegs and the countless clutter of city streets form a huge blazing pyramid—a fiery challenge and defiance. . . . Scouts, breathing hard, excited, scutter through a network of arms, legs and loot to report to Boolkie. I take my place next to Boolkie, as self-appointed adviser, strategist—anything—except fighter. In time I have made this position for myself, always playing the part that involves no personal danger and by sheer push, assertion and brass have become ex-officio everything. I no longer fight for petty leadership. I am a sort of prime minister of our gang state, and Boolkie kneads pliantly under my flattery. . . . The fire snaps, cackles, hisses

[35]

and flares a polyphonic accompaniment to the warriors'
cries, alarms and rampaging. . . . An uproar that
thrills. . . . The enemy is sighted. A block away at
Canal and Essex Streets a battalion of boys suddenly
flings into view and as quickly vanishes before a fusil-
lade of brickbats. . . . Our scouts apprehend Guerrilla
outposts at Ludlow and Hester Streets. Volleys are
exchanged. But Boolkie and I are unmoved even when
enemy forces are reported forming at a third point,
Canal and Orchard Streets. . . . Whence will the real
attack come to capture this little square which we have
denied to them for their baseball and "pussy-cat"
games? . . . Shimshin (Samson the strong), leader of
the Guerrillas, brags he will seize the square tonight. . . . Now there are flurries of fighting at the
three points of contact. The Guerrillas are prodigal
with their bottles, and they seem to be exploding everywhere. . . . It is time to start our manœuvres. . . . I
loose the pets of our forces, the gaming hawks, who
spread like opening wings towards Essex Street via
Canal Street, wheel and turn at the corner, hooting like
maddened night birds on the blood scent. . . . They
are pushing into Essex Street proper. . . . Our plan
is to distract the Guerrillas from Hester and Ludlow
Streets, where lies hidden in hallways and cellars the
main body of our effectives. . . . Our hawks hover,
and swoop and begin to meet with greater resistance.
We have irritated a sore spot in bringing the fight right
into the enemy's home territory. . . . He calls in his
men to repulse the stiff assault. . . . Now Hester
Street is deserted. . . . The enemy cheers. Our pets
are being squeezed out of Essex Street. But by this
time Boolkie has unleashed his hidden cohorts and in

person leads an unopposed charge upon the Guerrillas'
rear, and routs them to their cellars and roofs.

Our victorious gang parades the length of Essex
Street shouting insults and jeers. Seeing that victory
is complete and the fighting and danger over, I pop up
at Boolkie's side ready to demand and share the fruits
of the other fellows' fighting. The boys begin to tear
down the wooden signs fronting the stores. The shopkeepers plead with the vandals. It was then that I first
seized upon a plan that suggested to me the policy that
I followed throughout my career,—to make every situation return a profit. So I approach Jake Weingrad,
who has a woolen remnants store. He is wringing his
hands in impotent rage as the boys are pulling down
the long wooden sign under his show-window.

"Where are the police?" he cries in vain. Where
are they, indeed. They have learnt well the wisdom
of not being around when two gangs are embattled.

I take Mr. Weingrad aside, and throw out a hint that
a little payment will protect his sign. He cries out in
anguish, "Protection money!" and therewith coined a
name that became in the East Side a synonym for
extortion.

"Only twenty-five cents," I whisper, "and a new
sign costs much more. . . . " He is actually agape at
my audaciousness, but a ripping noise of wood and
nails coming apart arouses him to a practical conclusion.

I tell Boolkie, and he applauds the idea. The sign
destroyers now work under my orders, and I go among
the storekeepers and soon return to Boolkie with the
astounding sum of four dollars.

"Protection money," I cry, unconsciously echoing

Weingrad. "Protection money" is reiterated many times by the jubilant gangsters.

And in this way began the blackmail of small store-keepers that Boolkie and I later developed into a fine business, and in time this petty but wholesale extortion became one of the main income sources of gangsters.

IV

It was an early summer night, pleasantly warm, this night of civil war.

Then came the quiet that we call quiet in the city,— only an occasional rattle of an empty wagon and the clatter of hoofs, a moment's hush like a fevered sleeper's sigh, the rattle and jangle of car horses' bells to the slipping and grating of their iron shoes on the cobblestones of their bumpy treadmill; a cry, a greeting, now there is laughter, the saloon's ribald guffaw, doors shutting like the sounds of a slazey drum; cats sputtering and spitting over the garbage heaps in the gutter . . . the city's bedtime quiet. . . . But stilled are the cymbals of strife, the crashing and splintering of bottles thrown by the warring boys, and their strident battle cries. . . .

Now Boolkie and a little group of congenials are at the corner playing a deft and delicate game—picking one another's pockets. Peace hath its pastimes. . . . And I sit on the stoop of our house in a glow of pleasure over the four quarters that I have held out of the reckoning of collected tribute and which are hidden in my shoes. Ho, I put it over on them, all right. They battled, they were in danger, they did the footwork and handwork, but it was I who did a quick bit of headwork. The headwork! That's the stuff! . . . And how I fooled them with a little fumbling with my shoe laces while I shoved the coins into my shoes. And I was a hero, everybody said I was a smart guy and liked me because I got them a big boodle for a blowout

[39]

HAUNCH PAUNCH AND JOWL

of wurst and candy. I too feasted on spicy wurst and
hard candies—at their expense, but I had also money,
more money than I had ever had.

Snatches of conversation drift through my reverie.
Davie Solomon and Avrum Toledo are seated on the
lowest step. I suppose they greeted me, but I was too
engrossed in egotistical self-caressing to notice them.

My cronies at the corner break out in a jeering
chorus to a jerky stamping of feet, "Hippity-hop,
hippity-hop, look out, look out, here comes the cop."
And along came Reb Mendel Gerditsky, unconcerned,
dignified, lamely strutting, conscious of his office of
general factotum of the Grodno Synagogue, arch
enemy of all boys, whom he keeps in order during
prayers by applying his famous corkscrew pinch on
cheek, arm, thigh or any other part of squirming dis-
turbers. And his victims dubbed him *der hingkerdiker
shammos* (the limping beadle), always ridiculing him
in the street by calling public attention to his limp,
caused by one foot being shorter than the other. He
wears his famous frock coat, its skirts flapping about
his knees like windless sails. Neither the summer's
sweat, nor the winter's snow could divest him of his
official garb, which he carries with the pomp and
flourish of a senator's toga. Legend has it that The
Coat was of holy and reverent ancestry, an heirloom
from his grandfather, the chief Rabbi of Grodno. But
tonight there is a touch to his attire that betokens an
important event, a wedding or a funeral. Perched on
his head is a stove-pipe hat. Wallowing in his wake,
bobbing like a small boat in the trough of a large ship,
comes *Melamud* Mordecai, nobly trying to keep up with
the beadle.

The *shammos* stops to peer at us in the dark of the stoop. Avrum and Davie rise. The *melamud* pants for breath.

"Come, children," speaks the authoritative beadle, "come with us and earn the greatest *mitzvah* (blessing). Come and recite the psalms for the dying."

"Go, children, a great *mitzvah*, verily," says the *melamud*.

Avrum holds back, but yields to Davie's earnest plea to do a *mitzvah*.

The *shammos* leads the way to the top floor of an old three-story house on Hester Street and, as we climb the stairs, hear a weird jumble of lamenting voices. Boolkie and the others, very curious, have trailed along and now linger like restless imps in the hall as we enter the Schneider flat. Neighbors, synagogue brethren, and nine of the ten Schneider children pack the four little rooms. Only Ikey Schneider, the baby, is absent, called baby, although fifteen years old, because he is the youngest of the children.

"Find me my baby," wails Mrs. Schneider, wringing her hands. "Bring back the sinner to ask forgiveness of his dying father and receive his death-bed benediction. . . ."

She moves like a distracted creature among the people, whining *"Ikelle, mein Ikelle,* my poor baby is to be an orphan, *nebach* (pity)—an orphan."

Ikey is "on the bum," which is our idiomatic way of saying that a boy is not living at home. Ikey was proud when he reported to us—"My father chased me outa the house." His father said, "Until you were *bar mitzvah* (confirmed) I was responsible to God for your sins and to man for your acts. Now you must

[41]

bear your own burdens. You steal from me, you refuse to study and you refuse to learn the buttonhole trade. You act like an outcast, therefore be an outcast." So Ikey went out, rejoicing to sleep in hallways and beg or steal his daily meals.

I slip down to the hall and find Ikey larking with his fellow gangsters.

"Come on up," I say, "your father is croaking."

"What the hell I care, le' him croak," he answers, his swollen, pimply face awry with a stupid leer. He shifts his overgrown body nervously, the body that is man's size but governed by a feeble baby's mind. Ikey, who could learn nothing in school and *cheder,* learned one thing exceedingly well—how to steal bundles from wagons and bring them to Jake Weingrad's store and get a few pennies.

"G'wan up," commands Boolkie.

"Come'n up wi' me," whines Ikey.

"G'wan up, you dope," answers Boolkie, adding a few sharp prods in the ribs. Ikey, protesting, "Who you hittin'?" goes up the stairs, followed by Boolkie and his particulars.

Mrs. Schneider falls on the neck of her boy, but the *shammos* pulls him away to take him to his father's bedside.

The dying man is a terrible picture of emaciation. The *Gabbe* (president or headman) of the synagogue sits at the place of honor, near the head of the bed, shaking his head benignly. The *shammos* has distributed the *tillim* (psalm books) and we read them in a muted tone that becomes a thrumming and a murmuring as the bass and childish voices mingle. Ikey is thrust forward and stands dumbly looking down upon

[42]

his father's heaving chest. The father's eyes flicker open and after one glance at Ikey's face seems dismayed, as though, the *Gabbe* later said, he beheld the flaming vision of the angel of death.

Just then I looked around and saw my father come into the room—a frightened look upon his face. Schneider was dying of the shop sickness—consumption—and father had a dread of the shop sickness, the plague of Dollar Land. . . .

The candles are lighted. The man is dead. A wife grieves, and nine children mourn, but a tenth child says, "Momie, gimmie somethin' t' eat." Chairs are overturned and we sit on the rungs, while the bereaved family in stockinged feet sit on low boxes. A neighbor shrouds the mirrors, and through the night we keep vigil beside the corpse, droning the psalms. . . . The candles sputter. . . . An old man has fallen asleep and snores with an occasional rasping gasp. Boolkie sits near the door like a person waiting for something to happen, short, heavy set, named after the bulky breakfast rolls sold by the Ghetto bakers. Here is his mother, a professional mourner, puttering about the kitchen, every now and then releasing a prodigious sigh, more like the hiss of escaping steam. She is the beggarwoman who sits timelessly like a crouching bronze image in front of the Grodno Synagogue—only to arise and appear at funerals—rattling her beggar's tin box, mumbling benedictions on donors. Dago Jack's eager, curious face, swarthy and pinched, becomes like shining wax in the candle light, flits in the doorway. He is a *goy* (Gentile) and may not pass the threshold. A Sicilian lad, stunted, knock-kneed, a bravado, the glad doer of dangerous jobs, one of a

[43]

brood of twelve. His father tends a tiny peanut
and chestnut stand, and his brothers are newsboys and
bootblacks and his little sisters slaveys for the local
business men's wives. Sneak, thief, truant, a stiletto
artist, he acknowledges one God—To-Be-As-Tough-
As-Hell, and Boolkie is his prophet.

Avrum stares at the ceiling as though fascinated by
the cobwebby shadows cast by the flickering candles.
For the most part he has not made even a pretense at
reading. The *tillim* lies open upon his knees. But
Davie, leaning against his arm, has prayed, fearfully,
passionately. Avrum is a cold unbeliever, while Davie
believes, abjectly, in the *cheder* God of Vengeance.
Yet they are inseparable pals, called the one-and-a-half
twins because Davie, though he is Avrum's age, is
slight and small, while Avrum is long-limbed, sturdy
and well developed. They belong to the bookish clique,
detached dwellers in an ivory tower, have nothing to
do with the gang and are despised for sissies. Avrum
with his black hair, dark, smouldering eyes and olive
complexion suggests a Spanish young man, and Davie
with his white skin, blue eyes and golden hair suggests
a Polish boy of nine, his actual age being fifteen. . . .
Avrum is a new kind of Jewish boy in the Ghetto. He
came with his folks from the Balkans. At first the
neighbors thought they were not Jews because they did
not speak Yiddish. Their everyday speech was *Ladino,*
melodious Old Castilian garnished with Hebrew and
bits of the universal patois of Mediterranean ports.
It was the language of a great population of Jews in
Spain, who, when they were expelled by the Inquisition,
carried their dialect to the Balkans and Mediterranean
ports, and it survives to this day. . . . Avrum Toledo

is quite mature—a silky down, like little shadows, shows on his upper lip and cheeks. Years later when I looked upon Rembrandt's portrait of a Jew I thought I beheld my *Ladino* pal with clear wide brow, big brown eyes, reposeful, intelligent oval face, long shapely nose with its wide thin nostrils and ripe full-blown lips, a lover's mouth. . . . Avrum confides in Uncle Philip. They have but one thing in common, a hearty ridicule for God and all religion. Yet he is the son of a man whom Philip describes as a "double harness Jew," a man who is so pious that he prays wearing two sets of phylacteries. Avrum calls the fine long leathern straps that his father winds on his arm and head the shackles of superstition. But he is devoted to the ugly, stunted old man of swarthy face and queer woolly beard. Avrum sits many hours after school helping his mother and sisters make kimonos, which Avrum's father peddles from door to door. . . . And Davie Solomon, wan and winsome, clings to the stalwart dreamer like a delicate flower upon the trunk of a dark tree. He is the well-beloved of old Mordecai, for in Davie the *melamud* finds response rich and reverent. Davie's father, too, had died of the dread shop sickness and he is the only child of the little "horseradish widow," a shrunken young woman with gray, withered hair straggling from under her faded shawl. She has a small stand on Hester Street near Ludlow Street, where she plays a bitter tune on a horseradish mill and sells the ground root in little paper packets. Davie may be often seen sitting beside her, his beautiful head upon her breast, and as she turns the tiny handle of the doleful organ, Davie sings softly the mournful songs of an exiled folk locked within the Polish pale. . . . Archie Wotin is

[45]

getting restless. He has been pulling Ikey's coat from behind and Ikey is confused, looking about him, not knowing whom to blame. Archie is feeling better now that he is fooling someone, even if it is only a half-wit. His fingers are long, thin and nimble. Generations of needle-plying ancestors have endowed him with digits that are not an encumbrance to this descendant who has turned from stitching to snitching. Archie was a marvelous pickpocket. He was a versatile liar, a liar for lying's sake, told a lie even when the truth would do as well. He had roving little eyes set in a yellow, pinched face, and he looked like a sickly child when as a matter of fact his body was wiry, strong and active. He seemed afraid of only one thing—of being afraid. Fearlessness was his ideal. His father worked in a sweatshop and saw his son only when he was out of work. As Philip says, a worker and his children are strangers. He goes to work while the children are asleep, and in the evening he is too tired to do anything but go to sleep so as to be ready again for work at the break of day. So Boolkie had the bringing up of Archie, whose mother has the ceaseless care of four babies. . . . Boolkie thinks Ikey's bewilderment is great fun. Boolkie accuses Davie, who raises startled eyes from the *tillim* to find Ikey glaring at him. "Cut it out, you sissie," says Boolkie to Davie. But at this moment Ikey is again annoyed from another direction and he begins to splutter. . . . Harry Wotin, Archie's brother, until now sitting moodily against a wall, rises and begs Archie to stop. "It is wrong and a sin to harm an orphan." Archie is only fourteen and his brother is two years older. Archie snarls back at him: "You don't expect me to swallow that bunk." But

Ikey settles the matter by demanding of Harry, another one of the despised cult of book boys, "What the hell you buttin' in for. . . ." Avrum laughs. Harry's pimply face and scrawny neck flushes crimson as Boolkie remarks to Archie, "I betcha you could knock daylight outa him even if he is your big brother. . . ." Archie assures him that he could do it with both hands tied. . . . The *shammos* thunders, "What is this—a corner for tramps; have you no fear of holy occasions? . . ." Davie shudders and reads fervently, and even Boolkie mumbles a page or two. . . . At last the *shammos* tells us to go. His men have come to lay out the body for interment in the morning. The Schneiders, making a melancholy group, stand in the kitchen and are awakened to fresh outbursts of grief by these preparations. The reading of the *tillim* seemed to have hushed and soothed them. The two old men, the *shammos's* funeral assistants, went about their business with a great matter of fact manner, demanding of the *shammos,* "How is anything to be done? We can barely move about in such a crowd," meaning the mourners in the kitchen, who have been unable to make their beds because of the presence of so many people in every room.

V

All the boys in the gang were not thieves. Many remained petty thieves until stronger influences came along to lift them out of the ruck. It was the exceptional, almost abnormal boy who did not join the gang. The gang was romance, adventure, had the zest of banditry, the thrill of camp life, and the lure of hero-worship. An incident happened in the early part of this torrid summer that brought all the boy elements into the gangs and for the first time united the half dozen Jewish gangs in New York. . . . Feeling ran high when a Jewish peddler was killed by cobblestones thrown by an Irish gang on Grand Street near Gouverneur Street. A few of our boys were held up and badly beaten by the Jackson Street gang after our lads came out of the East River, where they had been swimming and poling logs. The Guerrillas had even fared worse, their leader's head was broken. Shimshin was personally brave, although not clever. He went into Gouverneur Street hospital long enough to have his head tied up and came out to defy the "Micks." He barely escaped with his life.

Jackson Street on the East River was the only spot that had a sort of a sand beach that made the bathing highly pleasurable. In fact, the whole river front was in Mick territory, and during the days when the Jew was a newcomer in this wild section of Manhattan the Irish hoodlums regarded him as legitimate prey. The summer was frightfully hot, and outside of the *schwitz mickvahs* (Russian sweat baths), the river was our only place for a bath. The gangs took up the Mick challenge gladly. It engendered that feverish, fanatical spirit that comes with religious war. The Irish lads shouted, "Kill the Christ killers," and the Jewish boys cried, "*Mopolize* the Micks." (A strange word, probably coming from the root of *mopel*, to abort. In any event it implied the direst punishment.) But the Micks were splendid fighters and the Jewish attacks were sporadic. It seems strange that there should ever have been this intense hostility between the Jews and the Irish, as later when they became acquainted they were amiable neighbors and the most powerful local gangs were made up of an admixture of Irish, Jews and Italians. However, the gangs in the main had one national predominance.

The Ludlow Streeters made a foray, but retreated ignominiously. Boolkie was furious with the humiliation. He had gibed Shimshin that we would give the Micks a good beating. The Micks were too numerous to be handled by a single gang. I suggested an alliance with the Guerrillas, and that very morning the two gangs, hot for revenge and without plan or preparation, invaded Gouverneur Street. We momentarily swept the Irish before us. Gouverneur Street is narrow. Our boys congested the street from sidewalk to sidewalk. We whistled and halooed gleefully, but in another moment fled from a downpour of bricks and mortar. The Gouverneur lads had simply retired to their roofs, dismantled a few chimneys, and rained the brickbats down upon us. Just then a gang of Micks coming from Henry Street attacked our panic-stricken ranks. Well, it was a pitiful debacle. You may imagine our chagrin, we who had rated ourselves unbeatable.

I felt deeply ashamed. My idea had not worked. It was up to me to save my face and the standing of our gang. Then there was that deep racial feeling. Our defeat was the talk of the Ghetto. For the first time our elders approved a gang fight. Here again was that vicious racial passion. The bookish boys rallied to our cause. The Stanton Street gang, a small contingent, called for a conference. They, too, had tasted the bitter dregs of defeat. I went to my home, saying to myself a few phrases that became my formula for every tight corner in which I would find myself. Use your head. Use your head. There's a way out—if you use your head. I was sitting in the kitchen. Mother was washing clothes. The wash boiler was on the stove simmering. Mother asked me to get the cover for the boiler from under the bed. I fetched out the cover by slipping my hand through the handle, and in this manner carried it to mother. Mother laughed at the way I held up the cover, saying that in the olden times the Jewish soldiers, the Maccabeans, fought with shields that looked like the cover of the washboiler. And then I used my head. I slipped out of the house with the cover and appeared before the gang flourishing it like a shield. "Come on," I shouted, "now we'll beat the Micks." Boolkie and Shimshin and other notables listened excitedly to my idea. Every boy was ordered to go and get his mother's washboiler cover. In a little time a grand army assembled on Canal Square with gleaming tin and copper shields. Other boys had climbed to the roofs of houses and torn off tin decorations which became armor helmets. A council was held. Stanton Street was summoned. A real campaign was outlined.

HAUNCH PAUNCH AND JOWL

Again we marched into Gouverneur Street. Again the Micks flew to roofs and started to pelt us with bricks, mortar and stones. But our clans were marching under a tin roof. We drove them from the roofs, administering cruel beatings to the captured. In this gang fight a revolver was used for the first time. Shimshin in a rage had bought a revolver and was determined to kill a few Micks. Fortunately, his bullets found no mark.

We marched down to the beach, planted guards and outposts and our hosts frolicked in the slimy waters of the East River.

How I enjoyed the triumph. My headwork had distinguished me. I was referred to as some wise guy. Everybody applauded my ingenuity. Neighbors congratulated my folks. It was war against the Gentiles. Everyone rejoiced that the oppressor was well trounced. Philip remarked casually, "Good ideas are good only if they show a profit. Bear in mind—have only profitable ideas." It was that evening that Uncle Philip, after long, silent ruminating, announced, "Meyer is going to be a lawyer."

VI

Looking back I try hard to remember when it was that we city street-bred boys had an age of innocence. It seems that we were born with a bit of apple from the tree of knowledge in our mouths. Things as they are were but rarely treated as anything else but as things as they are. Hymie Rubin's grandmother, who kept house for her widowed son and his children, would say to Hymie, "You were already a thief in your mother's belly." I mention this merely to say that we heard such things so often that they had no special effect upon our minds, but were just things that are. Hymie Rubin had a particular grudge against his grandmother. She had made him comically knock-kneed for life, and what greater injury can anyone have done to him than to be made comically deformed. When Hymie was born his grandmother, as was the fashion then, immediately swaddled his body with tight binders, but had erred in overtightening the binding about his knees. Hymie had no mother to look after him, his father was busy in the shop, and his grandmother, half-blind, spent the day grumbling and mumbling, having but one concern in life—to have a hot supper ready for her son, the breadgiver. Notwithstanding that she had crippled her grandchild for life, Hymie's grandmother officiated and advised at many births. Consequently Hymie, at twelve, was something of an authority on births. Yet he was one of the cleanest-minded boys I ever knew. And in the end it made

HAUNCH PAUNCH AND JOWL

Hymie decide to be a doctor. . . . And so it was . . . we just knew things. . . . Sometimes births took place under our eyes. Many a lad has lent a hand to a bustling midwife called at the last moment. . . . And then crowded quarters left nothing untold. . . . A multitude of men brought a plenteous supply. Seduction was commonplace, and many a man considered a trip across the ocean tantamount to a divorce. So there was much talk, and all a growing boy needs is a word here and there to piece together a pretty tale for his fellow adolescents.

Of sex mysteries there was none for me. The whole scheme of life was presented to me as preordained, and so what I saw and heard fitted in quite naturally. My advanced *cheder* studies embraced the rules and regulations of all human relations. It was not the sort of thing to disorder or inflame the mind. But then came the time of titters, and whispers and nudges. A personal, forbidden phase was presented. Scandalized murmurs, lewd references, bizarre narratives of individual experiences made us sharply curious of the newest Ghetto sensation, the Allen Street mysteries.

Allen Street, that shadowy lane living in the murk of smoke and rust and rumble of the elevated steam railroad, a stodgy home street, became in a day a thronged, roisterous thoroughfare.

A bare-faced and brazen-tongued crew of wastrels rented the lower floor of many houses on Allen Street and displayed colorful human wares in the windows. Even for the wide-open town that New York was at the time, the brazen and bare-faced desecration of a home street was shocking. Nothing concealed, no secrecy, no mystery. The hidden rites of the mystery

[53]

of mysteries became the crudest comedy. Panders in
the street bickered over a prospective customer. Boys
were welcomed and cajoled with cut-rates. The gaudy
window creatures winked and whistled a strange little
sound imported from the streets of Warsaw and Budapest, their trade clarion, which whistle and hiss in one
most of the boys soon learned and practiced. These
little tricks became one of the boys' games. Troops
of lads from every part of the East Side would slink
past to gape and wonder and end by jeering and laughing. A busy, noisy mart . . . highly profitable to
cadets, landlords, politicians and policemen.

Issy Weingrad, who invited bundle thieves to bring
their plunder to his father's store, introduced Ikey
Schneider into the Allen Street comedy. And so Ikey
had another reason for stealing. . . . Mike Rothstein,
the good-natured, easy-going fellow whose brothers
and sisters were models of good behavior and industry,
seemed to have no sense of wrong. He just did things.
When Issy told him where he might pick up some desirable stuff, Mike just went and stole it. And when
Ikey asked Mike to keep him company in Allen Street,
Mike drifted along, and in a short time drifted into a
hospital for a long tussle with disease. . . . But Mike's
disaster was no deterrent: soon it was a general thing
for the gang to visit Allen Street . . . and that, too,
became one of the things that are. And the things that
are are the things that are meant to be.

VII

Uncle Philip was not impressed with the news that the Grodno Synagogue had imported a *rov* (Rabbi) from its name city. A *rov*, he said, is a scholar a thousand years behind the times. Is the world startled by a new invention, a scientific discovery? Then the *rov* says disparagingly that it was known and tried before, generally showing by anagrams, cryptograms, hidden meanings, double meanings, that it was known to this prophet or that wise scholar or was one of the many things found as vain and futile by Solomon, the original Great-Know-It-All. The *rov* lives in a choked Talmudical jungle and dares not tear away as much as a little leaf to let in light. He is the supreme court of his congregation, presides as jurist in legal squabbles, arbitrates business disputes, adjusts neighborhood wrangles, regulates all ritual dictums, sets the spiritual standard and censors manners, morals and the arts.

The *rov*, Chiam Zucker, certainly raised the Grodno Synagogue's standing. He attracted many pious members, and rich business men paid high seat rentals for the honor of sitting near him. *Rov* Zucker set out to raise funds for the erection of a seminary. His slogan was, "Beware! this new land, with its freedoms, is but a snare and temptation to wean away your youth from Judaism." The *shammos* attended him everywhere as a fawning flunkey and entered the pledges in a bulky ledger.

Rov Zucker was easily a man of seventy. Tall, angular and erect, he carried himself with gracious dignity. He was like a patriarch of ancient times. His face seemed to shine transparently white, and his long flowing beard blew about his face like a fleecy cloud. His gray eyes were steady and farseeing. Serenely self-sufficient, he went about his duties and no man said him nay. Even Philip respected him and admired his ways. He said it was a pity that such a man should have been lost in an impassable jungle.

One day *Rov* Zucker discovered Allen Street. After the Saturday night service the Grodno Synagogue members remained to hold a business meeting. The *rov* asked a strange question. He wanted to know if any member of the Grodno Synagogue owned property on Allen Street. Harris Rittberg and Baruch Engel answered that they did. "And," asked the *rov*, "is any part of your property let out as brothels? . . . "

It was a stormy meeting. Rittberg and Engel were rich and influential members. They preferred to evade the *rov's* question—parried the thrust, saying they did not know what their tenants were doing, although it was common knowledge that certain tenants paid ten times as much as ordinary tenants. The *rov* did not urge the matter, but sat throughout the evening contemplatively, majestically silent.

The following day was Sunday, Allen Street's busiest day. About noon *Rov* Zucker stood at the corner of Canal and Allen Streets, a picturesque figure amid the shifting crowds. He then strode up and down the middle of Allen Street, his hands upraised as in prayer, and soon a number of men and boys collected around him.

He stood still and a hush fell upon the street. He

spoke in tones of exhortation and his words fell with the crushing cadence of Biblical curses.

"Hear ye, Children of Israel, heed the voice of the Lord and turn away from evil.

"Children of Israel, ye find yourselves in a new land, a stranger among strangers, and the heavy hand of judgment is always upon the stranger.

"Even so, ye find yourselves in a land of miracles, a land of life and liberty, where you may work how or where you will, a blessed land of free choice. You are not denied your God nor His house of worship. Here you are not confined, hampered nor oppressed.

"Here is the joy of the righteous, for here ye are not driven to extreme resorts to find bodily sustenance.

"In the name of the Almighty, I ask ye, search your soul, wherefore are ye in evil occupation?

"Turn away from evil, deck your shame and flee the sight and word of ill-fame.

"For even as one of ye is besmirched, all of ye will be named foul.

"Heed, or ye will bring down God's curse upon you in this fourth and last corner of the earth, the furthermost nook of your exile.

"Cease splattering slime and dung upon the Shield of David.

"Open your ears and heed, or cursed be your day.

"Cursed be your hour, your moment, your second.

"Cursed be unto eternity.

"May your eyes become as searing coals in your heads.

"May your tongues become as molten lead in your mouths and choke and stifle you, even a thousand times, a thousand times.

HAUNCH PAUNCH AND JOWL

"May your limbs wither and rot——"

Painted faces drew back and windows slammed shut. The street began to clear as shamefaced men sidled away and fled the fearsome consequences of a Rabbi's curse. Only a few open-mouthed boys lingered to watch the *rov*. . . . The *rov's* eyes, turned heavenward, did not see a hand clutching a blackjack strike out. Just one blow, well placed, and *Rov* Zucker toppled to the gutter. A wounded cry went up, not from the Rabbi, but from the onlooking people, as blood gushed from the old man's forehead.

VIII

Berel the harness fixer comes up for air. I was sitting on the steps to his cellar. I was crowded off the stoop by Philip and his friends, dubbed—the discussionists.

"Well, here we are again. The good old reliable hot summer. Every summer the people talk about the same thing. It's so hot. Every winter the people talk about the same thing. It's so cold. Bad weather is a fine thing. It's one thing people can talk about without getting angry."

Berel spoke in his gentle way, smiling and benevolent. It was easy to see that he was poking fun at Philip and his friends who were having an excited argument.

"You know, Meyer, I could hear them way down in my cellar and, mark you, Lutz was snoring."

Berel grabbed his head between his hands, exclaiming, "They will have to stop banging on my teapot."

Now it was Philip banging away, quick volleys of words,—derision, abuse, sneers. . . . Answers came, —quick, quivering, biting, insulting, pleading, reasoning, begging and softening, and then came a stillness as the one man spoke for whom the gathering had the respect that a quibbling group of intimates shows to a stranger. . . . The stranger is an American, and what is more, a Gentile, and his company was held as an honorary condescension. And how people knuckle under to a condescender, especially such fellows like Philip who defy the world. Philip defies the world so long as the world takes no notice of him.

HAUNCH PAUNCH AND JOWL

"Who is the *goy* (Gentile)?" asks Berel. "To me he looks like an Irisher, but it can't be. He's so quiet, got such nice ways—an educated man as I live: can't be an Irisher, I am sure."

Berel's acquaintance with the Irish was limited to a handful of hoodlums who thought it was fine sport and good citizenship to attack these outlandish newcomers, the dirty sheenies. Still, it was enough in Berel's eyes to condemn an entire people.

"Well, he is a real enough Irisher," I tell him. "His name is Barney Finn, a stranger in New York, comes from an American state called Vermont."

"Utt, that explains it," says Berel, "the wild ones are bred in this cursed city."

Barney Finn's talk is as casual as his long-legged gait, a mere amble that somehow covers a lot of ground.

"Take my word, folks, what you've been talking about is certainly important and interesting: Tolstoi, Marx, Kropotkin, Engles, Bakunin, their doctrines, formulas, theories, programs to make the world a better place. But that's where I feel moved to break in. I'm a down-to-the-ground fellow. My feet kind of get rooted to the spot I happen to be in. What about the acre of land I'm standing on! I'll clear it and cultivate it before I tackle the millions of other acres in the world. You fellows can't see any proposition or problem that's a mite smaller than the whole earth. . . . Here's our own little patch chockful of stink-weeds. . . . Folks, I refer to and mean that stinking shame—Allen Street. And I tell you straight out of my heart that Allen Street will be what it is as long as you folks stand for it. . . . I talked with the politicians. Oh, they don't make any shucks about it. They admit it's rotten, rancid stuff. They don't care, the politicians, because the people they're offending are not voters. They don't care so long as the greater number of East Siders are just immigrants, non-voting, docile greenhorns. They don't care how much they rile you—long as you haven't got the vote. They aim to please the regulars, and the regulars are the fellows who corral and deliver the voters on election day. And who are the regulars? The saloon keepers, disorderly house operators, shyster lawyers, professional gamblers, thieves, gangsters and cadets, and they are served by a pondful of smallfry—the petty favor seekers. They're nasty company, and a person with any self-respect shuns politics: so politics stays nasty. . . . Politicians know but one law,—if you're regular—you're right. Allen Street. The regulars want it,—so there it is. Rabbi Zucker's protest and broken head don't count. He don't control votes. . . . Do you want a decent community? It ain't the politicians' fault. They're willing enough. Soon as the bulk of votes is decent the politicians will become decent: after all, they've got the habit of officeholding, a comfortable habit that they won't want to get out of.''

I translate Barney Finn's talk to Berel, and he gives Barney high praise: "He don't bang on my teapot."

IX

Philip sees to it that my *bar mitzvah* (Confirmation; a sort of coming of religious age) is impressive. He and *Melamud* Mordecai prepare a learned address in Hebrew, a complicated thesis that I can't make head or tail of, but it is just involved and pedantic enough to satisfy the most critical. I commit it to memory. Philip tests me every morning before he leaves for work. He wakes me and before I can even brush the cobwebs of sleep from my eyes, plies me with review questions. I become letter perfect. The day of my confirmation falls on New Year's, a day made more holy by also being Saturday, the Sabbath. The synagogue is crowded and to everyone's delight I manage the intricate performance without a hitch or error. My mother is proud and happy. Philip doesn't complain, and that is praise indeed. Father seems just a dazed onlooker, and barely mumbles in reply to the congratulations.

My own feeling is elation. I am important, I am the center of interest. . . . I am important.

But back of my mind is a greater joy,—release from the confinement of the *cheder*. It is like saying good-bye to the bug-bear of religion, the religion that everlastingly thunders—fear, beware, be warned, be afraid of the God of Vengeance: a God eternally sitting in judgment. A mysterious, unseen, unseeable, unknowable and fearful thing—God. No wonder this religion is disagreeable, and unbelievable to us—pagans of the city wild. Little wonder we

[62]

rebelled against our daylong studies of Biblical lore with emphasis on the raw curses and chastisements, the subtle Apocryphal enlargement of the portrait of the God of Vengeance; the endless Rabbinical rules and rites and fasts and laments to appease that insatiable monster—God of Vengeance. No beauty. Nothing spiritual. You may vanquish or seduce a pagan with beauty; but fear—a pagan laughs at fear. This is how I translate today my feeling towards my religion, but on my confirmation day I simply felt,—I can't swallow that bunk: I puke it right back.

THIRD PERIOD

Bright and large eyed maidens like hidden pearls.

KORAN.

THIRD PERIOD

I

Girls exist. Rather, I have just become conscious of their existence. Until now it has been a Boys' World. Gorgeous flowers were blooming all around me, but I trod upon them. Good form of the Boys' World was to tease, insult and annoy these gangly things called girls. The sissies, only, had girl friends. As to the women we visited in Allen Street, well, they were not girls, they were a special species bred for a special purpose. At first we went out of curiosity and because we thought doing so made us mannish. One visit made quite a man of us.

Just about the time I put on my first pair of long pants I discovered the young ladies who were growing up around me, and my first notice found them in the beautiful budding spring time of their adolescence. My experience in Allen Street did not tend to make my interest in girls the vague, smouldering, undefined commotion such an interest generally is in a boy of fifteen. I saw, alluringly, busts, hips and legs, the rhythm of bodily form and movement. My interest was excited by the tales of affairs with girls, boastingly related by Ludlow Street Don Juans. I was not only sex-conscious but sex-sensitive. It was a relentless craving.

Nice girls dreaded the gang. They gave the corner hangout a wide berth. Boolkie and his regulars greeted them with outspoken intentions, and drove them away. But the gang had its female followers, who were admiringly called "tough babies." Though I was girl-crazy, I could not stand the tough babies. They were unfeminine little bummies, unkempt, harsh-spoken and utterly without the shy charm of the flower breaking out of the bud, the rare quality that drew me to the nice girls. The test of the matter, most likely, is that the tough baby was too ready to hand, and I was characteristically after the hard to get. The nice girls were elusive and dreadfully afraid of a bad name. Mothers let their boys run wild, but the girls had to account for every minute. The best I got was a few moments' passing talk on a stoop.

I was not crazy about any one girl—it was girls in general. Sam Rakowsky, Hymie Rubin and I formed a secretive clique of girl chasers. But we soon lost out as the nice girls told one another that we were inclined to be fresh. Fresh meant trying to kiss them. We kissed but a few times but tried often.

Sam got himself a job as an All Day Tramp, the name we gave to messenger boys whose soldier-like caps bore a brass plate with the initials A. D. T. (American District Telegraph). His worldly education grew in leaps and bounds. He was familiar with every joint in town. He was a directory of dives, brothels, resorts and theatres. He told racy stories of places and persons. A messenger boy sees and knows every-thing and everyone of interest.

Sam had an engaging manner and an inquisitive nature, which was a combination to get results. When in a tight corner Sam sang a song. He knew all the latest hits of the burlesque and variety stage and, if need be, could accompany them with a jig. He had

HAUNCH PAUNCH AND JOWL

ambitions as a song-and-dance artist. Sam's nosiness
once brought us pell-mell into the back room of a saloon
in Mulberry Bend. It was the headquarters of a mur-
derous gang. They were suspicious of us. It looked
threatening for the sheenies when Sam placed himself
in the middle of the room and broke out, strongly, in
song, a highly smutty thing he picked up in a black and
tan joint in Hell's Kitchen. He brought down the
house. We were welcomed as entertainers making
the rounds. Fortunately, Sam's ambitions had led us
to while away summer evenings in achieving certain
blends of harmonious effects of the latest rag tunes.
Emboldened by Sam's success, and the fact that the
roughnecks threw coins at Sam's feet, we put our heads
together in the approved quartet fashion and gave a
little concert. We left the place with several beers
inside of us and sixty cents in our pockets. Then Sam
remembered the place he wanted to take us to when
he stumbled into the back room. It was the Five Points
cellar places, where scrubwomen, mostly past middle
age, begrimed, frowsy, boozed up, were available to the
scanty purses of boys. Later, when tips were running
high, Sam introduced us to the fifty-cent houses on
Mott and Elizabeth Streets, where was beginning to de-
velop a large Italian colony. Pimps on the street pulled
at us, dragged us into doorways and cried their drawing card—"imported girlies, young—very young";
that was the attraction. And we found nothing mis-
leading in their advertisement. The girls were young,
very young, ten to fourteen years old, and imported,
imported by Italian padrones, importers of live-stock
only: pleasure girls, boy and girl street musicians,
children acrobats, crippled and deformed children for

[69]

begging; and when such importations were stopped only by the horrors exposed by their own excesses, they became respectable importers of mine and railroad peons. The Elizabeth Street joints were crude and dirty places, and Hymie Rubin, rather sensitive and soft-hearted, turned from them in disgust, saying he minded most the little girls' white, bewildered faces. He offended Sam Rakowsky terribly when he said the little girls made him think of Sam's sisters, of whom Sam had the small number of six. (Some ten years later Hymie married one of Sam's sisters.) Hymie preferred the Five Points scrubs because they were cheap and did not seem to be human beings.

II

"Don't think your education is finished. It has only begun."

In this wise Uncle Philip dampened my jubilant feelings when I brought home a diploma showing that I was a public school graduate. And that is Philip: nothing satisfies him. Yet I, too, should have realized how little my public school education amounted to. I found the school lessons one big cinch. It called for no effort to keep up with the classes that progressed at the pace set by the dozen or so slow pupils in a class of fifty. What we really got was a smattering knowledge on a variety of subjects. One teacher, alone, taught us for a half-year term. She spent five hours a day with fifty restless imps whom she was expected to instruct in everything from arithmetic to zoology. It was a heart-breaking task for the teacher and a dull session for the pupil. It became tiresome to hear day-long the same spiritless voice droning away at dates, sums, platitudes and scolding preachments. Every morning there was an assembly of classes before the principal, Dr. Berne, a gross, red-headed bully of a man, who, after reading a verse from the Scriptures, would fiercely demand excellent conduct, the high ideal of this schoolmaster.

Unruly boys were sent to the principal's office to be summarily dealt with by him. Dr. Berne wore a heavy signet ring on his little finger. The outlines of that ring were cruelly impressed on many boys' faces. But the boys won out in the end. The school had a shock-

[71]

ing number of truants and Dr. Berne's resignation followed upon a nervous breakdown brought on about the time Dago Jack drew a shining stiletto from his shirt and threatened him.

I expected to go to work after graduating from school. Father could not work much. He spent most of his time sitting by the window gasping for air. I knew extra earnings were badly needed, but Uncle Philip decreed City College.

"Don't forget, Meyer, do you hear!" he said, "you're going to be a lawyer."

City College was a shock after the easy snap I had at school. It was altogether different. City College . . . housed in the rusty old chapel on Twenty-third Street; vine-covered, with an air of scholarly detachment; of cloister quiet and dignity. Absent was the tedium of public school. Here we had to keep step with the brisk pace set by the teachers. Backward scholars were dropped by the way. . . . Every hour, with the taking up of a new subject, we marched to a different classroom and enjoyed a refreshing change of personality. There were no soft snaps: each study, directed by a specialized instructor, had to be known thoroughly.

III

The East Side is growing, looming up and spreading out. The small wooden houses with their slanting roofs, the Georgian brick houses with their garrets and the makeshift shop-buildings are being displaced by tall structures, great tenements reared side to side, back to back, with a tiny space between called airshafts, and no sooner are they ready than they are jammed with people. Ground is either sacred or costly. The builders are magicians. The houses spring up, as it were, overnight and the number of rooms per square foot is greater by tenfold. A small area set off by a thin wall of lathe and plaster is a room. And the miracle of paying the rents exacted is accomplished by the number of boarders you can crowd into the so-called rooms. Great big shop buildings are erected to take care of the fast-growing clothing contractors' business. Now we have sweatshops on a larger scale, but work is as scarce as ever. Every day brings its new flock of greenhorns, with little or no money, eager for a job at any pay at all.

I feel keenly responsive to all the flow and activity about me. I am thinking hard of how I am going to fit into it all. I try to be as impressive as I know how with the greenhorns. I like to think people look up to me. As I pass they look after me and I can feel them thinking: there goes Meyer Hirsch. He amounts to something. He is getting on. He carries himself manly, he's tall, got good shoulders, a handsome head and there's lots of brains in that head. How I thrill to it—what people think. I am convinced that is the big thing in life, there is nothing else; you are nothing but what people think you are. . . . The pious say, that's the clever lad who harangued the congregation in Hebrew so eloquently, read the portion of the Law fluently and without a single mistake, and, what's more, he can interpret a page of the Talmud! The worldly say, he's got a practical head, is a school graduate and now is in College: a boy who will get on in this world. The sentimental observe, he's a blessing to his parents, an only child, but such a talented child, a long life to him. . . . If they're not thinking these things, I am thinking them about myself . . . and it gives me a lot of pleasure.

These days I don't often show myself in the company of the Ludlow Streeters. The gang has grown in numbers and has taken a definite character. It is nothing more than a nest of thieves. I was thinking of dropping the gang until I thought out that here was a sizable asset to a young lawyer—a number of potential prisoners at the bar. I looked upon every one of these boastful fools as rich meat and drink for me,—still on the hoof and vine, but mine eventually. . . . Boolkie knew my ambition to be a lawyer. He said it will be a great thing for the gang to have its own mouthpiece. . . . So I keep in touch with their secrets and the tricks they are turning.

Davie Solomon has taken seriously to poetry. His face is melancholy and drawn, and he is like one who walks and yet dreams. He has become a disciple of one Walt Whitman, a sort of freebooter in poetry. This derisive description was applied to this Whitman by our English teacher in City College. I try to talk Davie

out of making a serious vocation of poetry. It doesn't
pay, and his mother, as it is, has a devilish time grinding out a living from her horseradish mill. However,
he may outgrow poetry as he sloughed off religion.
He is an atheist now and makes quite a fuss over it.
His mother is very unhappy about it, and *Melamud*
Mordecai is sure an evil spirit has lodged in him. Love
is Davie's God, and Beauty his handmaiden. He is in
love with Esther Brinn, or he merely uses her as a
target for his poems. Writing a poem to her seems to
satisfy him. . . . And Avrum Toledo talks to Esther
for hours. He, probably, is in love with her, too, and
is quite satisfied as long as she listens to his theories on
life as it-should-be-lived. He is a cross between a
philosophical anarchist and a single-taxing Socialist.
They won't mix, these doctrines, formulae, world-
righting schemes, he is assured by the catholic and
dogmatic discussionists, but Avrum carries on, earnestly, to his intellectual love. . . . I listen to Davie's
poems and Avrum's convolutions, but I find them hard
to bear, even for Esther's sake, for I, too, have my
passion, and it is not poetry or theories. It is just
Getting Something. Esther says, while she understands Davie and Avrum, she finds me a Mystery.

Esther Brinn is a girl of about sixteen whom we all
respect. She is natural. She is not afraid to talk with
boys and it is hard to imagine anyone getting fresh
with her. She has hardly begun to mature, physically,
and was not the kind of a girl to worry me, sexually.
Being a Mystery, she found me interesting. I was a
Mystery to Esther Brinn because her mind was mysti-
cized by the poetic and theoretical slants she got on life
from the Davies and Avrums, who were getting to be

as thick as flies around our way. They pictured a world that wasn't or couldn't be, and I was trying to get something in the world—that is. . . . Esther could not understand my being friends with Boolkie and the regulars, and she took me to task for being fresh with girls. . . . Yet I enjoyed being with Esther. . . . I suppose we egoists liked her because she was a good listener. Today she was but a slight, growing girl. It was a few years later that she sprang out of the chrysalis of the awkward age and dazzled our whole beings with her exquisite beauty, a beauty that tore Davie's heart, rent Avrum's soul and tantalized my every conscious moment. . . . But Davie was the prophet of Esther's beauty, for even now he described her in his poems as she was to be . . . perhaps he saw it now . . . poets are a mystery to me. . . . He saw her face, at any rate: he had no eyes for bodies then. He spoke of her features as having the delicately chiseled outlines of a rare cameo, a cameo shining in the sombre frame of her black hair . . . how her eyes glowed and shadowed like true agate . . . how her face had the pallor of marble in the first light of day. He saw her hands, frail and transparent; when in repose like Chinese lilies, and when moving, like snow-birds' wings aflutter in the moonlight, and heard her voice . . . like the kiss of a zephyr on a silver bell.

I am sure it is Lillie Rosenfeld, the Teaser, who told Esther I was fresh. Lillie is the kind of a girl who deliberately coquettes and then bitterly complains. She belongs to that class of sinners who fool their consciences by playing the rôle of injured innocence.

Lillie is unusual. She comes upon you like a summer sunbeam in a cool, dark room. . . . Golden hair, dark eyebrows, darker lashes, sea-green eyes, a pink and white complexion and luscious red lips have won her the name—French Baby Doll, and her dangerous game of tag earned her the private name—The Teaser. She is hardly older than sixteen, but is already in the high flare of womanhood, plump and well-rounded out. . . . She has a way of tossing her shimmering head, full-opening and then half-shutting her strange eyes,—and you begin to lose your balance,—but it is the undulating curves of her shapely body that make you dizzy. And so she tempts and leads you on. And she flies from you, flies from the public place of the stoop where there is security, flies to the dim recess of the hallway and corners herself under the staircase. Here you become delirious from inhaling a fragrant, ravishing incense, her panting breath near your mouth. . . . But—that is all. . . . She berates you and beats you off and you wake up to witness all the tricks of her stock scene of injured innocence. . . . And after each rebuff I vow, "I'll get you yet, French Baby Doll, you damned Teaser, I'll get you yet." . . . And I am not the only one.

Yetta Uditsky somehow always arrives in time to behold virtue triumphant in the person of Lillie lambasting the villain. The play is so much to her liking and so realistically performed that she jumps from the audience and joins the action, pushing me from the hallway, crying, "Go away, you loafer; I'll tell your father on you." Yetta we call the Queen of Sheba. Hymie Rubin once told her that she is so lovely that even though Solomon had eight hundred wives he would find her irresistible. As a matter of fact, Hymie meant that she was a big, slovenly, overgrown lump of a girl with dirty blonde hair whom no one would care to look upon a second time. Yetta grew up to help make woman suffrage history and lead the girl waist-makers' union to victory. She married a Gentile college professor and wrote the best part of his books on economics. But we thought Yetta an extremely dull girl: I guess because her hair did not shine. No boy bothered her, but she was busy fighting away boys from other girls.

Harry Wotin, Archie's brother, now a heavily serious young man of nineteen and a medical student, has been paying marked attention to Hannah Weingrad, daughter of Jake Weingrad, the fence for boy thieves. Weingrad ordered him to keep away from Hannah, calling him an unpedigreed *schnorrer* (beggar), and said he is onto Harry's game. "You nothing, you; you're looking for a girl to pay your way through college." . . . Besides Weingrad was doing an active business with Archie Wotin, and the respectable synagogue member did not want a thief's brother for son-in-law.

IV

Boolkie comes with bad news. Archie Wotin, Dopie Ikie Schneider and Dago Jack Marinari are under arrest. A little matter of burglary. Boolkie bewails most the loss of Archie the Gun.

"I'm good and sore on Archie," says the bereaved chieftain. "I puts him hep to easy money, makes him the best little dip (pickpocket) in the business, and why don't he stick to it? No, he don't listen to me but he follows that rat-faced sonofagun, Issie Weingrad, who wises him up to a store what they can get into by squeezing Archie through the fanlight, Archie being so skinny and quick with his body. Well, the bulls nailed him and the Dope and the Dago. And now they're going to ride. Aw, if Archie 'd stick to his line, and him as good as any Gun what ever snatched a poke, gee, he'd be a Cannon."

My erstwhile pals took a ride, a ferry-boat ride over the river. Being boys of no importance politically, of no family influence, without money to buy legal talent and bribe policemen, justice was meted out to them with striking swiftness. Such quick shrift was made of the three little nobodies' case that a week later Boolkie dolefully reported that his pals "got a bit in the Ref." . . . The court committed them for an eighteen months' minimum sojourn in the dreaded House of Refuge on Randall's Island.

I was peeved with myself that the gangsters' troubles did not in some way redound to my glory. It started my brain scheming. I began to haunt the en-

[79]

trance to Essex Market Magistrates' Court, the East
Side's police tribunal. . . . It was a busy mill of
agonized humanity. I eavesdropped and was pushed
away. . . . I lingered . . . and hurried away, busily
. . . returned, aimlessly, idly curious . . . but always
watching and listening, avidly . . . till I pieced together conversations, cases, important names, secrets
. . . observed the methods of the artful runners as
they snapped up dazed clients for their lawyer-
employers . . . watched out for the Who's Who of
bigwigs . . . studied the politicians, always smiling,
affable, cordial, handshaking, and after a while I smiled
and nodded and even shook hands with Highmuck-
amucks, for I soon got onto the fact that they did not
know everyone they were so friendly to . . . and I
showed off like a big gun before the ignorant and bewildered relatives of prisoners who waited at the
prison-yard gate. . . . It was here that I met Maxie
Freund, a boy about my own age, in America only two
years, and who also had ambitions leading to the legal
profession. He joined in the game with me . . . would
hurry away, return, whisper in my ear, and then I
would make an important entry in a notebook . . . and
we had a good time being impressive in the eyes of the
foreigners. . . . I tired of the make-believe. I wanted
the real thing. I just itched to get into the courtroom,
which was always jammed. I tried many times to get
in, but Black Riley, the fat cop doorman, barred my
way. So I began to cultivate Black Riley, a huge man,
mainly about the girth and neck, with great black mustaches and bushy eyebrows that compete with mustaches.

"Can I get you something, Captain?" I said, deferentially.

"What can the likes o' you get me, you little sheenie?" he asked.

"Anything you want," I pleaded.

"Very well, there's sumthing you can get me."

"Yes, Captain," I responded eagerly.

"*Get* the hell outa here," he roared.

"Yes, sir," I answered and marched off, only to return a few minutes later.

"And," said he, "did you get it?"

"Yes, Captain, I got it good and plenty"; which amuses him, and while he is busy laughing I walk past him into the courtroom and squeeze in between two women on a bench.

Mine is not a seat of vantage. I am oppressed by heavy elbows, elbows indignant at my sudden, discomforting intrusion. My view is blurred and barred by big round forms, the slow moving, heaving bodies of policemen, lawyers, detectives, and bondsmen. I wish they were not so well fed. . . . My first impression is a confusion of voices, gruff and shrill, harsh and squeaky: outside in the prison yard every little while an angry bell blares, a hoarse voice abuses stamping horses, and ironshod wheels detonate on irregular flagstones; a sharp click, a large steel key unleashes a rasping lock, rusty hinges groan . . . dragging, shuffling, weary footfalls . . . slam-bang, click, rasp, groan, the door of steel bars is flung back into its steel frame and made fast again . . . and prisoners and accusers, manhunters and defenders and prosecutors face the court to pule and whine, plead, denounce, impale, deny, mitigate and exaggerate in tones ranging from a mutter to

[81]

a peroration, and amid the babble and hubbub there comes to me an even, strong voice rising above the torrents of sound like the steady wind above a downpour of rain.

I see nothing but shifting backs. The dominating, leading voice must belong to the judge. He calls the next case. A husky voice cries the name. The attendant guarding the gate to the enclosure of the judge's bench takes up the name in bellowing tone, hurling it to the guard of the prisoners' pen, who shrieks it down a corridor and an affrighted defendant squeaks, "Me . . . me . . . my name." . . . An interminable reading turgid with legal phrases and repetitions . . . larceny . . . larceny. . . . Wherefore. . . . Wherefore . . . larceny . . . more jumbles of wherefores and whereofs. . . . Clothing. . . . Jewelry . . . familiar words . . . at last . . . and they cause a stirring and buzzing in the benches. . . . A woman rises . . . "Yes sir, mine, that's right . . . stole my jewelry. . . ." A gavel bangs. . . . The attendants shout: "Order in the court; keep still; sit down." . . .

A monotonous speaker . . . must be a lawyer . . . says the same thing many times and then ends up by asking for more time. . . . The judge marks the case off . . . an upheaval in the benches . . . protests against delay by accuser and her witnesses . . . a jam in the corridor. . . . "Keep moving; keep moving; hats off until you get out." . . . Protests and apologies, and the aisle is cleared, but in the meantime another case has been called. . . . A hair-pulling match. Two women playing dual rôles of plaintiff and defendant because of counter-charges . . . they lock horns, so to speak, and their children bawl and their respective husbands start a scrap on the sidelines. Both women claim victory and vindication: both have been found guilty and bound over to keep the peace. . . . A lively procession of cases all drowned in words . . . the interest wanes, and suddenly there is an electric murmur in the crowd—ah—a murder case. The most serious charge is disposed of quickest of all. . . . No bail. . . . Grand Jury. . . . Again starts the array of drunks and disorderlies, pushcart cases, assaults, larcenies and burglaries. . . . It is getting dark, the benches begin to clear. At last I get a full view of the judge. He was more impressive when I did not see him. His Honor was a little man with a whiskey-burned face, a completely bald head and the funniest pug nose. His intimates called him Pugsey Kelly from the Fourth Ward.

Maxie Freund awaits me. He marvels at my success in getting into the court and staying there so long. "I got a pull," I tell him, laconically.

A few days later a tearful woman stopped me and told me her husband was arrested for snatching a pocketbook containing seventy-one cents from a woman's hand. She said the charge was unbelievable; that her husband was a sober, steady buttonhole-maker, and she can't for anything understand why they picked on him. Anyway, she said, a thousand times innocent, it does not matter—he is in jail charged with the crime and she doesn't know what to do. It is near the courthouse and several of the runners edge up closer, scenting game in the offing. One of them tries to draw the woman aside, but I put myself in his way, whispering in his ear, "Lay off, I'm taking care of this for Black Riley." . . . He looks me over, and I turn my back on

him. I warn the woman to talk with no one, warn her
to be careful of the men around the courts, telling her
they are nothing more than spies for the police. When
she came to me, I told her, modestly, she was lucky, for
I had a pull with the court. I placed her on the steps
of the courthouse, bidding her to observe me. I stepped
up to Black Riley, begged his ear a moment, saying,
"Can you recommend me to a lawyer? I got a pickpocket case." . . . Riley pats my shoulder, saying,
"You've come to the right man. . . . Take your case
to Moe Levenson; you'll find him across the street in
the Silver Dollar Saloon. Tell him it's my case, and
I looks for my full split. . . . That's right, my boy, in
the back room, and keep me posted what he gets out
of it." . . . I take the woman aside and say, "Well,
it's a serious matter, have no doubt, but my friend, the
boss of the court, will help me out. The first thing to
do is to get the right lawyer, and the right lawyer
always is the personal friend of the judge." My last
remark was the stock in trade bait of the runners. I
didn't miss one of their cues. I guide her into the
back room of the Silver Dollar Saloon and look up Moe
Levenson, whom I find in a private room playing
pinochle. I inform him Black Riley has sent me to him
with a case. He thinks I am in trouble. But I mention, as though it were a long-established fact, that I
and Black Riley are working together. . . . Moe is not
very pleased, he's wondering how his own runner
missed the case.

Levenson talks with the woman, shakes his head
sadly, and says, "Terrible. Terrible. It's going to be
hard. It's going to be hard." The distracted woman
tears at her knotted handkerchief, and grows pale. He

turns to me, saying, "I leave it to you, how can I ask my friend the judge to help me out in a case of this kind, snatching a pocketbook from a woman's hand? Terrible." The woman pleads, able only to repeat one imploring word, "Please, please, please." Levenson strokes the side of his face and remarks, "It's going to cost a lot of money, yeh, a lot of money. . . . How much have you got?" The woman unties her handkerchief and places on the table crumpled bills amounting to twenty-six dollars. Levenson shows her a sorrowfully disappointed face. He says, "That money is nothing." The woman quivers. "Nothing!" she exclaims, "why that's all, every cent, we've got in the world." Levenson rises, absent-mindedly pockets the money, saying, "If you love your husband you will start out at once to beg, borrow or steal money. That's the only thing that will save him from a long term in prison. Remember, we are in America, money works and money talks in America." . . . The woman is thunderstruck. "But he is innocent," she cries. . . . "I know," says Levenson, dryly, "that's what they all say." . . . Levenson takes her in hand and counsels her to go out among her *landsleit* (country people) and make a collection for her husband's defense, tells her to go to relatives, pawn jewelry, sell household furniture, in short, do anything to raise money. . . . Levenson takes me aside and instructs me to stick close to her, not to overlook any good bets and to inspect her home and see what furniture she has. . . . I go home with the woman. The first thing that strikes my eye is a piano. I look at the piano, meaningly. The woman says, "We went without clothes, without many things to save up to buy this piano for our boy. He has talent. . . . It will break his heart to lose the piano . . . but we can't let his father sit in jail for the sake of a piano." She goes out to borrow money and I report back to Levenson. . . . "A piano," he muses, "that's all right, I'll take the piano for a part of the fee, my girl will need a piano pretty soon." Levenson sends me with truckmen to have the piano removed to his home. . . . The following morning Levenson appeared in court as counsel for the accused buttonhole-maker. Without inquiring into the merits of the case, he had it adjourned for a week. During the week that ensued the woman managed to borrow eleven dollars. Levenson again adjourned the case, and the following week he was satisfied that the nine dollars more that the woman brought him was the limit of this particular case's resources. It then turned out that the buttonhole-maker was caught among those running in the street when the stop thief cry was raised. The pocketbook was not found on him when arrested, and when the hearing was finally held the complainant said the buttonhole-maker did not in any wise resemble the man who tore the pocketbook from her hand. He was discharged, and the poor woman, who had spent her last dollar, sacrificed her boy's piano and borrowed from every person she could approach, felt satisfied that money bought her husband's release.

From time to time I picked up a case and brought it to Black Riley, who got his split from Levenson, who gave me a little rake-off. It was now two months since my pals were sentenced to the Ref, and one evening at the bar in the Silver Dollar Saloon I told Black Reilly about their fix. He consulted Levenson. He spoke about a little fixing in the right place, altering records, errors in commitment papers, and then effecting their release on technical writs. It would take a little money. Got to take care of the boys on both ends of the line. Well, a personal case. Three hundred might do it. I told Levenson the sum was even beyond imagining. He replied that it showed I had no imagination. Can't try a case without imagination. He then illustrated imaginative methods in case work.

Levenson said: "First thing to imagine in a case is, who don't want to be mixed up in the particular mess in hand? Next thing to imagine is, how can you mix up that person nice and messy? When your imagination carries you that far, you can imagine the rest. Now here's your case. Three boys. Thieves. Well, they're stealing something, ain't they? Who are they selling that something to? Somebody, no? Somebody's getting fat on their stealings. Easy to see that Somebody don't want a brass band announcing what's going on and he don't want to stop making easy money, and certainly he won't want no criminal charges. Well, Mr. Somebody will pay good to stop the noise, and that's what you call hush *gelt* (money). When you got all you can from Somebody, your imagination keeps on, if it's any good. The three thieves belong to a gang. A lot of pals feel sorry for them. If the pals ain't flush then they can go out to pull off a job to raise the money to get their pals out of trouble."

Levenson's hints fell on fruitful soil. I got right on the job. I talked it over with Boolkie. He shouted, "God damn him, Weingrad ought to put up to get the boys out. He's been getting the gravy out of all their jobs, and his son put them up to their last trick. I'm going in and make that old bum come across." I told

Boolkie to let me handle the matter. I said, apropos
of my teacher, "Boolkie, in these legal affairs you got
to have imagination. Leave it to me." . . . I went to
see Weingrad. I mentioned, after a little talk on many
subjects, that I was working around the courts and
that I had made many friends among the detectives.
I dropped my voice to a hissing whisper, saying,
"Weingrad, be careful. They're working on your
case." . . . His mouth dropped. He ejaculated:
"They! Who, who?" . . . I put up a defensive hand,
"Please," I said, "don't ask me any more." . . .
"Tell me, I beg you," he shouts. . . . I tell Weingrad
that I did not want to be mixed up in a criminal case,
that I had gone far enough in giving him the warning.
I added, "I can't help saying, Weingrad, it looks bad
for you, and you got to do something." . . . By this
time he is quite unnerved. He begs me to find out what
he can do to save himself, and I promise to report that
night. . . . Well, Weingrad was a hard giver-up. It
took three days of screwing him up with fear before
he came across with the necessary three hundred dollars. He did so when he was overwhelmingly convinced
that he and his son were about to be arrested upon the
evidence furnished by the imprisoned boys.

In about ten days Archie, Ikie and Jack returned to
old scenes, pastimes and practices. The gang rejoiced
and fêted them as heroes. I was hailed as a miracle
worker. . . . Maxie Freund has attached himself to
me as a sort of sounding board. He grimaces, winks,
and mysteriously hints that I have a secret tremendous
pull. He plays my game with rare cunning. Maxie is
a master of the art of implying and imputing anything
he may wish to put over without in any way committing

himself to a factual statement. He smells of the sub-
rosa and reeks of the skeleton closet. He irritates
Boolkie by appearing suddenly under his left shoulder.
Thieves hate to have anyone behind them. But Maxie
knows how to assuage him. He whispers, insinuat-
ingly, "I'm with you. I'm with you. It's all right,"
and thereby worries Boolkie that he has complete
knowledge of everything; whereas, he really knows
nothing. But it is a good way of surprising secrets
out of people.

A thief with a jail term to his credit has the standing
of a savant with an honorary degree. Archie now
speaks with sophomoric assurance. He says: "Say,
we're wised up to a lot of stuff now." The gang listens
intently to the wisdom learned in the reform school.
How to "roll a lush" (rob a drunken man), how to
practice the fine points of "stick up" (highway robbery), how to make a "getaway" under varying circumstances, how to "crack" a small safe, "can-
opener" fashion, or blow open a big safe with "soup"
(nitroglycerine), how to "jimmy" doors, drawers and
windows, how to snap a lock, how to use skeleton keys,
where to dispose of "swag" and where to buy burglar's tools, how to "fix" (bribe) cops and judges, and
many other delightful aids to a happy life of crime
and bravado. According to Archie his fellow students
in the reform school were busy planning jobs to pull
off upon their release, tipping each other off and working in concert to outwit the "screws" (keepers). He
recounted glibly the scandals of the menagerie and
told what happens when a number of young animals
are locked up together.

V

Berel and Barney have been teaching each other, swapping a Yiddish lesson for an English one. It is funny to hear them. Barney can't grind out the gutturals and Berel does weird things with the vowel sounds. . . . A gusty November evening. A cold drizzle drives the Discussionists to Berel's warm cellar. . . . Berel lights up the large lamp on the work bench and Barney Finn is revealed hunched up on the sagging couch. . . . Even Lutz laughs to hear Barney Finn, the lanky Irish Yankee, talk the sing-songy Yiddish of Berel's Bessarabia. . . . It doesn't take long for the ball of argument to start rolling. . . . Barney's hobby, Reform Laws, is being kicked about. . . . Legislation is Barney's Savior of Mankind. He would legislate light, air, water, paint, space, sanitary toilets, washtubs and bathtubs into tenement homes; justice for poor prisoners and litigants; clean streets, pavements, parks, playgrounds, libraries, night schools, clubs, nurseries and clinics; and better moral and industrial conditions. . . . He is answered. . . . Laws are futile . . . palliatives, expedients, soon discarded and forgotten . . . makeshifts . . . do not get at the roots of wrongs and evil . . . fine codes of laws existed from the time man became gregarious . . . make people evasive, hypocritical and criminal . . . made by the ruling class and are cruel and one-sided.

They think Barney is squelched, but he is unruffled and answers: "Let me get my laws passed and then I'll tell you whether they're futile."

HAUNCH PAUNCH AND JOWL

Barney says he learned Yiddish and lived in the Ghetto in an effort to understand the Jews. He confesses that the more he gets to know the Jews the more they puzzle him. He can't make them out; so many contradictions and contrasts; no two Jews seem alike. "You know," he confesses, "we outsiders think of the Jews of the world as one type." . . . By the time the Discussionists are done with him he is ready to revise another popular idea he holds, namely, that the Jews are unfailingly clannish, highly unified, and present, consistently, a solid front against the rest of the world.

Philip says, "Barney, you are simple-minded where the Jews are concerned. Solid front—bah! Clannish—puh! Unified—ha, ha! . . . Ask the Tsar's government: they torment and kill Jews, deny them the ordinary rights of education, trade and travel. But who do you think lends millions to the Tsar's government? Who—but the German, English and French Jews. Who lends money to the Roumanian government, which treats its Jews worse than dogs? English Jews, German Jews, Italian Jews."

Abe Lewkowitz, who is working his head off to organize a garment workers' union, adds angrily, "And who sweats and cheats the Jewish workman in America? Jewish contractors, Polish, Russian and Galician Jews."

"Who squeezes the contractors?" demands Philip, injecting his pet prejudice; "who but the German Jews?"

Michel Cahn chimes in, "And who cramps us in stinking, lousy holes and gouges us for big rents, eh, who?—American and German Jews."

HAUNCH PAUNCH AND JOWL

Bennie Finkelstein says, impatiently, "Well, boys, come make your point. The dollar knows no brother."

Simon Gordin rises and takes the floor. His contribution to a discussion is nothing less than a speech. He prefaces all his remarks with a statement that he views all subjects only against their historical background. He starts off in the minor key of a practiced orator and then rises to a crescendo of eloquence.

"I say to you, Barney Finn, would you understand the Jews? Then go out into the world, dwell in each land, and try to understand every people on the face of the earth. Jews are not Jews. They are Germans, Russians, Britons, Italians, Turks, Africans, and so on. They are nationals; narrow, broad, petty, big, noble, greedy, ideal, material, stupid, dull, ignorant, liberal, bigoted, intellectual and enlightened. They are the composite people of the world. They have all the high and low characteristics of the human race. They have the physical stigma of all the peoples of the world. . . . Go back through the ages, see the rush and sweep of conquering armies, Babylonian, Assyrian, Egyptian, Persian, Greek and Roman, bringing rapine's infusion of new blood into the veins of Israel; see the stamp of the conquerors' laws, customs, manners and cultures; see the wide range and horrors of the dispersal, see the excesses visited upon the exiles, the violence of the Crusaders and Inquisitors, all bringing more infusions of new blood. . . . Go out into the Ghetto and look upon the children of the Jews from all lands—and behold the peoples of the world."

VI

The Weingrads prosper. They have moved from the petty retailing of odds and ends to the dignity of the wholesale piece goods business, and comment is being made on their grand style of living since they employ a servant girl. . . . Weingrad's country people find his success as so much bitter vinegar in their teeth. They say, "Look at him—so puffed up. His father was a shoemaker in our village. But yesterday he himself peddled shoe laces and slept on a pushcart in Goldstein's stable." . . . But today, let us talk of today,— the despised shoemaker's daughter-in-law, herself the daughter of a tailor, which calling in the Russian Jewish Pale is next to a shoemaker in lowliness, puts on a magnificent air of a lady of ease as she sits in front of her husband's store. Albeit, the merchant's wife's dress is use-rumpled and stained, the hand-knitted woolen shawl around her hefty shoulders ravelled in many places, and her shoes worked out of shape and run down at the heels; upon her fat fingers and large red ears the blazons of wealth sprinkle, broadcast rosy, blue and icy gleams. Mrs. Weingrad's diamonds light up the drab lives of Essex Street housewives with the fires of vanity and envy; their sparks burn into the vitals of their husbands, who are asked: *"Nu,* when— let us already see when—you will buy me such *knockers* (sparklers) like Mrs. Weingrad's. Oi! Yoi! I think before I see that I will first live to see the Messiah. See you, now, such is the world. A few people have all the luck. Diamonds she has, and now she gets a servant girl. And why should she have all the luck——''

But my eyes are dazzled by the servant girl, Gretel Lipsky, a healthy, buxom greenhorn just off the ship, a sort of thirty-second cousin of the Weingrads. Her wages is her keep and Mrs. Weingrad's cast-off clothing—if the latter ever happens. She is lodged with the Bregsteins in our building because her employers cannot possibly squeeze her into their four-room flat, which is overcrowded with the parents and their six growing children.

I watch for Gretel. Her work begins at the break of day and ends at whatever time the Weingrads decide to go to bed. . . . I am dead gone on Gretel. She does not affect me like Lillie, who grips me only when I see her. As to Gretel, I just can't stop thinking of her. I wait for hours on the stoop to experience the thrilling moment that comes as she demurely slips by. I tremble and titillate like subject metal before a powerful magnet. Her mere passing makes me tingle all over. Blood rushes to my face. My heart pounds. My temples throb and my eyes ache from the concentrated stare I give her. And when she is gone the fire dies out of me, and I become base, inert iron. . . . And I have not said a word to her. I don't know what to say. . . . The rushing wind of desire sweeps the very breath out of me. . . . All I know is I want Gretel. She is for me—life and force; and without her I am lost. . . . I want Gretel, and what I want I must have. . . . Gretel . . . Gretel . . . Gretel. . . . She colors my consciousness with the radiant hues of a gorgeous sunset. . . . I know what I want, I know why I need Gretel so badly. I want her to save me from the menace of my lust. . . . Lately, a few of the fellows were badly burned . . . and I shuddered to think of my body eaten by vile disease. . . . I looked upon the whiteness, symmetry and soundness of my body as a holy thing. And I resolved to stay away from the fouling fires of the burning offal heaps in Elizabeth Street . . . not for my soul's sake, but for my body's. . . . And Gretel is a pure flame. . . .

Gretel is not a beauty in the ordinary sense. Her features are irregular. She has large feet and big hands. Her ample waist rests upon strong hips. Her bosom is full and firm. . . . She is as a young and sturdy tree. . . . Her deep-set eyes are a soft brown, like the color of a tree's bark after the warm rain. Her cheeks are like ripe apples, round and tinted. Her rough-hewn lips pucker provokingly, and her throat is as the ivory tower of the Song of Songs. Her luxuriant hair twines about her head like a thick garland of early sumach leaves.

Tonight I am lucky. Gretel and I meet on the stairs. Her breath whisks past my face like a breeze that has been philandering in lilac bushes. Her skirt flaps against my knees. I stop her. It is dark. I can feel her surprise. My hand rests upon her plump arm. She starts to go, and at last speech gushes from me, passionately.

"Gretel, Gretel . . . you always run away from me. Why? Have I done anything that you should dislike me? . . . Do you know,—night after night I wait and wait but to be near you for that second of your passing? Waiting and watching just for a second's sight of you. Gretel, I have died to talk with you, but there's no talking with you. You hurry away so. And I want to talk with you and tell you——"

I whisper musical Yiddish in her ear. I feel the warm flush of her face, hear her breath coming fast, and know her bust heaves in tumult. . . . She says she cannot understand . . . she cannot believe that I would stoop so low as to be friends with a servant girl . . . particularly, since she is a greenhorn and I, an American college boy. . . . And I tell her how I burn with love of her, and she puts her hand over my mouth, saying it is wrong for her to listen to such talk. . . . So—with time Gretel comes to tryst with me on the stairs, in the hallway, and the sweetest moments are the warm nights on the rooftop in the shadow of a chimney. . . .

VII

Our kitchen is packed with the Discussionists. Boris Udell, the pacifist-nonresistant-evolutionist-vegetarian-Tolstoian, brought his fiddle, no doubt intending to whistle away the stormy parts of the debate. But no tune could rise above tonight's raging topic.

DIE UNIE (the Union).

I am in bed, wondering when it will quiet down and let me fall asleep. Abe Lewkowitz, the ardent unionist, dominates the talk. He is frantically insistent: "We have talked enough. Act now! Act now!" He has raised another slogan that is too pathetic and appealing to be cried down. "A little better living—a little sweetness out of living—raise the standard of living—that's what the union will do for us and our fellow workers." . . . His emotion is respected . . . a moment's lull, just long enough for mother's timid, dry-voiced remark to creep in, "Maybe . . . if there was a union . . . maybe, my husband would be alive today, and not dead from the shop sickness." . . . I forgot to mention that father is dead: moved off like a shadow with the setting sun. Seems to me as though he were always dead. Another brooding shadow has taken his place; mother now sits in his corner.

"Well—aren't we going to try? What? Wait until we are sweated to death?" demands Lewkowitz.

Michel Cahn, the revolutionist, answers him:

"Yes: wait; wait until we are starved and sweated to the goading point, then shall we workers rise, rise like the hunger-driven masses of France, and destroy

[97]

the employing class. Don't prate unionism. Preach revolution. Prepare the workers for the class war. Bah—unionism. What is it—unionism—just a drug—a palliative—just something to sweeten the bitter cup—just something to make life a teeny bit better, just endurable—endurable enough to make the workers put up with wage slavery.''

Boris Ratnofsky, the mildest man in the gathering, is an anarchist. He speaks gently. Gently he describes the horrors of life, the cruelties that prevail, all because governments, institutions, rules, religion, marriage and traditions have imprisoned free expression. The union, he says, will be another hampering of free expression.

''I am for the union,'' breaks in Simon Gordin, the Socialist. ''It will teach the worker the force and logic of parliamentary action, train him to dispose of his problems in an organized, orderly fashion, and, in short, prepare him for Socialism. Socialism is not possible until we have an educated, self-disciplined proletariat.''

Boris Udell opens his mouth to speak, stops and instead tunes up his fiddle.

''That's it, men, tune up, that's what all you elements need—harmony. Play together, men, and each will get what he wants.''

Barney Finn has spoken. Berel is right. He does not bang on one's teapot.

How is it Uncle Philip, rabid Discussionist, has nothing to say? I have been waiting for him to set off verbal fireworks. . . . The unionist is pleading again . . . form a union . . . now . . . on this very spot . . . and still Uncle Philip has nothing to say. . . . ''Brother workers, who will join me?" . . . Lewkowitz's hands tremble as he prepares pencil and paper. . . . "Let me here put down the names of the organization and education committee to start the first garment-makers' union in America——"

"I——"

"Me."

"Put me down."

"And me."

Nonresistant, Socialist, revolutionist and anarchist volunteer in a harmonious chorus.

Now, I thought, Philip will give it to them . . . but, instead he bids them good night, quietly. . . . In the street, under our window, we hear cheers and cries—"Long live the union——" Lewkowitz's voice booms: "Brother workers, be prepared for many defeats. But an inch at a time is enough. Patience is power——"

Barney Finn stays on. . . . He must still expect to hear something interesting from Philip. Then I hear Bennie Finkelstein speak. He is always the silent one. I barely noticed his presence. He is, I suppose, some kind of an "ist," but has not as yet put a label on his views.

Philip shuts the door, saying, "Did you hear them—'Patience is power'—that's the worm's slogan."

Finkelstein says, "Mr. Finn, as we Jews have a way of saying, if you have patience enough you will also live to see the Messiah."

"Barney," says Philip, "you know Finkelstein, but let me introduce you again: this is Benjamin Finkelstein, capitalist."

So—that's the "ist" he is. A capitalist. . . . What in the name of "ists" is a capitalist!

"I should have said," adds Philip, "that tomorrow I and Finkelstein make our beginning as capitalists."

"And the worms," asks Finn, "the worms with the patience, I suppose, they'll fertilize the ground for you. But when your plants are up and growing, the worms, too, will want to eat of the plants."

"And we'll do what is always done with worms: we'll crush them and throw them out of the garden," answers Philip.

Barney Finn laughs his deep-chested laugh. "You're a frank chap, you are."

"And what is there to be ashamed of?" demands Philip. "I feel the earth under me as a hard fact. I see life as a grim truth of dog eat dog, man devour man. I don't see life as a poet's dream. I see that we live as long as we live, and there's nothing else, nothing, after we're done living: so *living* is the thing. I see that all we can get or have is what we can get from the other fellow. That's how the whole scheme of life works. There's nothing self-sustaining. Everything lives off something else. The stronger element absorbs the weaker. The weak lives only to nourish the strong. And that man is strong who believes he is strong: he is strong because he knows there's a world of weaklings to serve him."

I sat up. Philip was so sure and startling in what he was saying that the air seemed to vibrate: or, was it that mother moaned? . . .

Philip strides the room and the floor creaks under his nervous heel-taps; mother clasps and unclasps her hands with a cracking sound; Barney Finn crosses his legs and leans forward, astir with interest. And Finkelstein grins at Finn.

"Barney Finn," begins Philip, "we capitalists (uttered impressively), we who see life, the earth, its forces and elements, just for what they are, are going to organize and control the world. We will be kings of a new order: the empire of efficiency. We will be a driving force as merciless as nature for results. We will be the saviors of the dream-stupefied peoples. We will create industries, markets and wealth——"

Finkelstein interrupts, quaintly, "In short, tomorrow morning at six, Philip Gold and I begin as bosses—manufacturers of clothing. How do you like our firm name—New World Clothing Company?"

"Sounds smart," Finn replies.

"Bosses?" queries mother.

"Yes, your brother from now on is a boss."

"Yes, sister, I'm done being a slave to a machine; others will slave for me now."

"Bosses . . . machines . . . bosses——" mother mutters, ruefully shaking her head.

"Meyer!" Philip calls, "are you asleep?"

"No."

"Did you hear me, Meyer, I—your Uncle Philip is a boss."

There is an irrepressible question in my mind and I blurt it out—"A boss! on *what?*"

"Always practical, always digging into the guts of things: that's Meyer; that shows the shrewd lawyer making in him."

Finkelstein banters: "Looking for trade secrets. Maybe, you can't tell, maybe he wants to be a competitor."

"Meyer," says Philip, "on what? I'll tell you on what. On the backs of workers."

[101]

Mother's hands snap and crack. She cries out: "Only the workers, that's all, only the workers. You're a workman yourself, what do you want of the workers?"

"What did they want of me, what did they want of your husband? All they could get. That's what I want. All I can get!"

Mother's answer is a mournful sigh.

"Oh, what's the matter with you weaklings, you worms! That is the matter, dream-stupefied, you can't see the way life is organized."

Finn coughs. I know he sympathizes with mother. After all he is only a dreamer, whose illusion is that he has a practical cure for all the ills of the world—Reform Laws.

Philip throws back his head and exults: "I found out the secret of wealth. The road to wealth is paved with the backs of workers. I'll climb over those backs, the backs of workers; I'll climb higher and higher up the road to wealth till I reach the seats of the mighty—the German Jews. I take a leaf from the book of these damned nice, superior people, the German Jews: so good, so respectable, so proud: with their vaunted charities and rich temples which make you worms grovel before them. They are the ones who have been grinding you. But you don't want a change of masters. Your present masters are so swell, you're proud of them. . . . To me you say, you're a workman yourself, and what you mean is, worm,—squirm in the dust of your betters. But I am not a worm. I am as smart as the German Jews any time, and I found out the secret of their success. Simple. The quick turnover profits from cheap immigrant labor. Their pious dol-

lars, their charitable, respectable dollars are sweated
from your carcasses. But I'll go them one better. I'll
beat them at their own game. I'm not as elegant as
they are. I'm not veiling myself with hypocrisy. I'm
going to make money direct from the cheapest greenhorn labor I can find. The German Jews are too finicky
to have anything to do with cheap labor—direct. What
they don't see, they don't know of, so they say smugly,
they have nothing to do with sweat labor. They farm
out their work to contractors, and the contractors to
sub-contractors. And the German Jew is a good business man. A good business man makes the most of
competition. So he beats down, screws down the com-
peting contractors. Oh, no, the German Jew garment
magnates do not employ sweat labor. No, the contractors do. . . . That's how I'll beat them. I'll beat
them because I am unashamed, unafraid to face facts.
I'll have no middleman squeezer. I'll do my own driving, squeezing and sweating. I'll corral the poorest
greenhorns as they come through Castle Garden. I'll
work them, feed them and lodge them in my shop. . . .
And they'll be grateful. . . . And I'll work the women
and children in the tenements. They'll come to my
shop and be glad to get work to do at home. They'll
stitch and baste in their homes, and save me shop
space and shop rent, and they'll work for next to nothing, glad to earn a little extra money at home, and,
even so, they'll thank me.''

Mother, as always, awed by her strong-minded
brother, pleads humbly, ''Philip, you're a sweatshop
workman yourself. You see what it does. You saw
my husband sweated drop by drop into his grave——''

"And what would you have me do, eh?" he cuts in, savagely, sneeringly.

"Start a union shop," she says hopelessly.

Philip laughs uproariously, and mother shrinks from him.

"It's a good thing," he says, "this is a free country and I can exploit whom I like."

Finn starts to go, his head lowered, but when he gets to the doorway, looks up and states what he has been thinking. "It's usual to wish a fellow good luck when he starts a new venture. But I can't—for the life of me—wish luck to a sweater and exploiter." His mouth wrinkles into a smile, but his eyes are sad.

Philip sniffs, saying, "Barney Finn, wake up: you are dream-stupefied."

Finkelstein stays on, going over a multitude of details with Philip, and I can't sleep for the crisp click-clack of their talk.

Finally Finkelstein leaves. Mother climbs a chair, winds the wall clock, turns down the lamp and starts for the bedroom. Philip stops her. . . . "I'll tell you, Neshke, it's a good thing I've got the bringing up of your boy, or you'd make a worm of him like his father." . . . Mother bends her head, helpless against his inflexible will. . . . "You made a weakling of your husband—with your damned aching after respectableness. Your father set you a better example. . . ." Mother creeps off to bed. Philip blows out the light, throws himself upon the couch and calls out, "Meyer, respectableness is a lot of rot. . . . Say, did your mother ever tell you your grandfather was a horse thief? Yes, sir, grandfather—my father—may his soul rest in peace—was a clever horse thief." . . . The clock ticks, gloomily, and I guess the muffled sound I hear is mother's moaning. . . . "Meyer . . . in our town was a little boy. He was nobody's child—a doorstep bastard. He grew up and was smart, smart as a bastard, just as the saying goes,—smart as a bastard. . . . He bought stolen horses from grandfather, cornered the local farm products and in time was getting rich. People became jealous and taunted him, saying, 'You're nobody. You have no ancestors.' He said, 'That's all right, I don't need ancestors. I am going to be an ancestor myself.' . . . He's in America now . . . married into a rich, snobbish German Jewish family . . . he's rich and respected, and he'll be quite an ancestor for his children to look back to. . . ."

Philip yawned and turned over with a great crunching of straw and springs.

"Meyer, we've got nothing to look back to. It's up to us to be ancestors."

FOURTH PERIOD

I have unveiled my interior.
JEAN JACQUES ROUSSEAU.

FOURTH PERIOD

I

I wake, flat on my back, open-eyed, harkening to the spirited chirruping of sparrows. . . . After all—even here—even I feel—it is Spring . . . Spring—it means nothing to me, save the new Esther. . . . Yes: Esther's beauty was born with Spring; or, did Spring open my eyes to lovely Esther? . . . Esther. . . . The birds sing of Esther. . . . Last night Esther stood on the stoop. . . . A soft night . . . the air quick with whispers, perfumes and the stir of wings. . . . Davie put in words what we dimly wondered at. . . . And a warm-colored moon came out. . . . Avrum said, "See, the *Schina* shines about your head, Esther." . . . Harry Wotin sits on the bottom step, his hands clasping his head. Is he dreaming of his fat Hannah Weingrad, and her fatter dowry? . . . No: maybe he, too, has found the Spring with her exquisite Esther. . . . Davie murmurs Walt Whitman's "When Lilacs Last in the Door-Yard Bloom'd." . . . Davie and Avrum enshrine Esther. . . . but not I. . . . Last night I saw Esther the Goddess steal down from her pedestal and become flesh of the earth. She stretched out her arms to the moon. And Esther stood revealed to me—Woman for Man. . . . Esther asks Davie to recite his new poem and Davie with his head thrown back, his face aglow in the moonlight, speaks. . . . I sit at Esther's feet and breathe the fresh warmth of her body. I feel her body aquiver with new life. . . . And

she listens with closed eyes . . . opens them once to
look long and deep into my intent, burning eyes . . .
and her hand leaps to her breast. . . . And I think—
Esther, I am nearer to you than this poet and this
dreamer. . . . I know you are a woman and you know
I know. . . . Avrum has said that the new poetry—
Davie's kind—has only one measure,—the measure of
emotion. So I listen to Davie's poem:

> Silence.
> Not of the cloister cell,
> Sunless place of souls enslaved to fixed fear;
>
> Nor of the tomb, stark symbol of formal sorrow,
> Decadent with the dust of tears,
> Foul-sweet with the sighs of expiring flowers;
>
> Nor of the dungeon,
> Charged with clamorous quiet,
> Where swarm the vermin of melancholia;
> And time's a conscious treadmill;
>
> No.
> I mean
> Silence——
> Silence—
> Amidst the world's moil
> The struggle, the clash, the roar, the rush, the
>   lust of money and flesh,
> The silence
> That suspends you in timeless space:
> When first
> Truth flames across your heaven,
> When first
> Beauty is revealed,
> When first
> Love lives.

HAUNCH PAUNCH AND JOWL

A sentient hush. . . . Esther gives Davie a look that stirs him. . . . Avrum grasps his hand in silence. . . . Harry Wotin gets up and looks quizzically at Davie. . . . "A poet," says he, "is a bright-colored weed in a potato patch." . . . Avrum retorts, "As blind as a physician. Medicine is a backward science. It denies the value of imagination. So, it gets nowhere, stands still." . . . Harry says, "No room for dabblers and dreamers in medicine." . . . And Avrum answers, "Oh, Harry, I was hoping you would be different." . . . Harry, looking at Esther, says, "Up in college they knocked the dreams out of me. They have made me clear-eyed. Look at Davie. He takes up room and air and nourishment and gives nothing in return but an empty, flashing picture. Let him do something." . . . Esther speaks softly, "Harry, you are hard. Because you've been hard at it. Working hard to get money for your tuition and at the same time, studying hard. You are out of sympathy with anything else. Nothing seems worth while except medicine. But I tell you, Harry, poets are not weeds, useless parasites. They are very important to us. They are our eyes and ears to beauty." . . . Hymie Rubin comes looking for Harry, who is preparing him for the entrance exams to his medical school. . . . Harry looks about him and waves a contemptuous hand to the moon. He asks, "Why does the poet rejoice with the coming of Spring? Is Summer far away? The Summer here in the Ghetto, in the slum, in the dirty, crowded city. What is there to rejoice over! Where is his imagination, his eye for beauty? Does he see the beautiful babies? What of the Summer that brings hell to our babies? Summer complaint—that is Spring's beautiful promise to our babies. With the heat they'll die like flies. I know it is not beautiful to look ahead and see babies vomit and mess, turn blue with convulsions, become skinny and spavined, yellow and greenish, writhe and moan in distress, and fade and pass away under the eyes of agonized mothers." . . . Esther touches his arm and tells him, "It is beautiful and imaginative to look ahead and try to save them—" . . . Avrum says, "So you doctors think it is only a medical matter when the babies die like flies. I told you you have no imagination. . . . Would the babies get sick and suffer and die if they were not babies of work people living under the conditions of starvation wages? Doctors, infallible scientists that you are, tell me, do dark, hot, filthy tenements make nice Summer habitations for babies? Is cheap can milk and rotting foods—the leftovers of farm and dairy and market which the poor can afford— a healthful diet? Can the babies thrive when their mothers are underfed, run-down, overworked, and haven't even time for the babies? Oh, doctors dears, improve the wage and thereby improve the standard of living, and, presto, the medical miracle will happen, an improved standard of health." . . . Talk. Talk. Talk. And all I can do is look at Esther and desire her. . . . The evening passed in more talk, with Esther listening pensively, never looking at me, though she knows, I am sure, that I can't take my eyes off her. . . . And later I went to the roof where Gretel waited. She did not complain of the long wait. Her arms were ready for me and I found solace in the fiery peace of her embrace. . . . Yet with the kisses of Gretel still hot on my lips, I stole through the alleyway to the backyard of Esther's house, gripped my fingers on the sill of her window, drew myself up, bracing my knees against the bricks, and looked through the half closed shutters of Esther's little room. The moon had gone down behind the houses. It was dark. I could see nothing save an outline that suggested a bed. . . . I hesitated . . . heard a quiet breathing. . . . I dropped to the ground and went to my bed aflame with desire . . . slept feverishly . . . and awoke to the Spring call of the sparrows.

II

It is all settled. Harry is going to be a babies'
doctor, and Hymie a women's doctor—confinement
cases. They will have one office, a practical arrangement for the care of mother and child. Hymie is all
worked up over the idea; he has imbibed Harry's
enthusiasm. . . . He is telling us about it but breaks
off in dismay—"Where the hell am I going to get
tuition, books and everything?" . . . Harry has another year to go. The years of work and study have
told on him frightfully. He looks like a living skeleton.
Somebody once called him all neck. He has been working on knee pants every night till one in the morning
besides attending medical college. Harry says nothing,
he knows it is hell getting the money. . . . Sam Rakowsky says, "Don't worry, Hymie, I got an idea how to
get a lot of jack this summer." . . . Hymie does not
look pleased and makes no response. Sam's ways and
ideas are growing more and more distasteful to him.
Lately, Hymie has been coming under the influence of
the idealistic gang, and has been bitten by the cru-
sader's bug for education and amelioration of the
suffering masses. . . . Simon Adler threw away his
cigarette. . . . "Get a good graft," advises Simon,
who is working his way through Columbia Law School.
Simon has a cute little graft—stealing professors' and
students' overcoats with the help of Boolkie's experts.
Simon doesn't steal, he only spots the lay of the
plunder. . . . Now Sam loves Hymie and considers
his sensibilities. He says, "I got something good. On

the level stuff. And we'll clean up. Got to work it right.'' . . .

Sam has moved up from the messenger boy class nearer to the height of his ambition. He is an usher and fellow of all jobs in Tony Pastor's Variety Theatre on Fourteenth Street. He is smitten more than ever with the song and dance craze. Sam says, ''I got a new step. Regular crackerjack. It's gonna knock 'em dead. . . . I'll show it to you, but I'm waiting for a guy—gotta show it to him—Al Wolff, one wise gazabo. You musta seen him. He's the prize candy box bally-hoo in Miner's teayter.'' Every attendant of Miner's Burlesque Theatre knows the voluble between-the-acts speechmaker who convinces you that every ten-cent box of candy contains a val-oo-able prize soot-able for ladies and gents. Generally the gents found a minia-ture chemise or a tiny pair of unmentionables, and ladies often were lucky enough to find a small piece of shaving soap.

Al Wolff shows up. He is fat-faced and big-bellied. A stogie is stuck in a corner of his mouth and the belching weed is in dangerous proximity to his wide-brimmed western fedora, a head piece favored by show people. He was dressed in what Sam called hot-dog clothes. . . . Sam presents us and Al lets us touch his fat hand as he unctuously confides he is pleased to meetcha. . . . Al says to Sam, ''Do your stuff, kid.'' . . . Sam fishes a harmonica from a pocket and hands it to Al. . . . ''Now, Al, get this idea. I'm gonna come out made up as a Jew—'' . . . ''You don't need no make-up——,'' Simon's voice from the side-line. . . . ''No wise cracks,'' decrees Al with balloon-like omniscience. . . Sam continues: ''Whiskers, a

[115]

derby hat squeezed over my ears, a frock coat——" . . .
Al interrupts, offendedly, "Hey, you said you was
gonna show me new stuff——" . . . "Hold your
horses," admonishes Sam; "then I pulls I few wheezes
about the Irish and the Jews, you know, a couple of
good old Joe Millers for feelers out. Then I wants the
music to begin. Now get this: Al, this is the hard part
for you,—the music—" . . . Al says, "I never saw
the tune that I couldn't beat—" . . . "Well, see what
you can do with this—first an Irish reel, very zippy,
see, and when I am good and warmed up in the middle
of the Irish jig, giving the regular Irish steps, I wants
the music to slip into a Jewish wedding *kazzatzka*
(Russian-Jewish lively dance) with a barrel of snap,
and that's when I'm gonna show them a combination
step that's gonna knock them for a gool. . . . Get this
right, Al, I'm gonna give you the two airs and I'm
gonna show you how to join them up. But the hard
part is the windup—when you gotta get a medley of
the Irish reel and the Russian *kazzatzka*." . . . Sam
hums, beats his hands and feet in time and Al follows,
lamely, with the harmonica, but they keep it up,
patiently, for over an hour until the desired Irish-
Russian-Jewish potpourri is accomplished. The
tremolo and whining strains of the harmonica have
attracted a mixed audience. Mothers with babies in
carriages, a mob of kids pushing and shoving, Boolkie
and a bunch of Ludlow Streeters, Esther, Lillie and
Hannah on the stoop, Gretel looks out of the window,
a few pushcart peddlers have moved their vehicles
nearer the excitement and the Canal Street horse cars
wait while the conductors investigate and report back
to the drivers, and the passengers stick their heads

out of the windows, asking one another what is the matter. . . . Sam is happy . . . an audience! . . . Al looks around him in the masterful way of a leader accustomed to the gaze of mobs. . . . Sam signals, "Let her go—gimme a few bars—to open up, and then start her again and go right through." . . . Sam's dance begins . . . and the audience is noisily appreciative . . . and then came the knock-them-dead climax . . . it almost made us dizzy. Sam's feet don't seem to touch the ground. The windup is acrobatic. He does marvelous bodily contortions on his heels with original, difficult variations of the *kazzatzka* whirligig, and suddenly he leaps into an Irish jig in time with the music and then as suddenly twists himself into wild Russian back-breaking steps that seem impossible to do.

Al orders the mob dispersed. . . . "We gotta talk business," he says. . . . Sam selects Hymie, Davie, and myself to take part in the conference. . . . I lead them to Berel's cellar. . . . Al remarks, "Sam, you got the goods and all you need is a good manager to put you over," and we all knew he meant himself. He already had the flare and bluster and cocksuredness of a burlesque show impressario. . . . Al shakes hands with Berel with the assuring "pleased to meetcha" as he manipulates a stogie from one end of his mouth to the other with his tongue, teeth and lips. . . . Davie wonders what's it all about. Sam has confided to me the great scheme so near his heart. Hymie, who can think only of his career, worries about the possibility of dirty work. He is becoming one of those persons who fuss dreadfully about keeping clean. . . . Al asks Sam: "I suppose this is the balance of your quartet." . . . "Yop," answers Sam, "good talent, every one." . . . Al is skeptical, "You can think so, but they gotta show me—I'm from Miner's." . . . Sam points us out, "Now Davie, here, is my high tenor, got fine falsetto topnotchers; Hymie is comedy barry (baritone), Meyer is bass and I'm straight tenor." . . . Al calls on Hymie to oblige. Hymie is reluctant but yields to importunate Sam. . . . Hymie's was a nasal baritone. . . . Al pronounced it good for comedy stuff, and on the spot bestowed upon him his stage sobriquet— Hi Rube. "You'll come out wearing a sunbonnet with blue ribbons on it tied in big bow under your chin; and you'll carry a carpet-bag. We gotta give you some lines about a poor country girl in a big city. And you'll sing a hot-stuff song—a parody on a pop-oolar song— of what happened to an innercent gal in a wicked town. . . . Let's see you try to talk like a girl. . . . Use your nose, kid; use your nose." . . . Hymie balks. . . . Sam pleads. . . . Al says indignantly, "Don't do me no favors. You ain't the only nose barry in Noo Yawk." . . . Sam says, "Hymie, this is gonna give us work for the whole summer. You'll get enough kale to see you through college." . . . "What do you say, Meyer?" Hymie appeals to me. I advise him to try it out. "If there's money in it we'll stick along, otherwise we'll drop it. It's night work." . . . Al tries us out individually and then as a quartet. He withholds his approval and says we need a whole lot of polishing. . . . Davie submits, wonderingly, but when he learns that Al, our manager, is going to put us to work as singing waiters in a Chinatown dance hall, he flatly refuses. . . . Al gets sore. "Say," he demands in disgust, "you got a crust, bringing me a lot of sissies to do turns in a hell's-bells spielers' parlor." . . . Avrum arrives in time to convince Davie that work he must if he expects to continue college next term. . . . Everyone willing, at last, Al first begins to tell us of the difficulties in our path. We thought the jobs were ours for the taking. . . . Al arranges to sneak us into Miner's and for Sam to pass us into Tony Pastor's so that we may profit from professional excellence. And until summer comes we must rehearse without letup. Then he will arrange for gratis tryouts in back rooms and rathskellers. When the right time comes he will spring the quartet upon Frenchie Lavelle, who runs the largest dance hall in Chinatown. "You gotta be good to get past Frenchie," warns Al. . . . "Just about summer will be the right time: that's when some of his regular singing waiters go down to Coney Island fer big money in Paddy Ryan's joint. Maybe you'll get the jobs, and if you do, you're good for big money." . . . Before he leaves he entitles our "aggregation"—a favorite theatrical description for a variety turn numbering more than two persons—the East Side Four—Entertainers to the Four Hundred. He has designated Hymie as Hi Rube and now names Sam—Sid Raleigh, the human slide trombone; calls Davie—Dan Slater, the angel-voiced tenor, and describes me as Melville Hart, the only basso profundo in captivity. . . . Al amused us with his descriptions and assured us, most convincingly, that under his guidance we would become world-famous performers. Only leave it to him. I am perfectly satisfied so long as Al finds me the money to pay for my first year in law school.

III

Maxie Freund comes awhispering in my ear. He has found a place, downtown, near the courthouse, where second-hand law books are displayed on stalls in front of a book store. He hints they are bargains, great finds, indispensable; grasp the opportunity. It is Maxie's last thought, apparently, that the books be stolen. And he adds, significantly, Boolkie will be glad to get them for me. Boolkie assigns Little Joe and Big Joe, practicing and proficient shoplifters, to fetch me a few sample law books. Maxie seizes the volumes, runs through them with loving fingers and pronounces them highly satisfactory . . . In a short time Maxie and I acquired a considerable law library. . . . Maxie finds a law book fascinating reading and enjoys collecting and indexing what he terms cute little jokers in decisions. He likes cases of hair-splitting, and he can think and talk only in the ponderous jargon of the law. He says he finds law a cinch after the heart-breaking intricacies of the Talmud. Maxie, except for *cheder* studies in Russ-Poland, has never been to school, but every evening, after he leaves work in the shirt factory, grinds away in preparation for the State Regents' examination to earn enough counts to be permitted to take the law exams. When it is slack in the factory he sits through solid sessions of the Supreme Court, enjoying himself more than a boy at a circus. He is all alone in America, and has but one companion, a tomcat, upon whom he practices cross-examination. He tells me the more the cat snarls, backs up, claws and spits, the calmer he grows. After a while his intense, though quiet, unswerving but smooth talk, and a soothing motion of his index finger, sort of mesmermize the cat. . . . He says he is going to be a new kind of a lawyer, a quiet-spoken one, and he has an idea that this quality together with a hypnotizing intentness is going to make him the greatest cross-examiner that ever lived. . . . He suggests that we become partners. That we would make a great combination. I will get the cases, squeeze out every dollar in them, and he will prepare and try the cases. . . . The plan seems a good one.

Now and then I snare a sucker for Moe Levenson and in return for my occasional services he agrees to swear to my Clerkship, which will save me a year in law school.

I see little of Philip. He says nothing to me, except for an occasional sharp warning,—"Keep your nose to your studies." . . . He has no time for words now. He is up at the break of day, and often does not return until midnight. Only a burning ambition could keep him going. His former friends, the Discussionists, have excommunicated him. His shop is reputed to be the worst example of a sweater. And more, he is condemned for having started the system of farming out work to children and women to be done in their homes.

Barney Finn stalks the Ghetto streets like a melancholy Hamlet. . . . I look after him. I have just heard the queer news that he is in the freshman class of the Columbia Law School, his height and age making him quite conspicuous among the youngsters. . . . But I look after Barney Finn curiously. He is in love with Esther. She told me Finn took up law so that he could write his own reform laws and fight the poor's causes in the courts.

I never get much of a chance to be alone with Esther. She is busy taking a course in the Teachers' Training School. In the evening her short stay on the stoop finds her surrounded by girl friends or attended by Davie and Avrum. Lately, Barney Finn has joined the group. I am sure they are all in love with her, and to me they are strange lovers. They don't make love. Davie is inspired by her and his poems are indirect love tenders. Avrum seems to keep in the background, as though he wants to give Davie every opportunity. His act may be called the finest manifestation of unselfish friendship. I felt that virility and positiveness were lacking in Avrum's makeup. I often noticed that good-naturedness is another name for softness and weakness. . . . And Barney Finn looks into Esther's shadowing eyes and talks on hopefully of making a greater America out of the rough new materials from Europe. . . . Esther is their deity, before whose altar they offer their ideals for consecration. She exalts them into high resolve, but I try to reason with her not as a goddess but as a human being. I think idealism is the refuge of the incompetent. The real force of life is too much for them, and they dream of a softer existence. . . .

But I never get a chance to be alone with Esther. I believe that given the time and place alone with a woman she cannot resist me. . . . One Saturday afternoon I saw Esther's parents start strolling towards East Broadway, the Sabbath promenade boulevard of the Ghetto. I waited, and Esther did not follow. I knocked on her door. She opened it and I walked in, closing the door after me. She was too surprised and I acted too quickly for her to stop me. I asked for her father. She said he had just gone out. I stood looking at her. . . . Her beauty was too much for me. I fell to my knees. . . . I was worshipful, too. I adored the woman. She drew back . . . a pulse beat in her throat . . . her hands fluttered to her hair. I hobbled on my knees closer to her and embraced her legs, pressing my head against her knees. . . . Her whisper is terrified—"Meyer—Meyer—what are you doing?" . . . My pressure upon her legs was such that she was forced to kneel in front of me, and I grasped her wrists and talked close to her face. And Esther's kindness was almost her undoing . . . goodness . . . kindness . . . that is, weakness. She talked gently to me . . . her silver-bell-like voice inciting me more . . . I pressed her back on the floor, hanging over her head, speaking with all the passion raging in me. . . . Then I heard voices in the hallway, steps . . . the cautious man of this real world spoke to me—warned me of danger. . . . I let her up. . . . She looked at me wonderingly, even sympathetically, for she was Esther. It was her first experience with the violence of passion. . . .

And I go with my great hunger to Gretel. . . . And I leave her . . . hungrier for Esther. . . .

IV

Moods beset me like a swarm of fleas on a dog. . . .
I think Esther avoids me, loathes me . . . perhaps,
fears me. She is a puritan, and I surprised the woman
in her. Was that a responsive gleam of fire I saw in
her suddenly opened eyes that sought mine and fled
again behind fine screens of lashes? . . . No, no. The
puritan is supreme in her. She is not going to let herself think she is a woman. She prefers to be the
unfleshly ideal of the dream-stupefied blunderers. But
the woman of the earth is there, and I worry that she
favors Avrum, strong, handsome, eloquent and lov-
able. . . . Now I think it is Davie that takes her
womanly fancy, Davie with his curly blonde hair and
hazy blue eyes, a child of a man to ensnare the motherliness of a woman's heart, and I know motherliness
springs from the sex instinct. . . . Again I think it
is Barney Finn that may win her. He has the quiet
charm and repose of a Gentile, qualities that appeal to
the fine and high-strung East Side girl who seeks
escape from vulgarity and overemphasis of ego. . . .
These are the most pertinacious fleas, the gadflies of
jealousy, and they give me no peace. . . . And defeat—
what a terrible itch it leaves. But I deny defeat. Deny
it, but the itch does not let me sleep. . . .

It is Sunday morning. The quartet is rehearsing in
Berel's cellar. I follow along, mechanically. I try to
heed Al Wolff's injunction to zip it up . . . but everything is Esther. She draws me from all things. My
overmastering vanity fills me with hate, and I breathe

"damn her." . . . I remember a look in her face, a
look of pity. Pity—wait—wait, just wait, I will not
even show her pity. Pity is the greatest offense to
pride. And I vow she will yet crawl before me, abject,
begging for crumbs of my love. . . . Al is thundering,
"Bells, bells, bells! G'wan, try it again." . . . The
effect Al wants is of dissimilar toned bells, mingling
resonantly, receding, rising and swelling, and under
the gyrations of his stogie-baton our voices begin to
peal strangely symphonic. . . . Berel smacks his lips
and exclaims, "Such a year on me if it isn't better than
the Kishineff choir. Golden bells. Golden bells." . . .
Al's father, a cantor of renown, taught him the choral
art, but Al deserted the synagogue for the theatre and
became the scandal and grief of his parents' declining
days. . . . Over and over again we do the choruses,
solos, gags, nifties, buck and wing duets, grand ensem-
bles and specialties. . . . Davie makes a suggestion.
Al howls him down. He is witheringly scornful,
"What's that last remark? A few classical ballads?
So long, good-by, I kiss the whole shooting match
good-by. Classical ballads, say, where do you get that
stuff? Do you want to put a crimp in us? There's
only one thing goes in this game,—give the gang what
it wants, and if you want to get by, you gotta be better
than the next guy." . . . Davie inquires, quietly, "Tell
me, if you can, how do we know the people do not want
good music and good poetry, if no one will bring good
music and poetry before them." . . . Al says, "All
right, all right, call it a day. Remember, kiddo, I'm
the manager, and what I says, goes. What you want
to go looking for trouble for? That's what we man-
agers are for—we knows what the public wants and we

gives it to them." . . . Sam consoles Davie that it would be best not to think of trying any highbrow stuff. He says, "They won't get you. Them roughnecks would laugh you in the face and laugh you outta the show." . . . "Say," demands Al, "this is a nice time to come sashaying into the party with any-meeny-my tripe. I got it all fixed for the East Side Four to play a date, Saturday night coming, in the Dutch Village Rathskeller. You'd make a bum outta us with your classical bushwah. Forget it, now, forget it. And you fellers don't quit working out every chance you get. Saturday night is our tryout, and I'm fixing it to have Frenchie Lavelle come and give us the once over."

Sam is agog. The dream of his life begins to merge into realization. But his face turns gloomy. He whispers, "Say, Meyer, what are we gonna do? Al don't know we ain't got the price for makeups. What are we gonna do?" . . . Before I can answer I give myself a number of mental shakeups, tossing about the tormenting fleas, so that I may begin to grapple with Sam's problem. And then I remembered a little plan of my own that would need money. Al liked my idea; in fact, he averred with managerial aplomb, that he had counted on such a scheme himself. I meant to salt the rathskeller audience with a sprinkling of Ludlow Streeters to stimulate applause, and our claque would have to have money for drinks and coins to throw to the entertainers.

Berel greets a newcomer. It is Lewkowitz, the tireless and oft-defeated union organizer, come on an errand of mercy. He offers a pasteboard to Berel. "And, what is it?" asks Berel. Lewkowitz tells him it is a raffle ticket for a gold watch for the benefit of a consumptive union member whom they want to send to Denver. . . . An excellent idea, I think, and I then and there conceive the plan of running a raffle for a non-existent gold watch. It is one thing to run a raffle, but another matter entirely to sell tickets and fail to present the prize to the lucky number holder.

So I wander about, with Sam at my heels, asking his unhappy question, "What are we gonna do?" . . . Davie has hold of my arm and is dilating upon art for the masses. The people will not reject the beautiful, he argues. Avrum comes and relieves me of Davie. And then I come upon Boolkie eating a sandwich. In the shelter of an upturned pushcart a passionate crap game is in progress. Dago Jack is rolling the dice and he prays, "Come, baby, come, be nice to papa." Little Joe says, "Them dice knows who's fadin' you and they'll never, never come to you." The dice roll to a great snapping of fingers, and a disgusted howl advises me that Dago Jack failed to make his point. . . . Boolkie gets my wink signal and saunters off with me. "Now, Boolkie," I begin, "here is a nice, easy way to get a little change for both of us and give the boys a big time Saturday night in the Dutch Village Rathskeller. We are going to run a raffle, see. We print tickets: Raffle for a sick friend. A gold watch to the lucky number. Twenty-five cents a chance. Get the gang to hold up the storekeepers, landlords, standholders and peddlers to buy raffle tickets. They know it's wise to keep on the right side of you. They got to come across with protection money once in a while. Next time we'll run some kind of a racket, a dance or something. Get them in the habit of coming across with protection money." Boolkie likes the idea well enough to make the rounds himself. On the following day I brought him the printed tickets, and in a few hours he disposed of one hundred at twenty-five cents each. We made a fifty-fifty split, Boolkie agreeing to stand treat to favored members of the gang on Saturday night in the Rathskeller. . . .

And Sam and I spent a happy evening bargaining with the Houston Street costume storekeepers for our various makeups. Little Joe accompanied us and stole a fine beard for Sam and a splendid set of mustaches and goatees for me. Little Joe's system of stealing was side-splitting to us. He simply took things right under your eyes. It was so preposterous that no one ever watched or suspected him. He is never from under your eyes, true enough, but the hand, gentlemen, as the sideshow ballyhoo will tell you, is quicker than the eye. Little Joe's gifts were not for long wasted on petty shoplifting. He got a fat job in "Honest John's" gambling house as a dealer. Little Joe's lightning manipulations helped to maintain "Honest John" Brook's high reputation for square dealing.

New York town's vice is always self-conscious, like the bad manners of a growing boy. Its symbol and guiding beacon is the red light, which shines, resplendently, tonight, Saturday, the big pay night, and flush time of Manhattan's pleasure places. There is no pretense or hypocritical disguise, no game of hide and seek of outward order and decency. The lid is off. The town is wide open. The red lamp glowers in the doorway and says, I am sin, and the people drink and sing and love, boastfully, as though to say, See—I sin.

Are you pleasure bent? Look for the color of red. If you are color blind, ask a cabby or a policeman. If

you are not overfinicky, ask a child. Everybody
knows. . . . The Tenderloin is a bright lobster pink.
Allen Street has the hue and smell of a red herring.
Elizabeth Street reeks, blood-red, tart and fulsome like
overdoses of cheap Chianti. And the Five Points'
crimson lamp blinks sickeningly under its mottlings
of mud.

The Dutch Village is a dazzling ruby on the Tenderloin's gory breast. It is an uptown, expensive place,
divided in two parts. Upstairs there is a meretricious
atmosphere of refinement. It goes in for the good taste
trimmings of the day. Pink lights, palms, carpeted
aisles, tablecloths, full dressed waiters and a string
orchestra. Strikingly dressed women, chosen for their
statuesqueness, today's standard of pulchritude, loll
past your table, tinkling their satin petticoats and dif-
fusing heavy perfumes, and ask, quietly and modestly,
if you desire their company. . . . Meanwhile there is a
strumming, politely restrained, by the string orchestra
stuck up on a shelf-like balcony. And then a wind-
broken tenor with an ill-fitting wig and waxed mustaches, and an old soprano desperately painted against
her manifest years and with a remarkably buttressed
figure, together, or individually, cook up an operatic
farrago of overworked and mangled arias made
already unbearably familiar by hurdy-gurdies. . . .
But downstairs in the Rathskeller it is different. Here
there are no carpets or tablecloths. It has a rough
and ready, good-fellow, you're-welcome-any-way-you-
come air. Instead of tenors, sopranos, and a dulcet
string orchestra, we have roof-reverberating coon
shouters and a whiz-bang ragtime band, made up of a
piano, fiddle and drum, mostly drum. The girls who

[129]

seek your company are not so toney, and their style not so spiffy, but their manner is cordial and naturally New-Yorkese. They sit down at your table, give or receive a quip, and if not wanted, move along to the next one. Here you have an intimate good time, and you may stay as long as your money lasts. The Dutch Village never closes.

Al times our début for the midnight hour. He wants a well-filled place and an audience that has become mellowly convivial. . . . He points out Frenchie Lavelle, sitting in a corner, and we look at the huge man with a saturnine face, whose eyes seem scratched out by crows' feet. . . . "Don't play to him," Al advises; "it won't do no good. Frenchie looks for one thing—the way you hit the mob. Now g'wan and hit 'em for a bull's-eye."

The drummer beats a prolonged roll call. Al mounts the performers' platform. He is recognized. Every patron of Miner's knows him. . . . "What are you giving away tonight?" . . . "A prize in every package." . . . "Only a dime, the tenth part of a dollar." . . . Al's fat face creases in happy smiles at the good-natured sallies. . . . "Do your stuff, kid." . . . Al motions the drummer and he beats again a roll call, and Al begins, "Ladies an' gents——" A cat-call. An exaggerated sneeze. A mock baby-crying. Al puts up a tolerant hand against the familiar friendly buffoonery. . . . Cries of "give him a chance" spurt out here and there, mostly from planted Ludlow Streeters. "He's good." . . . Al launches into his speech, his voice carrying above an occasional interruption.

"Ladies an' gents, I'm gonna take a few minutes of

your time." . . . "It's all right, long as you don't take our watches." . . . "He can do that, too." . . . "Take a year off." . . . "I hope the judge gives him ten years." . . . "On bee-have of the manigment, I takes pleasure in arnouncing a brand new fee-ture for tonight's entertainment, an added attrackshun, which they has got at great expense, and will be shown to the public for the first time anywhere. I takes pleasure in arnouncing the East Side Four, kwartet, buck an' wing and comedy artists, introducing numberous nowelties, all bein' under the pursonel direckshun of A. Wolff, Esquire. Ladies an' gents, I now calls upon the East Side Four, entertainers to the Four Hundred, to show you their stuff." . . . We filed to the platform, and Al identified us, individually, by our stage names. . . . Applause broke out, no doubt started by our claque, and then it became general. Everybody was in good spirits.

Al took the piano and played the introductory bars of Sam's medley song and dance. To the onlookers' delight, Sam put on his makeup right out front. It was something new. As he put on his beard and frock coat, and squeezed down the squat derby over his ears, he kept up a rapid fire of familiar Irish-Jewish wheezes, connected up in a story, to which Al tinkled an accompaniment. Then Sam began the dance, saying, "Now watch the national dance of New York. Irish-Jewish." . . . Loud applause. . . . The difficult dance, with its weird intermixture of Irish reel and Yiddish *kazzatzka,* brought down the house, and there were long calls of "do it again, kid." . . . The comment ran, generally, "It's hot stuff." To give Sam a chance to catch his breath, the quartet sang the chorus of

HAUNCH PAUNCH AND JOWL

"Paddy Reilly Does the Jewish Wedding Dance,"
music by Sam Rakowsky, words by Al Wolff. . . . Big
applause. Our quartet was really well trained and
capably blended, and the effect of bells impressed our
hearers, for New York was at this time quartet
crazy. . . . The drummer and fiddler caught the easy
tune, really nothing more than the familiar Irish reel
melody and Jewish wedding music, rearranged and
joined. Sam did his dance again, and by the time he
started the back-breaking heel dance the audience broke
out in surprised enthusiastic applause. Then Al played
an introduction that called for Davie's appearance.
He had no makeup on, but his wan beauty and ethereal
expression brought cries of "Oh sister, does mamma
know you're out tonight?" . . . "Hoo, La, La." . . .
"Sweet baby." "Cut the comedy." . . . "Give him
a chanst." . . . Davie began to sing. His pure-toned,
deep and richly sweet voice hushed the crowd. He sang
a sentimental ballad, a mother song, full of flourishes
that music hall gods doted on, into which he put tenderness and appeal, and when his voice broke in sobs during the pathetic finale—one of Al's touches—the house
went wild. The quartet took up the chorus, trying several of Al's shadings, and the resultant table rappings
and feet poundings attested to our success. . . . Hi
Rube almost gave the bunch hysterics when he
appeared in a sunbonnet and a wrapper that showed
his pants legs. He carried a carpet bag. His mincing
steps and squeaky voice were well done. He sang an
original bit of thing that couldn't bear repeating even
in a frank book. I was the author of the words, which
I fitted to a popular tune of the day. The title of the
song was, "Something Tells Me If It Happened Once

[132]

It Will Happen Again." And Hymie made his narration so woeful that he achieved high comedy results. And under Al's tutelage, he got down among the audience, and went from table to table, and spoke the lines to music, "Won't you tell me, please, I'm only a country gal in a big city, if it happened once, will it happen again?" . . . Bringing the audience into the show was an example of Al's craftsmanship. It was the beginning of that kind of entertainment in New York. I had no specialty number. My voice was used only for bass effects in the quartet. They made quite a fuss over us. Coins dropped at our feet, especially during Davie's second song, "Mother's Broken Heart." . . . We were treated to drinks, and at last Frenchie gave the good word to Al. And we jumped for joy. We were engaged as regular singing waiters beginning Monday night.

While the regular coon-shouters did their turns we mingled with the audience and worked for the house. Working for the house means ordering expensive drinks whenever we were treated. Sam and Hymie were quite drunk and by the time dawn came they had to be put behind the piano to sleep it off. Al stuck to beer and was always himself. We now knew the secret of his being able to get us a date to play the Dutch Village Rathskeller. Mazie Lou, premier coon-shouter, was stuck on him. And in this little world of abandon when a woman loves you she shows it in an exaggerated way. We think it is exaggerated. It is rather the metier of their morals. Mazie Lou, a little drunk now, kept asking everyone, looking ecstatically at Beefy Al, moist and bedewed with sweat, "Ain't he grand! Ain't he grand! Ain't he got the grandest act you ever seen!" . . . There was a girl wandering about the

place and she reminded me of Esther. It was more
striking when I saw that she had taken a decided fancy
to Davie. This girl was called Billie. She had turned
down a number of invitations for the night, and just
hovered around Davie. Her resemblance to Esther
inflamed my jealousy against Davie. But Davie was
dazed in these surroundings, and a bottle of wine he
had drunk made him star-eyed and moodily uplifted.
He barely noticed Billie. She was a great favorite and
had an Irish temper. She got it into her head that
Davie was studiously ignoring and insulting her. In a
rage she slapped his face. A glass rolled off the table
and splintered on the floor. The piano stopped. A
drunken hush fell over the place. It was the drifting
dawn time, when even noisy revellers begin to whisper.
Davie rose and held out his hand, and asked pleadingly,
"What have I done——?" . . . Billie flung herself to
her knees. "I didn't mean it. . . . I couldn't help
it. . . . I've gone crazy listening to your golden
voice." . . . Davie helped her up, placed her in a chair
and sat down beside her. . . . The comment ran that
Billie had gone nuts again. There was a little gossip
that she came of good people . . . that some day she
would get hers . . . too much temper and independ-
ence for a street walker . . . and, besides, she did not
have the protection of a pimp . . . and she wasn't a
regular feller. . . . The other girls made nasty remarks about her. They were jealous of her distinctive
good looks and refined bearing . . . most of all they
resented that the better class of frequenters, the good
spenders, all tried to pick up Billie. . . . Billie was the
first choice. . . . Boolkie was ponderously intoxicated.
He had tried to make Billie, and I guess he was pretty

sore at her. He waddled over to her and asked her what she meant by hauling off and slapping a friend of his. He said he had a good mind to squash in her face for her. Billie opened her handbag and took out a small-barreled revolver, and said, "Go ahead and try it, you big bully." . . . Davie was distressed. He begged for peace, said it was nothing, and Boolkie retired in face of the revolver, saying, to save his face, "It's all right, 's long as my friend says so." . . . I watched to see what would happen to the pure idealist in the hands of an infatuated harlot. Davie was drinking another bottle of wine. Billie was sipping iced absinthe. She took another, while Davie mooned over his second glass. And Billie now gulped down an absinthe plain. The ivory pallor of her face deepened. Her slender, long-fingered hands moved restlessly, erratically across the table. She asked Davie to sing. The wine had gone to his head. He sang "Drink to Me Only With Thine Eyes," and the audience wanted to know what the hell he was pulling off, though they were charmed by the feeling and beauty of his voice. Billie seemed lost in a rapturous trance, and her slate-gray eyes filled with tears. . . . And Davie sang again, wonder of wonders, a Schubert love song, which made the audience go wild with enthusiasm. . . . Al said that the audience was drunk enough to like anything once they liked you when they were sober. . . . And Billie drank absinthe. . . . The other girls said, "Look out for her when she hits that stuff hard. She goes nuts." . . . I took my whiskey straight, like grandfather-horse-thief. I found it made me morose and thoughtful. I took the liquor thinking that maybe it would cheer me up, but instead thoughts of Esther kept shooting through my brain like red-hot needles. And there was Billie to remind me of her. . . . I took a seat at Davie's table. He was either frightfully innocent or deliciously drunk. He was reciting Walt Whitman to Billie, who listened with an intense face, showing intense absorption or intense bewilderment. . . . And Davie was explaining Walt Whitman to her. He told her Whitman loved all people, and because he loved them he could understand them and reach their soul-beings. She asked, "And do you think he could understand me—me—and love me and see the soul of me——" . . . And then Davie, whom I thought but a baby of the world, spoke to her Whitman's lines addressed to a street walker for an appointment. . . . And Billie drank her absinthe, and I swallowed the raw booze, while Davie spoke of the poet he was going to be. . . . "I have been precocious, but I shall lose all that as I get to know and love people. I shall get the swing and measure of life. I will move like the swell of the sea, I will fly on the wings of emotion, I will pant with the consumptive, swelter and pine with the prisoner in his cell, I will agonize on the wheel of industry, I will reel with the drunken man, drunk with his despair or his joy, I will thrill with the mother who suckles her babe and the father who looks on, I will walk the streets with the homeless, the pariahs and wantons and love them and be with them, I will sing their song, their lilt, their pæan, their dirge; my beat will be the beat of their hearts, the beat of their tired and halt steps, the pulse of their wrongs and angers and passions——"

Now is the sodden hour. The waiters are busy with their own breakfasts. Henry Meckelheimer, the proprietor, comes to look over the cash receipts. It is morning. The air clears. A young girl's voice calls out—"Papa." . . . Meckelheimer answers, "Here I am, downstairs." . . . A flaxen-haired girl appears, fresh-eyed, and brisk. It is Henrietta Meckelheimer. I look at her, wondering how a morning glory grows in a garbage can. The Meckelheimers have an apartment over the Dutch Village. . . . But I saw Henrietta Meckelheimer again—twenty years later. She was brought before me, and I sat in judgment upon her. She was convicted of robbing a man in a panel game. She was friendless, without home or money, and a hopeless morphine addict. I sent her to State's Prison. . . . They started to mop the floors and we roused up Hymie and Sam. We squeezed them into a hansom cab, and followed in a barouche. Billie watched us leave, and when the barouche started off she called out, "So long, boys, I'll see you down Frenchie Lavelle's place."

I remarked to Davie, "She is coming to see you—no one else." And the gadflies of jealousy tormented me. . . . Davie answered, "I think she enjoys our work. . . . I will be glad to see her. . . . Ah . . . look, Meyer—Homer wasn't the only one to see the rosy-fingered dawn." . . . The barouche swung into Sixth Avenue and there the dawn died.

V

Monday morning Al leads the way down the Bowery, past the succession of saloons, bedhouses, two-cent coffee places, second-hand clothing stores, oyster stands, rescue missions, and second-hand shoe cellars. . . . Underfoot it is slippery with chew-tobacco juice. Everybody is busy spitting. The old-timers, the right-at-home bums sun themselves in the doorways of lodging houses and at the corners. Panhandlers look for live ones. Fake cripples and blind men, offering pencils or shoe laces, whine for pennies. One drunk mutters, another speechifies, one sings or curses, and another lies prone in everybody's way and nobody pays him the least notice. Sailors, stevedores, oilers, stokers, firemen, hobos and street walkers crowd the sidewalks. Country boys, threadbare and hungry-eyed, fortune seekers stranded in the big city, and tired-looking, jobless men from everywhere, wander in this land of the down and out. . . . Here is the city's backwash of sewerage. . . . Into Park Row, continuation of the Bowery, at Doyers Street, where Chinatown begins, is Frenchie Lavelle's bar-room and dance hall.

It is too early for Frenchie. His barkeep expects us and admits us to the dance hall. It is cavernously dark, except for one light, a blue and yellow gas jet at the farther end over a piano. We see a creased bald head with uneven fringes of white hair bending over the piano keys. A full glass of whiskey stands on the music rest. The head is motionless. Hands creep soundlessly, searchingly across the keyboard. . . . A few notes, aimless; and again silence. The door shuts behind us. Music begins. . . . Al whispers, "Wait a minute. He don't know nobody is here; that's when he plays like you never heard anybody play. . . . God— how that man can play." . . . Davie whispers, "He is improvising." . . . The music: drops of water upon a still pool; fugitive themes, alighting, fleeing; crashing gusts of despair, anger, protest; fantastic humors; shifting moods, cold, harsh, bitter, abandoned; and again drops of water on a still pool. . . . Davie is moved. He says, "I know what he is doing: he is thinking in music." . . . The barkeep comes in carrying a glass of whiskey. "A little oil for the music box," he remarks. We follow him to the piano. The old man drinks up the whiskey before him and the barkeep places the full glass on the music rest. . . . So this is the marvelous "Piano" O'Brien whose playing Al cannot praise enough. He never uses music. Whiskey is his score, and he won't play unless the whiskey is before him.

Piano O'Brien rises, gives us a gallant bow and says, "Good morning, gentlemen. I have been expecting you." . . . Al shakes his hand and introduces us. . . . And that evening we began as singing waiters.

The art of a singing waiter is in a class by itself. It consists of carrying a song over a multitude of busy doings, remarks, orders, servings, making change and cleaning tables, all done during the song. Occasionally you interrupt the song to sing out the order, and then you must immediately take up the last word and note where you left off. Try singing in a changing crowd—

HAUNCH PAUNCH AND JOWL

" 'I loved you, Nellie'—'Draw two!'—'as I never'—'Make it two more!'—'loved before.' " . . . During the heartrending moments of the piece you may have to make change for a two-dollar bill and reckon up the amount due, put down the change, receive your tip, move to the next table, mop its surface dry, remove empty glasses on a tray, call at the little door for your ordered drinks, pass out the right brass tags to the checker, show people to the tables, smile to known frequenters, laugh at a friendly gibe and stoop to pick up a coin thrown as a compliment to your vocal efforts. And then when the second chorus is reached, the four of us, no matter how far apart we may be, do our quartet stunts.

Piano O'Brien's deft signals holds us in key, time and place. He is more than an accompanist. He is our guiding genius, attending our every move with telepathic accord. And so he sits the whole night, slightly stooped, at the piano, accompanying the singers, playing a vagrant, restful interlude, or joining the fiddler, cornetist and drummer in banging out the dance music of the day. And his eyes seem drowned in the eternal well of whiskey on the music rest. He appears as tireless and detached as an automaton. He is a pale-faced drunkard, as though the very blood in him has turned into high-proof spirits. . . . Drunk unceasingly for many years, yet he is never the drunken man. His repose is deathlike, but gruesome in the midst of life. His eyes are like small clams congealed in alcohol. He has thin lips that compress into a purple straight line. His skin, drawn taut over forehead, cheek bones and jaw bone, seems petrified. His hands, only, seem limber and living, but the hands become as part of the piano. To the world he has no personality or being or self except as the thing of the piano. So he is known as Piano O'Brien. His secrets seem hidden behind the glaze of his eyes. No man knows his history. A word, a whisper here and there, has had it that he is an unfrocked Jesuit. . . . But Davie Solomon evoked glimmerings of the man he may have once been. He found sympathy in Davie, and it unsealed the years of silence. . . . Once he spoke in Hebrew, a scholarly, meticulous Hebrew. . . . Hymie, always curious, saluted him in Latin. And O'Brien let us listen to a Latin parable as crisp and clear as the new pages of a classic. . . . Maxie Freund, who sometimes came with me to rehearsals and who regarded Latin as the holy tongue of law, turned some of the rehearsals into a Latin lyceum. O'Brien was a happy teacher. Maxie said he was better than a thousand text-books. And then Sam, who until now had hobbled across a pianoforte with two heavy fingers, learned to use all his fingers under O'Brien's instructions.

The world comes to Lavelle's—a world of men.

The East Side and West Side, uptown and downtown, drift in, singly, and in merry batches . . . curious lads, feeling adventurously grown up . . . young men with cigarettes dangling from their lips, careless-mannered, desperately affecting the nonchalance of rakes . . . little cliques of married men, thrillingly frisky and wicked with the matrimonial yoke cast off for a night . . . old men seeking youth at the fountain of folly . . . clean-faced college boys furiously living "the life" . . . swaggering gunmen, guerrillas and gangsters who give the place a tone . . . chummy groups of sailor boys and marines after a long practice

cruise with faces as free and fresh as the open sea,
consciously on a hell-raising shore leave . . . race
track hangers-on and touts and jockeys in loud-
patterned clothes . . . seafaring men picturing
the nations of the world, flush with back-pay and
pent up desire . . . pimps aflash with jewelry
and nobby clothes . . . puffed up one-horse politicians . . . cheap gamblers, loaded dice and cold deck
artists . . . cappers . . . sneak thieves, hold-up and
second-story men . . . husky yeggs . . . roving panhandlers . . . kerosene circuit actors . . . dope peddlers . . . steerers to gambling and bawdy houses . . .
flitting, temperamental fairies, the queer effeminate
men . . . slumming parties, distinguished by their full
dress . . . a world of men.

Of course, the main attraction is the girls, who
wind in and out the table spaces like a garland of
strangely strung and varied flowers. The garland has
dragged in the dust of many roads. . . . But flowers
are flowers . . . what if they are rumpled and faded,
soiled and drooping with rough handling . . . anyway
there is left the suggestion of fragrance and charm
and beauty . . . but they are not the posies they once
were. Now they are downtown flowers—who came
Chinatown way after being discarded by uptown. . . .
Tenderloin gets the fresh-cut flowers . . . later the
gutter wash drifts them down to Fourteenth Street,
and then the changing tide flings them on to the mud
flats of the Bowery and Lavelle's, where they stay until
dumped into the garbage cans of Five Points, Mulberry
Bend and the waterfront back rooms. . . . The trench
in Potter's Field is the last stop.

Lavelle's is better than street-walking. The bright

lights, music, drinks, songs and jollity of good-time crowds help them forget that they are on their way to the dump heaps. . . . And now this life takes on the sameness of the factory and department store life they gave up because it was dull and drab and always the same . . . this unending, inescapable sameness becomes the horror that may be forgotten with dope and booze's specious aid. Desperate people know how to be hilariously, extravagantly happy. And the place rings with their high-pitched, desperate merriment. They shriek over our smutty songs, our double-meaning gags; weep over our sentimental ballads; drink deeply, chatter and smoke without letup; dance with vim and abandon and march off with their snared john to a filthy bedhouse with the gayety of a schoolgirl off to a picnic. . . . Their incessant smile, ringing laugh, good cheer, sparkling eyes, what are they but the habits of their workaday life? . . . But Davie says they are sparks from their souls to light the world . . . that they are the stars of dark desire. . . . "Whatever that may mean," I put in slurringly. "Let me tell you what I mean," persists Davie, "I mean it is the soul force ever working to exalt all human conduct." . . .

O'Brien hears Davie and asks him, "Who are you— what are you that you love and excuse everyone?" . . .

"I learned comradeship, understanding from Walt Whitman, love from Jesus and forgiveness from Tolstoi." . . .

O'Brien ruminates on the piano keys . . . fitful thoughts . . . again he is as one alone in a dark forest and listens to drops of water on a still pool. . . . He murmurs, "You Jews—how many Christs are among you?——" . . . Sam frowns at such heresy. Hymie muses and smiles. He has told me that since he became a freethinker he feels a thousand pounds lighter. . . . Davie smiles, saying, "I hope—no more Christs. Christ was a dreamer, but without strength and sanity. Adoration of a superstitious mob turned his head; he succumbed to the hypnotism of their belief that he sprang from the godhead." . . . O'Brien rises, leaning against the piano, as though falling back, and he hears Davie remark in the most matter of fact tone, "The hope of a better world is in the destruction of the god-delusion."

It is the petering out hour, morning. The lights have been put out except for the one over the piano. Here and there a drunken boy or man has fallen asleep over the tables. An old Chinese woman with a wizened face and a childish form comes and stands meekly near the piano. She is O'Brien's wife, punctually arriving every morning to lead her husband home. O'Brien is nearly blind. Davie bows to her, and she jerkily bends her body. The scraping of a chair, quick catlike treads and Billie appears under the arc of gas light. She has come every morning for a month. Her eyes are like stars in a fog, and her face has the radiant whiteness of sun-filtered morning mist.

As Davie speaks, I think I hear his master, Avrum Toledo. . . . "Destroy the god-delusion. Then we won't have a supreme being to blame, appease, and look to. God's will—there's the answer to war and horror, disease and suffering, injustice and tyranny. God's will. Accept all in God's name in God's world, the best world of all possible worlds. Yield. Submit. We go on living in an ugly world of hate and pain and grief, comforting ourselves in a vision of a God's hereafter. Destroy the god-delusion, and man will account to himself." . . .

Billie steps forward. She has not listened. She asks the question she has put every morning, "Dave, are you going home with me?" . . . The question always makes me laugh inwardly. Everybody has a home. Even Billie, the temperamental street-walker. Her home, most likely the barest kind of a furnished room somewhere in Hell's Kitchen. And every morning Davie answers, kindly, patiently, "My mother, Billie, I can't leave my mother." . . . Now she asks, "Are you on the level, you tin-Jesus; are you on the level, or are you just stringing me?" . . . Davie laughs, gently, and moves close to Billie. She looks up into his face, and her eyelids flutter. Her hands are clutched at her breasts. I can see nothing else in her except the heightened lust of a depraved creature for a pure thing. But Davie, although he has rid himself of the god-delusion, has replaced it, as we always do, with another delusion. No matter what happens to the body, the soul force remains untainted. . . . Davie took Billie in his arms and said, "Believe me, Billie, I love you." . . . It was very simple. Davie loved Billie because she needed him. . . . Billie flung her arms around his neck, whispering passionately, "Try me, Dave, I'd do anything for you. Try me, Dave." . . .

VI

Ragtime has the whole country jogging. From the World's Fair in Chicago it sent syncopated waves bounding across the length and breadth of the land. The negroes had given America its music. Soon the white man started stealing the negro's music and making it his own. There was money in the negro's music. Cultured people snickered at it. Boston, which at this time still claimed to be the center of culture, stuffed its ears. Musicians, who ruled and confined their art with religious dogma, raised their hands and voices in horror and denunciation. The élite, the elect, the polite, the ultra-fashionable, and their aping followers, despised ragtime and complacently decreed its early doom. But ragtime had the vitality of a people's music and the whole country hummed, sang, whistled, two-stepped and cried for more doggerels and maddening tunes.

The ragtime craze helped to fill Lavelle's every night. I took pains to let Lavelle know that it was the superior work of the quartet with its many improvements and innovations that had made Lavelle's usually dull season the busiest he had ever known. Slumming parties of full-dressed men and evening-gowned women came regularly in greater numbers, and they were welcome as big spenders. At my suggestion Lavelle printed a special wine list with higher prices for their benefit. It was about this time that Al and I took over the management of the place on a percentage basis. Al took care of entertainment and I had charge of general matters.

HAUNCH PAUNCH AND JOWL

Al added a trombone to the dance orchestra. He made every musician a performer. He showed the drummer how to throw his stick in the air and catch it without losing a beat. He made the cornetist go through contortions while playing, and taught him the trick of over-riding cacophony. He got interesting effects by making the cornetist hold a derby hat at the end of his horn, and got bizarre blare effects by placing glazed paper over the end of the trombone. The fiddler had to imitate the famous Rigo, a gypsy violinist. He made him wear a crazy wig and a short red plush jacket. O'Brien heightened the tempo and suddenly slowed it, surprising and delighting the dancers. This kind of music started a new kind of dancing. Al introduced the Bowery Wriggle, a dance perfectly suited to the eccentric rhythm. It was the father and forerunner of the Turkey Trot and modern dancing. Often Al led the band, making the players a part of the hilarious dance. Until then dancing was done with the feet. We started the dance of the body as a thrill for the sightseers, and, to continue to draw them, we made the dances more and more animalistic. Al picked up Ivan Orloff, a down-and-out straggler on the Bowery, who had been a pupil of the St. Petersburg school of the ballet. He trained Orloff and Billie, a sinuous and graceful dancer, to give exhibition dances of the Bowery Wriggle. Before long everybody was doing the Wriggle. Militant clergymen, sensationalists who called themselves sociologists, who visited our place, instituted a campaign of sermons against Lavelle's, describing it as the modern Sodom and Gomorrah. They succeeded in advertising our place extensively among their congregations and in the newspapers and we soon got fat returns from their attacks.

Al and Sam were busy creating original ragtime songs and dances. O'Brien encouraged them, saying its flexibility offered infinite possibilities. He urged them to make use of the negro plantation, levee and spiritual songs with their pulsating African rhythm and ornament them with Semitic colors and figures. . . . Davie said that the boys ought to try for originality. O'Brien said there was nothing original in music. Man understood only a few sounds. He sneered at musisians' technical flourishes and intricacies, declaring it was not music but rather a limited parlor game. A melody, a tune, was music; nothing else. And all musical writings were differentiations of the few tunes known to man. He sketched the history of music. He took as an example church music. He jokingly referred to the musical reformer, Palestrina, the sixteenth century choirmaster and composer for the Pope, and declared his grand and solemn church music was nothing more than lewd tavern songs and troubadour chanties rearranged to meet the Sistine Chapel's needs. . . . It sounded unbelievable. Davie asked, "Do you mean he could make a solemn mass cantata of such a song as Sweet Rosie O'Grady?" . . . We laughed. What could be more ridiculous? Sweet Rosie O'Grady, the simplest little love song that somehow had the widest popular appeal. It had a nursery and sugary refrain. . . . O'Brien did not reply. Instead he played Sweet Rosie O'Grady as it is usually played. Then he began to weave its strains until there was left only a remote suggestion, an elusive reminiscence of the hackneyed tune. He stopped and Hymie took down a Latin translation of the words as

O'Brien dictated. . . . Latin words to music that rang magnificently sacerdotal. We caught O'Brien's idea. Al said it was great stuff for a choir and started rehearsing us. We mastered the words and tempo. We enjoyed their solemn, strange cadence. Although we had watched it developing, the final effect was exotic and startling. During the choruses I was instructed to set up a sombre background of hallelujahs, and it was long before Al was satisfied that I gave each hallelujah a proper bell-like intonation as thrown against Davie's silvery flutelike tinkles. Sam fell in robustiously, and Hymie droned like an organ. O'Brien was pleased with the fun of the thing. He congratulated Al on his choir handling, saying he had the Palestrinian method of throwing dissimilar toned voices against each other and obtaining an harmonious whole. . . . "Palestrina, me eye," scoffed Al; "that's my old man's method. He is a *chazan*. You know what that is, a cantor. He got the method from his father, and his father from his father, and so on. Say, Palestrina must be some four-flusher. The method is as old as the Jews."

We decided to try out Latinized and Palistrinated Sweet Rosie O'Grady on the mixed gathering in Lavelle's. Nobody took it for the original, although not a note was changed. It was received as a tremendous piece of blasphemy and the foul deed of O'Brien, who, they were convinced, was a renegade, mocking priest. . . . A few of the girls wept as though at a solemn mass, and several drunken men became vociferously conscience-stricken. A man tried to hit O'Brien with a chair. The slummers thought the mass music a great jest, but it nearly caused a riot. I saw at once

it was a mistake. Where religion is concerned no one
has a sense of humor. Drinking people are the
most unreasonable when a religious question comes
up. Most bar-room fights begin in religious discus-
sions. . . . My bouncers surrounded me, ready for the
signal that would start their celebrated bum's rush.
Each bouncer, a professional bruiser, selected a
troublesome fellow, made a quick dash, gripped him
by collar and scruff and the seat of his pants, ran him
across the floor, gaining momentum near the door,
where a properly placed kick sent the rowdy reeling
and sprawling into the gutter.

We are making money. Drinkers are liberal tippers.
Drunken men submit to being overcharged and short-
changed. The slummers paid high prices gladly; they
would not have liked it nearly so much if it were not
expensive. Every night we reckoned up our percentage of the gate and were elated with the profits.
Lavelle was a good sport and freely conceded that we
had drummed up a fine business. Al and Sam wanted
me to join them in a song publishing enterprise. I decided to bank my money to pay my way through law
school. Yet had I invested in their publishing business,
my money would have earned in ten years close to a
quarter of a million dollars. Al and Sam became the
richest publishers of popular songs. They cooked up
the music for musical comedies; stars paid them fabulous royalties for exclusive songs, and then came the
phonograph to grind out more royalties. They really
owed their success to O'Brien. He opened up to them
the storehouse of the world's best melodies. He played
for them for hours, and Sam and Al followed him and
picked out the tuneful bits from the works of the mas-

ters. These tasteful bits they wove into ragtime hits. And their music became the music of America, and its leading motive was always the throbbing African rhythm. Davie said their music appealed because it had the beat-time of the living body's blood.

We found that Lavelle's receipts swelled as we attracted the respectable citizens, who spent as lavishly as they were proportionately shocked. They wanted to see the life and excitement that they imagined was a continuous phantasmagoria of depravity, license and murder. So I decided to treat them to an occasional picturesque murder. I staged the scene near the piano. Billie and Ivan, completely disguised by queer costumes and make-up, had just finished the Wriggle to a tumult of applause. It was sensual and fleshly enough to satisfy the cravings of the most respectable curiosity. They seated themselves at a table that I had pushed out on the dance floor. Dago Jack, dressed in clothes that would gratify the sightseers' notion of what a cutthroat should wear, staggered across the floor. Billie, on seeing him approach, rose and screamed. . . . In the meantime my bouncers stood at the doors to keep timid people from running out in a panic. . . . Dago Jack was instructed to speak lines that would keep the character true to the popular idea of a tough guy. "Cull," hissed Jack, "when I sez lays off me moll, I means lays off, lays off, see." . . . Ivan jumped up dramatically and drew a dirk from his shirt. The dirk had a bright colored handle that flashed in the gaslight. Dago Jack snarled and with a swift shift of his arm flung out a long-bladed stiletto which he caught high in the air. . . . Ivan backed out on the dance floor with Jack following. They slowly circled around each other, while the surprised onlookers watched with bated breath. Dago Jack made a cat-like leap and a desperate lunge, barely missing Ivan. Billie screamed. Men gasped, and a number of girls shrieked. . . . Now Jack has Ivan on the run. Billie is on her knees imploring Jack. Jack makes another drive with the stiletto and everyone sees the blade slowly sink into Ivan's back. Ivan stumbles, raises agonized hands, totters towards Billie and falls face-forward across the table, sending glasses splintering to the floor, and to everyone's horror the stiletto remains sticking in Ivan's back. Jack surveys his prostrate victim with a sneer on his face, stoops and picks up a derby hat from the floor and hangs it on the handle protruding from the dead man's back. Jack pulls his cap over his eyes and starts strutting across the floor. Near the door he calls out, "Stay where youse are, youse guzzlers and lobbygows, youse lousy tripe, don't move. Youse seen what happened to dat spieler, well, culls, look out dat don't happen to youse." And he darted out. Buzzes of conversation, craning necks, frightened glances. The band starts a rollicking Wriggle. Two bouncers swiftly cross the floor, carelessly lift up the supposedly dead Ivan and carry him off. And the dancing starts as though nothing had happened, and soon Ivan returns minus his exaggerated make-up and no one knows him for the recently assassinated dancer. Billie also returns without her crazy clothes and wild make-up and the nice tragedy is kept intact in the minds of the thrill seekers.

Then I hired three Chinamen with particularly yellow and malevolent faces to sit at a table smoking very fancy opium pipes. I instructed them to glower at the passing girls, who ordinarily would not be frightened by a thousand Chinamen, but, at my hint, they shrink back and cry out in alarm.

There was a little bit of a girl called Millie the Stray. She had the frame and height of a twelve-year-old girl and a thin face with deep-set eyes that helped along the picture of girlishness. Millie joined our little play with gusto. As she passed the Chinamen's table, one of them leaped up and placed his taloned fingers around her neck. She drew back, of course to the center of the dance floor so that the slummers would miss nothing, and apparently the Chinaman was choking to death a little girl of twelve. It was a good sadistic picture. Finally the Chinaman dropped Millie to the floor, where she lay in a convulsed heap. She cried out, "Don't kill me, Ly Chee, don't kill me. I'll bring you all the money next time." Ly Chee was an intelligent fellow and could speak a pretty fair English but for this occasion he spoke pidgin English. "Me killee lou, me killee lou, bling allee timee allee money, no floget, me killee lou."

I staged police raids, fights between two girls over a man, a hold-up and other divertisements for the gullible.

Hymie is happy. He sees a clear way through medical college. Meantime, Lavelle's is a clinic to him. He tries to win the confidence of the girls and learn the causes of their downfall. He listened to many romantic stories. He said only one girl had told him the truth, and she was Billie. She ascribed her downfall to curiosity. He then began making notes of the girls' statements, the general trend of their talk, their tastes and manners, and then came to the conclusion that the greater part of the girls came from respectable middle class homes. He said he was trying to arrive at their psychological index number. It was as a result of his inquiries in Lavelle's, coupled with his years of experience in gynecological clinics, that he arrived at his finding that passionate women do not become prostitutes. He said that the ecstatic, vibrant quality of a passionate woman's love life is so holy to her that she cannot give herself promiscuously. It is the woman, he reasoned, to whom the physical relationship is not beautiful and glorious, who finds it easy to give her body freely.

VII

It was long past noon. I slept heavily after a busy night in Lavelle's. Through my sleep swam the figure of Esther, always above me, always eluding me. I woke slowly to a heavy pounding on the door. The pounding kept up. Mother was out, and I got up and opened the door. Dopie Ikie was there with a message that a couple of guys wanted to see me down in the Talkers' Café. I dressed and started down the stairs. Half way down I collided with Lillie the Teaser. I forgot all about the message that had been brought me and grabbed Lillie in my arms. She asked what I was doing, but I noticed she made no effort to free herself. I kissed her many times and then she whispered, "Meyer, people will see us here." . . . I took her hand and led her up the stairs, and when we came to my door she asked, "Where are you taking me?" . . . Lillie was ambitious to go on the stage. She had heard I was manager of Lavelle's and that we were making a big success. So I told her I wanted to talk with her about going on the stage. She went into the house with me. I locked the door and she said nothing. She stood trembling near the table. I looked at her golden loveliness and my brain seemed to swim. One thought came into my mind. I remembered Hymie's phrase. I had put my finger on Lillie's psychological index number. Her eyes were dilated and her breast moved rapidly. The egotist was always supreme in me and I cried out, "Lillie, do you love me?" . . . Her words came out in little gasps: "Meyer—Meyer, do you love me?" . . .

We sat on the couch. Lillie's nervous fingers were trying to put up her jumbled hair. Tears ran down her flaming face and her body shook. She turned her head away from me. A knock on the door. Lillie shuddered and I shot my hand out, covering her mouth. I called out, "Who is it?" . . . "It's me, Dopie. Didn't I tell you a couple of guys is waitin' for you?" . . . "All right. Tell them I'll be right down."

VIII

The Talkers' Café is on Division Street, facing our
little square. It is a tea house, a rendezvous for the
freethinkers of the Ghetto. Avrum, Davie and Hymie
are seated at a table near the window. I sit down and
look out on the cobbled square, aswarm with half-naked
children playing in the hot July sun. Hymie is looking
through a big text-book and Davie is writing on the
back of a soiled menu card. Avrum regards Davie
with anxious eyes. The place is full of talking, gesticu-
lating men. A poster on the wall announces a *Yom
Kippur* (Day of Atonement) picnic to be given by the
Truth and Light Bund. It is a gesture of contempt
and defiance. The young Jews wish to show the extent
of their emancipation by feasting and revelling on the
orthodox Jews' holiest fast day. I remember that
Avrum is against the freethinkers holding the picnic.
He is a pacifist. He thinks no good is done by antago-
nizing people; that we should reason patiently with
the unenlightened.

Avrum sent for me. He has not wanted to leave
Davie alone. He tells me Davie has decided to marry
Billie. Avrum thinks Davie's act is prompted by his
desire to atone to Billie for the wrong man in general
has done to her. Avrum thinks no good will be done
to Billie by sinking Davie's life and career with hers.
Avrum says Davie has the sacrifice mania. . . . Hymie
looks up. It is the sort of analysis that tickles him.
Davie smiles shyly at Avrum. . . . "The Christ
mania." . . . He starts to tear the menu in small

[157]

pieces. . . . "No," Davie continues, "I am not so noble. . . . I think you will notice that people love in two ways. One kind loves the person he needs for his happiness, the other kind loves the person who needs him. First I was drawn to Billie because she needed me. I suppose it is a compliment hard to resist. . . . Now it has become so that I need Billie. She is beautiful. She is an artist. She has a good mind. I tell you it matters nothing to me what she has been." . . . I start to speak, "She is not normal. The normal, every-day existence will not hold her. She is intense. She will take you——" . . . Avrum holds up his hand. He says, "There is nothing more to say. I feel now that Davie loves her. It may not be as you think, Meyer." He smiles, apologetically, and says, "Meyer, you know you are something of a hard realist; you have a one way mind." . . . I remark casually, "All right, have it your way, it's none of my funeral." . . . Across the street I see Esther turning into Ludlow Street. . . . Esther has lost Davie. I am glad of that, the egotist in me rejoices. And now you have lost me, Esther, I tell myself; but I am not quite so sure that Lillie can make me forget Esther. Gretel could not do it. . . . And there is Lillie talking with Esther at the corner. She is smiling and gay. . . . I thought Lillie would be hiding somewhere, crying her heart out. . . . I had forgotten Lillie was a good actress . . . and I think, maybe, she is happy because she loves me. That is a pleasing thought. . . .

On my way down to Lavelle's that evening I found Lillie at the corner, waiting for me. Esther is on the stoop, and I try not to think of her. Gretel looks after me out of the window. I have just left her. I think to

myself, Gretel is just like a wife. No matter what I do,
I come back to her. She seems to round out the day
for me. I realized years later that between Gretel and
me there was a happy physical affinity.

I suggest a matinée, next Saturday afternoon; Lillie
agrees with a nod and I tell her where to meet me. . . .
I took her to a burlesque show and then to a furnished
room house. . . . Lillie is just good to look at, but one
cannot everlastingly look at a face. She is dull, pas-
sionless, complaisant. . . . So, a few years later, when
Sam fell in love with Lillie, I advised her to marry him.
She was not in the least offended by my suggestion. In
time she became engaged to Sam and married him. I
think she was torpidly true to her husband and was
likely to stay so unless a forceful person came along
and annoyed her into changing her mind.

IX

O'Brien's piano is like a waterfall in a cavern that takes the colors and reflections of the advancing day's humors and melts into a living murmur of night. Harmonies ripple from his fingers, changeful scores from the world's masterpieces, which Al and Sam heed with the rapture of treasure hunters. Sam shouts in glee that he can twist a blareful, stirring Wagnerian fugue into nigger jazbo stuff. Al tells him, "Well, kid, jazz her up." It was the beginning of their use of the word "jazz." Whenever they appropriated a melody or strain they simply jazzed it up into one of their syncopated hodgepodges.

Now Billie, whimpering, runs like a frightened creature from Davie to O'Brien. She is as one who has wandered in dark places and suddenly comes upon a brilliant sunrise. And she whimpers, "He wants to marry me." Orloff's cloudy face turns ashen. His eyes blink in the glorious light. O'Brien turns his head. But Al and Sam are lost in the meshes of the colorful embroiderings of their musical tapestry.

"He wants to marry me." Billie weeps on O'Brien's shoulder. . . . "Hey, girlie," cries Al, "you're making a bum outta the rehearsal." . . . Soon the rehearsal starts again, but first there is Davie's idea of a wedding. He takes Billie's hand, saying, "Before the world I take you as my wife, my mate. Do you take me as your husband, your mate?" . . . And in this wise Billie and Davie were married.

[160]

HAUNCH PAUNCH AND JOWL

A barfly stumbles among the tables, lighting up the place. Orloff fingers a slim-bodied glass that had held Billie's last absinthe potion. He muses with Russ retrospection: a woman becomes desired by many as soon as one man wants to marry her. . . . Now he understands why Billie would have nothing to do with him. . . . He speaks of himself as a playboy of the world's pleasure marts. . . . Like most educated Russians, his keenest interest in life is analyzing emotions. He observes with a mixture of contempt and amusement that there is none so faithful and straitlaced as a courtesan when she finds respectable love. She is beyond the temptation of mere flesh. Fed-up people find it easy to forswear fleshpots. The simple fare of virtue has an exotic flavor. Tired out roués become home-loving husbands. The sex problem begins *after* marriage for the man who has been chaste. Marriage awakens his sex life. After marriage his eyes and thoughts follow attractive women. If you don't sow your wild oats before marriage, you are likely to sow them after. So he thinks Billie's heartaches will be many. Davie is too good-looking, and Billie will be tortured with jealousy. People always judge others to be at least as bad as they themselves are. Ask any prostitute. She will tell you that there isn't a single virtuous woman in the whole world. She knows—her self is the gauge. . . . In short, Orloff reasons Billie would have been better off with him. Orloff is right. The trouble with the world is that people can't get away from justifying themselves.

The summer is drawing to a close. I have seen little of Esther. Harry Wotin interested her in a milk station for sickly babies, where she works as an interpreter and assistant to the doctors. The milk station was Harry's idea. Barney Finn got his spinster aunt to finance the place. Esther, Barney and Harry are as happy as only people can be who think they are succoring a dying world.

One day I persuaded Esther to take a day off. We made a gala holiday of it on the beach of Coney Island. I showed off like a schoolboy, displaying all the aquatic tricks I had learned as an East River wharf rat, and Esther, who timidly lingered in the surf, was impressed with my strength and daring. Most of the day we frolicked in the water. The only chance we had to talk was when we lunched on the sand under the boardwalk. She spoke of Davie. It came like a black cloud to darken the day. . . . "Is he happy? Has he kept on with his poetry? He must have loved her with a rare love to have taken her." . . . I said I did not want to talk of anyone but Esther. And she answered, "Then there is nothing to talk about." . . . I began to sulk. . . . "Meyer, please let us be good friends. I don't want any lovemaking. I don't want anything to take my mind off what I have set out to do." . . . I had it. Esther was heartbroken over Davie, and she was looking for forgetfulness and consolation in giving her life to the children of the East Side. Esther looked out on the water, and my spirits sank as I saw the calm repose of her face and her eyes alight with joy at the beauty of the sky and sea. And she was more baffling than ever to me. . . .

Late that afternoon we returned to Ludlow Street. To my great surprise I found Billie sitting on my stoop. Her face was convulsed with held-back tears. Her eyes were wild with fear and she spoke in a hollow

voice. "Meyer, they took him away in an ambulance."
Esther's face blanched and she cried out, "Oh, Davie—
what happened to him?" . . . The two girls stood
looking at each other. I sent a little boy running to
fetch Avrum. . . . Billie turned her back to Esther.

"We were sleeping this morning, me cuddled up like
a baby under his arm. And Davie started to toss, and
I heard his breath puff in little gasps, and his hands
began pulling at me like he was trying to save himself
from going under. When I sat up I saw blood bubbling
from his mouth, running down his white neck like
burns. And I screamed. People came, and a cop. He
rung for an ambulance and the doc said he was in a
bad way, and they took him away over the river to that
pest house on Blackwell's Island, the place they call
City Hospital. I went there and they wouldn't let me
near him; said visiting days was only twice a week;
nearest one is two days off. All they would tell me,
he's very sick. The con and something else. The
something else—they wouldn't tell me what that was.
What am I gonna do? Meyer, what am I gonna do?
I got to see him. I just got to see him."

Her face softened under the flood of tears. "I guess
I got to let his mother know. I guess it's only right I
should." . . . Esther spoke to her quietly, "Please
don't tell his mother. Wait until we know something
more. Maybe then we will have better news."

"You're Esther, ain't you? You're the girl he
thinks so much of."

Avrum came. He shook hands with Billie, and
stroked her arm. "Hold fast," he said, "it might not
be so bad as you think. We will do everything, everything for Davie. Everybody loves Davie." Billie

smiled and looked around, saying, "Everybody. Guess that's right. There's nothing else to do but love him. There's no harm or hate or bad in him. He feels for everything and everyone. I guess that's why he could take up with me."

Avrum and I took Billie to see Lavelle, who brought us to see Big Jim Hallorhan, the political boss of the lower end of Manhattan. Hallorhan owned the building which housed Lavelle's dance hall, and Hallorhan's ownership put Lavelle's place beyond police interference. Hallorhan towered over us. He had a pink, fleshy round face supported by a bull neck that rested on bulging shoulders. He heard Billie's story. He rang for a bartender. Hallorhan's office was in the back room of a Bowery saloon. The bartender brought paper and pencil. Hallorhan with a big, clumsy hand wrote, "Dinty Shea shake hands with bearer Meyer Hirsch a regular fellow he's one of the boys Jim Hallorhan." Hallorhan told me to take the note over to the City Hospital and see Dinty Shea. "He'll fix you up."

Hallorhan's note worked wonders. Dinty Shea said Davie would be put in a private room with a special nurse and have the best of everything. Billie begged to be allowed to stay with him. Dinty said, "I'll do anythin' for Big Jim." Then we were taken up to see Davie. He was lying in a long ward congested with beds, where all the sick men and boys seemed to be complaining and groaning at one time. A nurse put a screen around his bed and the three of us sat down and looked at Davie, sunk in a heavy, perspiring slumber. Billie whispered, "Look at my boy, laying there all give out like a baby. Look at his golden curls laying on his head like they was tired out, too." His face had the color of refined wax with just a tinge of yellow. His eyes opened and he lay there looking at the ceiling without seeing us. Then Billie sobbed. Davie was too spent to move. He called out in a whisper, "Don't cry, Billie, I'm all right." And Billie laid her wet cheek on his hand. Avrum stood up, smiling in Davie's face. "See, Billie," said Davie, "there's Avrum, like a ray of sunshine. Tell her, Avrum, people get sick and people get well."

We waited while Davie was being transferred to a private room. The doctor, a young interne, trying to be as matter-of-fact as possible, told us that Davie was suffering from a bad case of pulmonary tuberculosis, to say nothing of some other serious complication. He said, "There's no use filling you with false hope. He can't last long."

Billie moaned, "I done for him. I done for him." . . . She paced up and down the corridor. . . . "Say—God—God—what did you want to do it for! I thought you sent me Davie to make me go straight and clean. No, you sent him to punish me. You saved up all the dirt to give the first clean man I met, the first man I loved, the first man who loved me." . . . She leaned against the wall. "I know why you done it, God. You wanted to get even with me for what I done to my mother. Now, God, I'm punished enough. Let my Davie get better, give him back, I pray God, give me back my Davie. Without him I'll be a drifter again."

Davie did not get better. Even an interne may be right. Everybody knew Davie was dying except Billie. In her extreme grief she turned to prayer. The burden of her prayer was, "Let up, God, don't you see I am punished enough." But Davie had another hemorrhage. So the time came that his mother had to be told. Mrs. Solomon had begun asking anxiously after him. He had not come to spend the last Sabbath day with her. It was the one day of the week he gave to his mother after his marriage. I brought her to the hospital, making it easier for her to bear by saying his illness was inevitable. Davie's father had died of the shop sickness, and I convinced her that consumption was the one inheritance the father had left the son. She did not so much as look at Billie. When the neighbors heard that Davie had married a Gentile they urged the mother to disown her son, and never see him again. But in her eyes her son could do no wrong and she stopped all discussion about his marriage. . . . "Mamma," said Davie, "here is my wife, Billie." . . . Mrs. Solomon looked at him, distraught and constricted. . . . "She don't want to know the likes of me," said Billie. . . . And all the mother could do was to stand alongside of the bed and look and look and look at her baby who was fading away under her eyes. . . . Esther and Avrum came. We were all silent and solemn. Only the object of our commiseration was smiling and cheerful. Little pink spots burned under his eyes, which were steadily glassy. He seemed to sense in our silence, not so much distress over his condition, as a unanimous censure upon Billie for his condition. . . . "Billie," said he, "come sit on the bed so that my head may rest upon your breast. I want you close to me, so that when I go I shall feel that I am passing into your wondrous heart. Billie, I bequeath—to you a memory . . . and this is

the memory: I love you, believe in you . . . you gave
me fulfillment and happiness. . . . Do many men die
happy in the fulfillment of their belief? . . . Friends,
I leave you a heritage—believe in the soul in people—
the soul is incorruptible. If I could tell you the fulfillment my well-beloved showed me. . . . If I could
tell. . . . Inexpression: stillborn . . . yet racked with
the aches of creation . . . tortured thoughts . . . tortured . . . in travail for expression . . . feeling, feeling, fine and fierce . . . immured in the sealed sepul-
chre of inexpression." . . . And so Davie died with a
poem on his lips.

Davie's death stirred anew the scandal of his marriage to a *schicksie* (Gentile girl). Mrs. Solomon went
to the *shammos* to arrange for his interment in the
synagogue's burial ground. Mendel Gerditsky bal-
anced himself on his good limb and told her that
Davie's marriage had excommunicated him, and therefore he could not be placed in the congregation's con-
secrated burial plot. His presence would defile the
sanctity of the place. However, he would call a meeting of the trustees to consider the matter. The refusal
to bury Davie in the Grodno Cemetery brought all the
members to the trustee's meeting. The synagogue was
crowded. *Rov* Zucker sat up front to the right of the
Torah cabinet. The *gabbe*, Jake Weingrad, recently
elected because of his generous contributions of a new
Torah and a new coat of paint for the benches, stood
by the prayer stand in front of the *Torah* cabinet and
presided over the buzzing meeting. In Jake Weingrad's opinion the matter was a simple one. Davie
could not be buried in holy ground. He would disturb
the peace of the dead. The matter seemed settled.

HAUNCH PAUNCH AND JOWL

Rov Zucker stroked his beard, and turned the pages of a large volume. Trustee after trustee, glad of a chance to make a fervent speech, denounced Davie and his terrible sin. Mrs. Solomon pulled her shawl tight around her shoulders, left the woman's compartment and mounted the central service platform. She spoke, and the congregation was shocked into silence by the temerity of a woman intruding in the men's part of the synagogue. "Here is my spot," she said, "here I will remain until death overtakes me, until my son is laid to rest by his father's side among his own people." . . . At this point I nudged Maxie Freund to raise the technical questions that he and I decided upon in order to confuse *gabbe* Weingrad. He strode down the aisle and addressed the *gabbe*. "Who says the deceased is married to a Gentile! Who can prove it? You are condemning his soul to eternal wandering by refusing to inter him in hallowed ground. What proof is there of his marriage? Who can show one tittle of evidence that the deceased was married to any woman in a constituted tribunal, church or synagogue?" *Rov* Zucker shook his head, commendingly. Maxie continued, "It is therefore that I suggest that you call upon a student of our own laws, who at the same time is a student of the American law, to tell us what evidence, if any, there is of a marriage. Let Mr. Meyer Hirsch tell of the painstaking inquiry he has made of this unfortunate affair." . . . Maxie delivered the speech we had cooked up together, in his quiet yet compelling style. I got upon the service platform and asked permission of my elders to present the known facts of the case. I decided upon a formula of repetition. I knew that an oft-repeated statement

[168]

gathers strength and intimidates. I demanded, "Who among you can say of his own knowledge that the deceased was married? No one. Who will dare to fasten a wife, a forbidden alliance, upon the poor boy now silenced until judgment day? No one. Nobody knows of his own knowledge that Davie Solomon was married. Are we women in the market place that we heed every rumor? No, we are men concerned with actualities and facts. Davie Solomon is not married. Who can produce the wife? No one. There is no wife. He is not married, no woman can claim him according to the law of this land and least of all according to the law of Israel. I have seen the deceased every day for the past ten years, every day I have seen him, and I can say that he is unmarried according to all legal understanding. He is not married! And no one can prove the contrary! He is not married!"

Many heads were shaken from side to side in surprise at my eloquence. They recalled my confirmation harangue. Whispers flew about, started by Maxie, that I was a remarkable lawyer in the making.

Gabbe Weingrad was nonplussed. He appealed to the Rabbi for an opinion.

Rov Zucker spoke thus: "I have heard many grown men say, do not bury the dead young man, he is married to a *schicksie*. Yet not one of these grown men have told us how they know that the young man was married. I have heard a youth declare he is unmarried. Can anyone contradict him, contradict him with proof?"

The trustees decided to bury Davie. In the meantime Avrum had told the hospital authorities that Davie had requested him to leave his body in the hospital to be dissected by medical students. But Mendel Gerditsky, the redoubtable beadle, raised a great storm in the office of the hospital and Davie's remains, slightly hacked here and there, were turned over to him.

The funeral was interesting. The dispute over his burial brought throngs of curious. The Ludlow Streeters turned out in a body in honor of their pal. They had considered him a pal ever since he made a hit in the toughest joint in the city. The Essex Street Guerrillas came in six carriages which Shimshin had blackmailed a local livery stableman into providing. O'Brien was led in by his Chinese wife to peer at Davie's face with his dim eyes. Frenchie Lavelle, inopportunely, came with a wreath, which I hid under the stairs. Bartenders, burglars, pimps, Davie's City College and school teachers and many others who had known the strange boy and loved him, squeezed into the small flat to look upon him for the last time. Soon Ludlow Street became an immovable mass. As the crowd grew, everybody for blocks around came to see what brought such a gathering. And it was with great difficulty that the funeral procession started for the Grand Street ferry en route to the cemetery in Brooklyn. But, in all that great conclave, Billie could not be found. And Davie was buried with all the ceremony he despised, and, with his passing, his bride of fulfillment disappeared as though she, too, were swallowed up by the earth.

X

"Aren't you going to *schule* (synagogue)?" mother asked. She has just finished lighting and blessing the candles. A *yahrzeit* (death anniversary) candle lamp burned on the shelf over the stove in father's memory. It was the eve of sacred *Yom Kippur*.

I hardly heard her question, so engrossed was I in a book on criminal law. The door opened and Maxie Freund pussyfooted into the kitchen. He had just passed his Regents' examination with great ease—after paying one of the examiners twenty-five dollars, thereby sparing himself another year's preparation. Big Jim Hallorhan put me next to the examiner, and I arranged the easing detail for Maxie.

Maxie greeted Uncle Philip, who was lying stretched out upon the couch, smoking a pipe. Philip now used a pipe because it was more economical than cigarettes. It seems the more money he made, the more frugal he became. . . . "Good evening, Herr Capitalist, may your fast be a light one." . . . "May your fasts be many and heavy," responded Philip. Maxie wished mother a good year and a light fast, and then saluted me with "Good evening, Judge." . . . Philip puffed stentoriously, blowing little clouds of smoke over his head. Mother remonstrated with him: "Philip, what will the neighbors think and say to see you smoking on *Yom Kippur?*" To which Philip replied, "Let them shut their eyes, the scared jackasses."

Mother again pleads, "Meyer, please go to *schule*. It is *Yom Kippur*. Every Jew, no matter what an *Epikaros* (Epicurean) he may be the rest of the year,

[171]

goes to *schule* one day—on *Yom Kippur*. Please, if only for my sake, go to *schule*." . . . I tell mother that I plan to spend the holy day in study, as law school opens the following week. Whereupon Maxie interposes in the singsong of the Talmudist, "On the other hand, your honor, I think attendance at the synagogue may be properly classified as part of your preparation for lawyership." . . . "How do you make that out?" inquires Philip, who credits Maxie with sharp wits. And Maxie reasons in this wise: "To begin with it keeps him before the eyes of a lot of people. It stamps him a solid, respectable member of the community. It gives him a chance to impress a number of people. Everybody needs a lawyer some time, and the man before their eyes is the most likely one they'll think of when that time comes." So Philip says, "Get off to *schule*, Meyer. Hereafter be a regular attendant, mind. Maxie is right. Strut before them. They'll take you to be the man you say you are. Impress them. Make yourself their lawyer, the only lawyer they'll think of. Stick your oar into their congregational affairs. Advertise yourself. Start off with giving them free advice. They'll pay well later on. Do things for them. Get them used to having *you* do things for them." . . . After which I and Maxie became regular *schule*-goers.

Yom Kippur morning I accompanied mother to *schule*. I noticed a crowd in front of the Talkers' Café. The onlookers were highly scandalized and offended. The Ghetto freeminded elements were publicly eating on the most sacred of sacred fast days. The superstitious expected to see the traducers stricken on the spot. The tolerant deplored their bad taste. In the window a large poster invited the public to come to a *Yom Kippur* picnic at North Beach. The Talkers' Café was the only restaurant open in the entire East Side. The news of the open, defiant sacrilege spread, and, by noontime, when I left the *schule* for a breath of air, I found a dense mob in front of the café. Indignation grew as the hungry fasters beheld the impudent unbelievers dine with ostentation. . . . Soon Boolkie and his lads used the ready contents of overflowing garbage cans with which to pelt the men and women who went in and out of the café. The dodging and fleeing of the calumniators amused the crowd. Boolkie, spurred by popular approval, then hurled a cobblestone which smashed the large plate-glass window. This was received with an uproar of acclaim. Then began a shower of stones, bricks and any missile that came to hand, and the café became untenable. When the freethinkers rushed out of the bombarded position the crowd pursued them until they were dispersed in all directions. A few were caught and severely drubbed and the café was completely wrecked.

By this time the exercise and excitement had made the gangsters good and hungry. They could get nothing to eat at home. They had just stoned men and women who dared to eat openly on a holy fast day, and they themselves were now thinking of ways and means of getting food. Everybody is agreed that consistency is the height of cruelty. . . . Big Joe reported that he had a line on a lot of good stuff. Mrs. Weingrad, he said, was in *schule* and her ice-box was crammed full of "yum-yum, boys." And he licked his chops, making everybody's mouth water as he described each delectable, giving us to understand his representations were as per tasted sample. It was too much for Boolkie. He hastened a detail of youngsters to raid the ice-box and bring the stuff to a secluded backyard in Canal Street. They returned forthwith with a large roast duck, *gefülte fisch,* white holiday bread, the light and toothsome *challah,* a variety of fruit and a big honey cake. Everybody cried out, " 'Yum-yum, boys,' is right; Yum-yum." So the champions of the fast observance made an excellent meal from the Weingrads' larder, fattened for an after-the-fast-feast.

All of which reminded me that I was ravenously hungry and there was nothing to be had at home. I met Lillie and asked her if she were hungry. She just laughed. Lillie never did anything. She was the kind that was always made to do the thing. I told her to slip up to the station of the Third Avenue elevated, where I would wait for her. She just laughed, as much as to imply, well, the sin is on you, you're making me do it.

We got off at Fourteenth Street, where there were a number of Gentile restaurants. We could not get into any one of them. They were packed with my hungry co-religionists, and the waiters told me that *Yom Kippur* was their busiest day of the year. We had to walk up to Twenty-eighth Street before we could find an eating place with a free table. How we enjoyed the hearty meal! A fast day always puts an edge on an appetite. And Lillie just laughed when I took her again to the furnished room house. . . . I hurried back to the synagogue and was in time for the solemn closing services. In all it was an interesting day.

XI

Came brisk October evenings with electioneering's
carnival confusion. Brass bands; fireworks; red splut-
tering torches; bonfires; ringing bombasts; button-
holings; cigar-giving and whiskey swilling; monster
mass meetings; parades; streamers; picture buttons;
badges; gaudy and glittering banners snapping in the
wind; walls, windows, fences, ash cans and packing
cases plastered with posters screaming slogans and
promises and showing the heavily postured likenesses
of the candidates. And the wind swirls the torn and
discarded multi-colored campaign literature high in the
air like so much confetti. At the corners, crowds gather
to hear cart-tail orators. Their faces are like burnished
copper under the kerosene flare lamps. The speakers
blare as usual the annual ass-solo of balderdash and
buncombe, so sweet to the ears of jackasses. They
listen in the same open-mouthed, naïvely spellbound
way, clap their hands and cheer in the ready fashion
of the habitually gullible.

Maxie and I attended the political meetings to get
lessons in public speaking. The excitement was catch-
ing, and it seemed so easy to sway the multitude that
I just itched for a chance to try my powers over them.
Besides, Maxie said, the best way to learn public speaking was to take the stump yourself. Then we considered what party would be best for us to join. . . . The
Jewish business men were disposed to vote Republican.
They felt after Cleveland's disastrous free trade administration that a Republican high tariff wall would

keep out hard times. At this time, however, the bulk
of the East Side, politically, was negligible. Many
were not in the country long enough to become citizens.
Many who could qualify for citizenship could not spare
the time. It took several precious mornings to become
a citizen. By making these men citizens and control-
ling their votes, but a few years later, I was able to ask
the older bosses to reckon with me as a political somebody. I got my idea from the Socialists, who were constantly urging the workmen to become citizens and
make themselves felt in the parliamentary functioning
of their country. I went them one better. I arranged
for a quick and easy process in the courts to change
them from aliens to citizens, flattered the new citizens
into joining my club, did them trifling favors and paid
them a few dollars on election day. The secret of
political power and swinging local districts to success
is told in a few words. The average man under our
system of pull and favoritism believes that any day
he may need a favor, and it is for this possible favor he
puts his franchise in pawn. . . . The Socialists had
put a ticket in the field and except for a great deal of
pre-election oratory confined to the Ghetto—elsewhere
they were beaten off—they were considered permanently insignificant because their total vote on election
day was one of the jokes of the times. . . . So Maxie
and I looked over the political prospect for personal
opportunity only. We were concerned with no other
issue but just what we could get out of it. It was manifest to us that the lawyers who succeeded in court were
those with pull. And it was evident that Tammany
ruled the city, although the Republicans held national
sway. So we decided to become Democrats. We

attached ourselves to Big Jim Hallorhan's club. I
gave up singing in Lavelle's, only giving a couple of
hours a night to getting things running. Al reorgan-
ized the quartet after Davie's death and after Hymie
dropped out to take up studies at medical school.

I made my maiden speech in Big Jim's clubrooms.
As the meeting was attended mostly by his Irish constituents, I made it a fulsome piece of adulation of the
philanthropies of the Big Boss, the pee-pul's one and
only friend. His eleemosynary works consisted of giving out a few dozen shoes in the winter, free Thanks-
giving baskets and a free picnic for women and
children in the summer.

Big Jim told me to tackle the East Side. He wanted
to put a crimp in the Republicans, and he was the only
man at that time who foresaw the growth of the Socialist vote among the Jews. He was also worried about
the Italians. He thought their warm blood would
respond to the Socialistic appeal. Big Jim was shrewd.
I organized a flying squadron of youthful spellbinders,
and we made a rousing campaign. Maxie instructed
the speakers to stress the few points that we made our
political stock in trade. We represented the Democrats
as the common people's party, painted the Republicans as the silk-stockinged bluebloods, and lied atro-
ciously about the Socialists. We fastened upon them
every crime of radicalism, called them freethinkers,
free lovers, enemies of God and the sanctity of the
family. We gave them an odor that they have been
unable to shake off to this day. We used rough-house
tactics in breaking up their meetings, and even rotten-
egged Republican rallies. The hoodlums and the police
were with us. I recruited Boolkie and his gang, im-

[177]

pressing upon them that political pull afforded police immunity.

The day before election was "dough day," the day each district captain received a roll of money for judicious use on election day. The price of a vote in those days was two dollars, and to a poor man, who saw no farther than his instant belly needs, this was a lot of money. When I saw the money circulating, I confided to Big Jim that I had a gang of strong-arm men working for me and that they were ready for his orders. Big Jim assigned his lieutenant, Red Mike Dooley, to put the boys to work. Red Mike conferred with various district captains and then handed me cards bearing the names and addresses of voters and their districts. My boys were to vote in the names of these citizens, who were known Republicans and doubtful Democrats. Red Mike accompanied the gang, pointed them out to the election inspectors as the right guys and then the boys entered the booths, voting straight and regular. They were armed with clubs and blackjacks to overcome such slight opposition as they might encounter. The Ludlow Streeters spent an hilarious day dashing about town in carriages, voting willy-nilly, stealing ballot boxes with the connivance of policemen and substituting others in their place. I paid the boys ten dollars and I pocketed one hundred dollars as fair compensation for generalship.

Tammany, as usual, swept the city. There was a big celebration on election night, and I led the Ludlow Streeters and others in a local torchlight parade. We carried brooms as a symbol of the clean sweep. The parade stopped in front of Big Jim's club. I instructed Maxie to stay with the paraders and stimulate their cheering while I went in to felicitate Big Jim. He was surrounded by a large gathering of drinking men, and I noticed he was the only one who did not take a drop. I shook hands with him. Our band was playing "A Hot Time in the Old Town Tonight," and when it stopped our fellows began to cheer under Maxie's leadership. Many cheers were given for Big Jim. Then the name of Meyer Hirsch was cheered. "Who's the bunch outside?" asked Big Jim, cordially. "That's my club, Boss," I told him. Then Red Mike told the boss that my boys had done a good day's work, and Big Jim said he was glad to hear it, adding, "Come around and see me if there's any little thing I can do for the boys."

We then marched down to Lavelle's, where we had a riotous time.

Early in the morning I crept into bed. I was tired but could not fall asleep. I spent hours picturing to myself the honors, glories and profits that would accrue to me from a political career. I saw now very clearly how it was that in my city lowbrows ruled in high places, and I saw myself with my brains and astuteness reaching dizzy heights. . . .

FIFTH PERIOD

Woe unto you lawyers also! for ye load men with burdens grievous to be borne, and ye yourselves touch not the burdens with one of your fingers.

St. Luke.

FIFTH PERIOD

I

As I pass it seems as though the very tenements bow
in deference. The pushcart peddlers humbly tip their
hats. I am their protector and advisor. The gang
greets me as boss. Even Shimshin and his tough eggs
look up to me as their guardian saint. Business men
greet me, respectfully, as their accelerator in certain
affairs. Everywhere I meet respect and gratitude.
The bearded orthodox *schule* people praise my faithful
attendance and the way I serve the *schule* and the poor
without pay in legal matters. My policy is to put as
many people as I can under obligation to me. They
are the straw for the bricks of my political structure.

So we have come up in the world. I am a lawyer,
politician, champion of Jewry and member of a dozen
Jewish lodges, societies and charity organizations. I
became a Professional Jew in emulation of the successful Irish politician whose principal capital is being a
Professional Irishman. . . . By this time Philip feels
himself solidly on his feet as a manufacturer. No one
knows how much money he has made. At any rate, he
has the biggest sweatshop in the East Side. We live on
Canal Street in the upper part of a private house that
boasts running water, gas light, washtubs and a bath-
room.

I begin to be mindful of good repute. I don't bother
with Lillie. Sam is courting her in earnest. But Lillie
doesn't draw or hold me. It is easy to drop her. But

Gretel is so different, she seems to be my physical complement. I cannot give her up. . . . And I suggest to mother that we get a servant girl. She says she likes to keep busy, wouldn't know what to do with herself without housework, and there really was not much to do. . . . Philip knows what is back of my mind. He insists that we get a servant girl. I tell mother that Gretel, Weingrad's maid of all work, is a good worker and has agreed to work for us. Mother gives in, as usual, afraid to oppose her brother. That evening Gretel came, ostensibly to be our servant girl.

In the morning mother woke early as was her habit. She went to Gretel's little hallroom to call her. She was not there. . . .

Philip called to mother to serve breakfast. Gretel watched mother, nervously, and then sat down at the table. Then I followed, also giving everything a matter-of-fact, taken-for-granted air and joined them at the table. Mother stood still by the stove looking at us in bewilderment and anger.

Philip again demanded his breakfast.

Mother spoke in a dry voice. "What is this——"

Philip was impatient. He was always the business first, business-as-usual man. He snapped: "Serve breakfast and ask questions later."

We ate in silence. Gretel looked abashed. She was never bold. Mother finally burst out, "It's a fine servant girl you have brought me. Where is she—the servant girl? . . . Is your mother the servant girl? That's it, I am a servant girl to a——" . . . Gretel, blushing, slipped into her room. . . . Philip told mother to be sensible, make the best of it. Philip lit one of my cigars and left for his shop.

HAUNCH PAUNCH AND JOWL

Mother came close and looked at me. Her face showed that she believed I was outraging every decency. She wept quietly and asked how I could offer my own mother such an insult as to ask her to live under the same roof with Gretel—and worse, expect her to serve her. I told mother Gretel was not a bad woman, and so she asked, "Then, if she is a good girl it is your duty to marry her." . . . So I tried to explain to her that I had my career to think of, that some day I would be able to command a large dowry and the daughter of a fine family . . . in the meantime . . . I am but a man, and this arrangement was better than chasing around. . . . I warned her to mind that to the outside world Gretel was our servant girl and nothing more.

Mother cried again. She ended up by saying, "It cannot be that you are my child. You are so unfeeling—you must be the goat's child." . . . And during many years that followed mother never spoke as much as one word to Gretel . . . not until her craving for decency was gratified . . . but that should be told later, in its place.

II

There is a cloud that comes to darken my world. Esther hides the sun of my greatness. When I am with her she makes me feel . . . extinguished . . . sort of blotted out. She seems to live in a world wholly apart from mine. She teaches school and directs girls' clubs in the little social settlement Barney Finn started with his aunt's money. She trains with the intelligentsia . . . the *welt schmerz* droop-eyed, the hollow-cheeked idealists, the long-winded radicals and the hands-raised-in-horror parlor and Pecksniffian reformers. . . . Mine is a busy, pushing, pulling, scheming, contriving life, but I cannot put Esther out of my mind. She is the only defeat in my life . . . and just what I want of her I do not know. When I am with her she obscures my other world. My eyes are filled with her loveliness. Her sentient charm takes me away from Meyer Hirsch, ever present before my eyes in a Narcissus reflection. I quail before her clear, broad understanding . . . and to talk with her is a refreshing relief from the humdrum rot of my daily doings. . . . And yet I do not for a second think of marrying her. I have come to know one thing. Ambition is my undying desire. Marriage must socially and financially further my ambition. . . . It is always just before I fall asleep that Esther comes before me. . . . I want her love, her blind approval of everything I do. . . . I want to be her supreme being . . . but if Esther should come suppliant, adoringly lost in me, then she would not be the Esther that wrenches me from myself. . . .

HAUNCH PAUNCH AND JOWL

I came to the little office in the settlement house. I was determined to prove to myself that Esther did not count. I was going to put her out of my mind, nothing would mar the perfect picture I made of myself. . . . Esther was alone. Her willowy form draped in a one-pieced dark dress was silhouetted against the white-washed wall. Her face had that luminous quality that Davie described so long ago—like marble in the first light of day. Her beautiful hands, I thought, moved towards me as I came into the room. I looked at her and knew that the beauty of Esther would ever lurk in my being and never let me rest. . . . I meant to say just a few passing words, wasn't going to show I cared or was interested . . . but I stammered as I lost myself in the shadows of her eyes. . . . I asked her to come to the opera. Her face brightened with pleasure. Her answer tinkled in my ears like the silver bells Davie told about—little silver bells chiming to the kisses of zephyrs. . . . "You know, Meyer, I have never been to the opera . . . you are making a dream-wish come true." . . . I had never been to the opera but . . . it would be unlike me to make such an admission.

"Then let us go tonight—tonight, Esther." . . . Stimulating is her quick assent, and gratifying. Perhaps, after all, there is a little place in her heart for Meyer Hirsch. . . . Impulsively, I speak—surprised on the instant at the surrender I was making,—"You don't know—you know, you feel, you must know—how much I enjoy being with you. I can't tell you why, or what it is—it just is . . . I suppose it is love. I love you, I love—" . . . Pulling at my sleeve is my acquired extra sense, caution, become an apprehensive

[187]

instinct against self-commitment under any circumstances. Now, there is a shouting in my consciousness: hey there! don't involve yourself! Career. Ambition. Greatness. Honor. Wealth. High Places. Look out! A dream-stupefied girl. Nowhere: that's where you will get with her. Nowhere. Nowhere. . . . But I do not heed the warning din. I shut my eyes to the conjuring high places. . . . I put out my hand. All that I held precious—those jewels I had crystallized from life—lay in my hand, held out to her. What if Esther had taken it . . . would I now be writing a different history of Meyer Hirsch? . . . Ignoring my appeal, disdainful of what I had to proffer, she drew herself away. Rather, she shut herself from me. I could hear the snap and click of steel fastenings made against me. And, as always, the more she resisted me, the more I desired her. Denial, difficulties, defeat fired the lust of conquest, the sheer call and lure of the hunt.

"Do you know what they are going to sing tonight?" she asked, pulling on her gloves with jerky tugs. Far from calm was Esther. I caught at little clues for comfort. Surely, she was disturbed. Had she not put on her gloves before her coat and hat? She didn't look at me with her characteristic face-forwardness. And her breath came quicker. As she reached near me for her hat, I caught her arm, crying, "Esther, Esther, I wish they would sing a love song for me that would reach your heart." . . . A smile lighted up her face, and shaped her mouth for a kiss . . . so I thought . . . and her eyes full opened right under mine as though to let me see what was working in her mind and heart . . . as if she herself knew. Does anyone ever know, know anything except the pull and response of blood? . . . Swiftly, I bent down and kissed her. Her lips seemed to melt in my mouth. Like a boy, tasting love's first kiss, passion's first thrill, I was quivering all over, fair to swoon. Startled, overwhelmed but for a lightning-illumined moment, Esther quickly recovered and moved towards the door. I turned, expecting to find her gone, but there she was framed in the panel-like doorway, a picture of a lifetime balancing on the threshold of fate. She had put on her hat, a white soft beaver, and, when she uplifted her head, it looked like a halo made of little white flowers. Her face was soft and white and her lips, moist, hurt and crushed-looking. But there were her eyes, clear, unflinching, and, to me, like frozen pools in the light of a wintry sky. . . . I had touched the body, and the body yielded, but the spirit, the spirit was untouched. I saw it . . . the spirit could not bear with me . . . the spirit which I chose to name— puritanism. Anyway, I have something of Esther's. I tasted of her lips, a drop of wine squeezed from the rarest passion fruit, so potent, one drop made my senses reel. But, in my heart, I am sick of a vague disappointment. . . . I cannot let Esther go. It is early. Later, troubled by a prudish reflex, she might not want to meet the man who took the swift body-surprising kiss.

I looked at my watch and said, "Esther, it is a little after five. Come uptown with me and we'll find a nice restaurant where we'll have a leisurely dinner before the opera. There's a good deal I want to talk about—" Quietly, amazed, perhaps, at her own doubt as to what to do, she studied me, seeming to probe her instincts for a searching light to throw upon me

She took her little bag from the writing stand, looked at me with a smiling, composed face and said, unemotionally, "Come Meyer, let us go." Her eyes were clear and unafraid.

As we tread our way through thronged Chrystie Street, which is the narrow mouth to Second Avenue, Esther's hand nestled on my arm and I was glad of the chance to have her close to me. It was Esther who suggested that we walk a winding way uptown in and around the quaint and quiet streets of Stuyvesant, Gramercy and Madison Squares where old New York was making its last stand against the push and swarm of business and immigration. She liked the reposeful byways with their Georgian brick and brown stone houses of subdued elegance, fitting grand manner and soothing good taste. It is her favorite walk, and a key to what she wants.

Coming upon the wide walks of the boulevard—Second Avenue was our grand avenue of the promenade—Esther took her hand away and strode beside me in the independent, upstanding, free-swinging way of hers. "Don't take your chummy hand away," I pleaded. She replaced her hand with a comradely taunt—"Come along, little boy, are you afraid of getting lost?" My exhilaration was that of a schoolboy on a lark, the exhilaration of camaraderie. For the moment my head was clear of the passion-wine. I too, skipped along, freed from the dead weight of flesh-heavy desire. But, when the hand lying next to my ribs began to warm, penetratingly, I tingled. . . . Within I began to boil and rage and anathemize the spirit, the sacred spirit that hides behind an ice barrier and is adamant against my strongest flame.

HAUNCH PAUNCH AND JOWL

A cheery, familiarly nasal greeting roused me from my mood of bitter chagrin.

"Hey there, where are you two rushing off to? Wow, where's the fire?"

I daresay our walk kept time with the charging rush and torment of my thoughts.

We turned around and found we had been seen and followed by Hymie Rubin and Harry Wotin, both doctors now. With them was a tall good-looking young man with a weather-tanned face.

"Give us a chance to say, 'How do,' won't you?" demanded Hymie, jocularly. "Haven't seen you in a year and a Wednesday." . . .

"Meet Dr. Lionel Crane." . . . Where did he get the bang-up snobbish name—doesn't go with his face. I mulled with distemper the cognomen—too smart-sounding this Lionel Crane to be anything else but a cognomen—that ill-fitted his handsome but pronouncedly Jewish physiognomy. Possibly I was prejudiced by an instantaneous shock of jealousy. There actually wasn't anything outstandingly Jewish about him except his nose, and that feature, the after-truth to tell, was a fine example of a Roman proboscis. . . . On the spot I disliked him, this Lionel Crane, *ne* (Harvard matriculation) plain, vulgar, Lazarus Cohen. Like velvet rubbed the wrong way, sickeningly soft, creepily irritating, was his meticulous, modulated speech with its heavy Harvard accent. It cloyed. Inconsonant in *him,* not his by right, therefore an affectation, I felt, as were his distinguished manners—a nicety of deportment shaming mine and calling attention to my *gaucherie.* Anyway, I was ill at ease, upset, mentally tied up, so to speak, by a short circuit of my emotional

wires. . . . I wanted to drag Esther away. Here was
a cross-current, Dr. Lionel Crane, whom I feared. . . .
"On a visit to New York. . . . Looking around . . .
tremendously interested . . . gripping developments
. . . growing into a national problem . . . big field. . . .
Yes . . . might stay on. No; wasn't going in for
straight medicine. Nor for surgery. Something new."
. . . Superior something or other. Very. Very.
Superior. . . . He didn't say it—but his bearing's impress brings out his superiority. . . . Perplexing,
whatever it is. . . . "Race psychopathology. Serious.
Very. Race Psychopathology." . . . What a name for
—the Jewish Problem! . . . . "Yes: in America . . .
Certain of it. Bound to spring up, spread like a pesti-
lence, the Jewish Question. . . ." I catch snips of
talk, snatches of an idea. I don't like this overbearing
fop in his English cut clothes, his simple cane, pince-
nez with its thin little black streamer disappearing
somewhere in his collar, his finesse, ease, superiority
and self-command. I see him taking Esther away from
me, probably appeals to her like a Gramercy Square
house. She bends, absorbed, interested, to his talk,
his personality.

At last relief comes when Hymie breaks in with a
jest. He has turned out to be a rotund little man, sug-
gesting a plump boy despite the disguise of a spade
beard. "How do you like my whiskers, Esther? Going to let them grow long enough to hide my knock
knees."

"You look terribly dignified and doctorish," vouches
Esther, merrily.

"Raised the hirsute thingamajig out of self-defense.

Countenance too cherubic. Can't look innocent and be a doctor. Got to look like a doctor to be one."

Even sombre-visaged Harry jokes about the beard. "Doctors," says he, "owe a duty to the germs who give them so much business. When they chase the germs out of the patient it's only fair that they provide them a convenient hiding place. That's why doctors wear beards."

"I'm a doctor all right, here's the Van Dyke to prove it." So Hymie prattled away, saying he feels like a boy on the first day of vacation. He has just ended his long internship in a maternity hospital, and was planning to take a part of Harry's so-called office, two bare rooms with the minimum of doctoral contraptions to impress patients. How can a man be a doctor without imposing cabinets of instruments, a library-like sitting room, pictures, hangings, medicinal odors and the hush of teetering agony—without even a suggestion of the traditional doctor's office? No wonder Harry can't make a start. He knows babies and wants to treat them. But when the mothers come to his stark office, where there is nothing but conscientiousness and scientific knowledge, which they can't see, they are appalled. He can't be a good doctor, they reason. He has nothing himself. Here is Harry. His ambition reached after years of diligent study and racking midnight toil on knee pants. He has had his dingy Forsythe Street office open two years, hardly ever gets a paying patient, and looks as shabby and starved out as ever. Everybody wonders how he gets along. Does he still make knee pants during the secret hours of the night? I daresay, if his mother didn't fetch him an occasional meal he would starve to death. And he muddles on,—

the idealist; and what is he getting, I gloat, with and
for his idealism—nothing! He stumbles on because he
is dream-stupefied. Why doesn't he get wise to himself and know the world he's living in, the world he's
got to contend with? He knows a doctor without money
can make his start in only one of two ways, marry a
rich girl to tide him over the first getting-acquainted
period, or perform abortions. I suggested a few off
color cases to Harry, but he turned from them in horror. Just dream-stupefied. I can't make out Harry
at all. There's his brother, a clever pickpocket who
has so grown in the esteem of the light-fingered fra-
ternity that they have raised his rating from Archie
the Gun to Archie the Cannon.

"Tomorrow I begin the practice of medicine. Look
me up in the swell doctors' row on Forsythe Street.
Don't fall over the garbage cans and don't trip over
the tomcats. Forsythe Street has more tomcats than
any other place in the world."

"My congratulations and best wishes, Dr. Rubin,"
Esther shakes his chubby hand.

"Good luck to you, Hymie," I mumble.

"Thanks, Esther. Much obliged, Meyer. I need
good wishes—and patients. I bet Harry is glad to
have company. Won't be so tough and lonely now
that he'll have someone else starving alongside of
him. . . ." We all laughed. Even Harry. Hymie is
droll even when he doesn't say anything that's intrinsi-
cally funny. But the shadow of a cloud settles on
Harry's face when Hymie's jocularity touches a sensitive spot.

"The only way to make a start as a doctor is to get
a rich father-in-law. Meyer, old boy, find me a *shidach*

HAUNCH PAUNCH AND JOWL

(a match) with a dowry big enough to fit up a classy office and carry me along the first five years."

Harry is thinking of his Fanny Weingrad, whom, people say, he wants to marry for her father's money. . . . Now, Dr. Crane swings the talk into a serious channel.

"Dr. Rubin, there's a great truth lurking in your jest. The State should endow a physician the first five years of his practice."

Whereupon another discussion starts on that Second Avenue corner, and it seems to me as I sweep my eyes up and down the street that Second Avenue is dotted with little groups of Discussionists. Just when I have decided that they would rather talk than eat, Hymie, bubbling over in his festive mood, asks, "Say, when do we eat?"

There is no getting away from ebullient Hymie, who is like a college lad on a spree. So I have plenty of company at the dinner I had planned for Esther and myself, for confidings and communings, for the pleasure of having her alone, near me, before my eager eyes.

Hymie takes us to a foggy goulash joint, a Hungarian cellar restaurant on St. Marks Place, just off Second Avenue. Everybody is smoking in the poorly ventilated place, which accounts for the fog. My impression is of a misty sea with bobbing heads as buoys and waving hands as sails; laden schooners, waiters, carrying remarkable numbers of dishes in both arms, cruise through the aisle-channels; and one of these waiters takes us in tow and gives us a crowded berth at a small table in a corner. The unceasing talk is like the wash of the tide around our wharf. . . . "Best

[195]

goulash in the world, and oh boy! their schnitzels are schnitzels.'' Hymie is making amends for the stuffy, noisy surroundings. "And you can get real Pilsener and Culmbacher and *pischinger torte* and French pancakes *à la Wein,* Sauerkraut and Furters, and the Sauerkraut—sweet as the dew on the morning's rose.'' The way he ecstasized over the dishes awakened gustatory sensations. The proprietor, a Bohemian, round as one of his kegs of native beer, came to shake hands with Herr Doktor, and listened delightedly to the praise of his cookery.

"I will serve you myself," he announced with princely grandeur. He showed us further honor by ordering a timidly hovering omnibus boy to spread a clean tablecloth and bring his proprietorship's personal dinner service. . . . Although it was a good dinner in every respect, Dr. Harry Wotin and I sat through it in moody silence. I know Harry is thinking of Fanny Weingrad, whom he may count as lost to him, for next week she is to be married to a business man of her father's choosing.

Shammos Mendel Gerditsky was the *shadchan* (marriage broker) who arranged the match. The *shammos* supplements his meager earnings as beadle by being a matrimonial commission merchant, and a peddler of ritual wines. This morning the *shammos* had laid before me the details of the affair, as he wanted to sue Weingrad, who questioned the amount of his commission for finding a desirable husband for his daughter. I called in Weingrad and effected a settlement. The *shammos,* who liked Harry, said it was a sad affair that would mend itself. No one, in his opinion, ever died of love. Dying of love was a grandmother's tale. Yet in his own way he felt sorry for poor Hannah, who looked woebegone with her puffed fat face soiled and distorted with crying. She was short and big-bodied and pined for her spavined-looking, pinched-faced *schnorrer* doctor. The *shammos* praised her for a dutiful daughter. She would make the sensible marriage, though her heart wasn't in it, just to please her parents.

"It will mend itself, no one need fret, it will mend itself," Gerditsky reiterated, but added, a little wistfully, "Harry is a dear young man, but no one seems to see it." . . . So Harry sits brooding over his lost Fanny, and I note with growing dismay that Esther and Dr. Crane are hitting it off like long lost, joyously restored kindred spirits.

With twinkling eyes, twitting lips, between bites and munching mouthfuls, Hymie darts from table to table greeting fellow students; young physicians; acquaintances of the free guild of radical-minded; young old men, keen Discussionists of *welt politik;* old young men who are grayed and aged by their first discoveries of the grim and harsh realities of life; and the regular coffee-house hounds, who had transplanted themselves from the amiable idleness of Vienna, Budapest, Prague and Berlin to a similar ground and atmosphere in the new world, who live on remittances, borrowings, card-playing, peddling of pawn tickets, cleaning soiled cards and reselling them, doing any odd little what not, except work: a motley, queer, happy-go-lucky collection of humanity.

I heed Crane's elegant enunciation. . . . There has been a lively debate between him and Esther. He says,

"Please do not deceive yourself." . . . She has just declared that the Jewish question will simply wither away in the free, pure air of America. . . . But Crane counters deftly, opening deeper and deeper the flesh of the subject with swift, knowing scalpel-thrusts.

"The Jews will create a Jewish Question in America as long as they cling to their bizarre Jewishness. . . . What calls immediate, curious attention to the Jews . . . his outlandish ways and attire—his beards and ear-locks. . . . He is always the repellent foreigner awakening unpleasant associations of the historically misrepresented Jew . . . his slovenly, baggy clothes, or his overdressed, bejewelled, flashy appearance; his blatancy and vulgarity . . . antipathetic assertiveness . . . his maddening infallible belief in himself as being better, wiser, cleaner, more moral, shrewder, greater; the chosen of the One and Only God, worshiped in the One and Only true way—his way . . . his contempt of all others, their ways, living, believing, stupidity . . . and he becomes hateful, unbearable, undesirable. . . . Are you shocked— angered—— But those are the things we have been letting the outside world see. Here in America the Jew can show that he is something else than the marked, harried creature he seems . . . or the grasping, merciless, self-centred Shylock of popular imagination. . . . Now in America the Professional Jews stir up rumpuses, alarms, furors over every fancied grievance, insult and reflection. They focus a spotlight upon the Jews. Their self-righteous rantings in the circulation-seeking press, in pulpits, on the political stump, in mass meetings and legislative halls, do more to raise up the spectre of the Jewish question in America than all the sneers, insinuations and charges of the rabid Anti-Semites. . . . The Professional Jew is making his people more and more a delicate political problem. He forbids all criticism.

"And that is what we need here—criticism, and more criticism from within—a self-consciousness of shortcomings. . . . But who dares criticize the Jews for resorting in America to Old World ways of gaining a livelihood? Necessary, the last resorts of a hampered, hemmed in people, and, so, we understand that they were excusable—in the Old World. But here, in America, shall we condone usury, faginism, receiving stolen goods, corrupting officials, procuring, brothel-keeping, sharp-dealing, legitimatizing the cheating and overcharging of Gentiles, labor-sweating? . . . And they are but a handful comparatively, this riffraff, this scum of the wretched, cynical Continental civilization.

"Because the Professional Jews won't permit criticism and house-cleaning this handful of riffraff is made representative of the great population of poverty-stricken, hard-working, clean-living, simple, law-abiding Jews. . . . So they stifle criticism, these Professional Jews who are doing nothing but working on their lucrative jobs of appealing to the racial vanity of their people. . . . What if the criticism pierces like the probing, cleansing lancet, and burns and pains like antiseptic poured on festering sores? . . . The Jews——"

Why are there tears in Harry's eyes? Hymie has taken his seat at the table and listens, soberly. And Esther, well, her eyes have not been off his face for even a fleeting, wavering second. Crane's face is composed; his eyes have a far-away look, as though passing over a resumé of what he has said. The coffee and French pancakes are served and we eat in silence. After the table is cleared we sit without speaking, looking at Crane, expecting the tank to fill and again spill cascades of ideas. In me there is a rising, personal anger. I want to retort, choke him with strong patriotic answers. But my wires are crossed. I can't function. . . . Like the far-away boom of the surf, crawling, menacing, ominous . . . Crane's pronunciamento. . . .

"The Jews . . . only the Jews themselves . . . can solve the Jewish Question. But it has been made a closed subject. Its door has become a trap. He who ventures to open it is caught and crushed in the jaws of the guardian dogs of Jewry, the Professional Jews. They call themselves the protectors of their people. But in reality they are the jailors of their people, keeping them from enlightenment and self-liberation. Undiscussable—the unwritten law of the Professional Jew. Non-discussable. The Jew is non-discussable, a forbidden subject.

"But I will discuss it. *I will take the sick ego of my people to the clinic.* I know I will be called the enemy of my people, hounded, cursed, spat upon, disowned even by my own family, ridiculed, called a renegade, turn-coat, the paid tool of the Anti-Semites . . . excoriated . . . left without peace. . . . But I have got to go ahead, see ahead. . . . *I will take the sick ego of my people to the clinic.*"

Crane lights a cigarette. I think that here is my chance to call a halt and remind Esther that she wants to walk. But Esther says, "Please, don't stop, **Dr. Crane.**"

HAUNCH PAUNCH AND JOWL

"Yes, yes, go on," urges Harry in a dry voice, fingering his throat; while Hymie urges him to get it off his chest.

Crane smiles at Hymie and then looks into Esther's eyes. I do not seem to exist. . . .

"There is no question of religion. . . . Worship as you please, when and where you please. But get rid of the foul fungus of the Ghetto. If you do not become an integral, euphonious part of the American nation you will again isolate yourself and stand out yellow-badged among the people of the New World . . . again . . . alien, wandering, strange figures . . . again . . . distrust, dislike, persecution. . . . The Jew must take himself in hand, see himself as the world sees him. Face historical facts. Face scientific truths. Face medical and pathological findings. Treat himself. . . . I know when the outsider criticizes the Jew, the Jew withdraws behind the ramparts of his Ghetto and his religion, throws himself blindly into his consoling faith, a faith that has given our race a paranoiac tendency, the faith that he is God's Chosen People. . . . God will deliver His Chosen People from the oppressors and smite the oppressors . . . and His Chosen People will rule the world . . . some day . . . some day. . . . We are hysterical, overwrought, high-strung . . . we need the sedative of repose, selflessness. . . . We are neurasthenics . . . look at the greater ratio of insanity and feeblemindedness among our people. . . . We suffer from racial paranoia . . . believe in our racial supremacy, assert it, boast it; flaunt it in all our actions. . . . There has been too much inbreeding in the fastnesses of the Ghetto, so there are insanity and feeblemindedness, and diabetes. . . . I know the Jew

[201]

has been forced to use his brain-machine until it is
jolted out of gear . . . that living in dread and fear
of the oppressor has made us hysterical and neuras-
thenic . . . but here in America . . . it is different . . .
should be different . . . we can make it different. . . .
Tear down the walls, let out the pent-up people to
mingle and mix. Let intermarriage bring in the saving
tonic of new blood. . . . End the isolation——''

I don't know how much longer he would have continued. I looked at my watch and reminded Esther
that we would be late. We bade them good-bye, hurriedly, and Esther asked Dr. Crane to visit Finn's
social settlement. . . . She wanted to see more of him,
hear more of his crazy race psychopathology.

I called a cab, and we rode uptown without talking.
I saw Esther was lost in thought and it seemed to me
that Crane had vastly widened the distance between us.

I got tickets for the little balcony under the gallery.
Hardly had we taken our seats than the lights went out
and the orchestra showed dimly beneath the footlights.
The overture began . . . Aïda. . . . I did not hear the
music. . . . I could feel only that Esther, who sat next
to me, was in spirit far removed from me. I had
touched her hand and she pulled it away sharply. . . .
For a moment I thought I could fling myself from the
balcony. . . . But egotism came to my rescue. I sat
dreaming through the music, carried away by the
imaginings of the High Places I would reach. . . .
Esther would be an impediment. . . . She would make
me dream-stupefied. . . . I don't remember what
Esther said. . . . I kept my eyes towards the High
Places. . . . The odor of perfumed warm bodies rose
to my nostrils. I saw the white circle of shoulders in

the boxes, and I told myself I would sit in the white circle, honored, sought after, charmed, loved . . . voluptuously happy.

I left Esther at her door, bade her a crisp good night, walked vigorously to my home and ran up the stairs. I was running away from the pull of Esther.

I found Gretel waiting up for me.

III

HIRSCH & FREUND
Counsellors at Law

Thus read the large gilt letters on the expansive
plate-glass window of the store in which we make our
offices. And a swinging yellow and black sign, high
above the door, to catch the roving eyes from all points,
is more to the point. It bears a one-word legend, in
three languages, English, Yiddish and Russian, black
gaping out of yellow:

LAWYER

Mine has been a bad night. My mood is in the throes
of misgiving. Here is my office. But yesterday, I
pridefully beheld it, and today, I see it shamefacedly
as a pirates' ship. . . . I am in terror of the dream-
stupefied. I have breathed the scents of their poppy
fields.

Our pirate ship, flying its skull and bones and plague
colors, lay, so to speak, at the mouth of the lagoon.
Across the way is the Essex Market Courthouse. All
vessels in distress, alimp, leaky, in tow, must pass our
runners and steerers, pilots for the predatory crew of
Hirsch & Freund, who are adept and daring with
the grappling irons, and perfect ferrets for smelling
out worth-while plunder.

Little groups of men and women wait in front of our
office. They are the overflow of our already filled to
capacity sitting room. People like to patronize a

crowded shop. It is the herd instinct, the fear to be alone, act alone; the fear to try the new. . . . Deferential good mornings, stepping back and making way, raising of hats, eager, solicitous glances, servile holding out of hands, and awed whispers of "here he comes," are balm to my sick, drooping spirit. I pass through the congested sitting room. It is like being bathed with healing oils. . . . I plunge into a sea of troubles, other people's troubles, and peace comes to my soul. My brain clears. The poppy scents are dissipated. I am again Meyer Hirsch.

The little glazed door, which connects Maxie's office with mine, opens an inch. I get rid of the client who has my ear. I shut my outer door with a bang by way of signal to Maxie that the coast is clear. Immediately Maxie enters, followed by a stalwart, lumbering fellow with an inflamed face. . . . "Judge Duffy, I want you to meet my partner, Meyer Hirsch, a regular feller." . . . "Glad to know you, Mr. Hirsch." . . . A few minutes of small, awkward talk, and then His Honor departs. . . . Maxie smiles. He looks like a cat laughing in his whiskers as he remarks, "That's my fifth one. Laying the hooks and lines. . . . Well, bread on water, hey Mike? . . . Just took up Duffy's notes for two thousand. Told him not to worry about them. Pay when convenient. You know, when convenient. Won't bother me if he never pays." . . . Chuckling, Maxie makes an entry in a small black book which he has taken from his vest pocket. . . . "Charged it off to profit and loss." . . . I simply grin. Maxie's facial expression is an attempt at cuteness. It is very unbecoming. But I did not pick my partner for good looks. He is viciously clever, but loyal and above-board with me. I keep the political irons hot, fix the cops, do all the backing and filling in connection with the criminal cases. I split fees with court clerks, attendants, keepers, detectives, policemen, their superiors, saloonkeepers—anybody who will bring us cases. I take care of the boys all the way down the line from the judge on the bench to the bootblack in the criminal courts' hallway. Maxie's province is the civil courts, and his skill and subtlety as a cross-examiner along new lines have already earned him a reputation. But Maxie knows that legal knowledge only, on the part of a lawyer, even plus cleverness and preparation—entitles a lawyer to starve in New York courts. So he keeps his hand in the political grab-bag and is a note broker; only judges' notes. Like most of the judges, Judge Duffy was heavily in debt—in the beginning of his term. . . . So it was in that hurly-burly time of New York's nineties: A nomination or appointment to judgeship cost a stated sum; judgeships had their regular scale of prices. The market price for a Supreme Court place was $35,000. The average salary for the term fixed the price for the job. . . . Maxie's system was simple. All he wanted was the good will of the jurist. He did not ask any outright preference from the finicky and the fourflushers, just wanted the shade on his side. Soon the judges found it was safe to rule in his favor. For Maxie was not crude. He came into court prepared, bristling with facts, a-sparkle with decisions, and pointed like a porcupine with technicalities. First, he had won the gratitude of the judges, and then he proceeded to exact their respect for a thoroughly and cleverly prepared case—which gave them an essential sense of security.

HAUNCH PAUNCH AND JOWL

So the judge did not have to fear making a raw decision, and incur a rebuking reversal. Maxie saw to it that the case was punched full of loopholes. The judges liked him. He did not throw the full brunt upon them. He steered the case into a safe channel, tied it up in such a way that no one knew where it started or where it should land. Presently there circulated one of those quietly notorious facts that Maxie even wrote the decisions for the judges, wherein you learn how Maxie created a good many legal precedents—the secret twists of which he alone knew. . . . In time, when a big matter was broached to a judge, he feared to move unless Maxie was taken in as trial counsel. Then the Judge felt he was safe in throwing the case. . . . So, the notes bore fruits of perennial bloom. Judges became our steerers.

Steadily, with unremitting purposefulness, I was creating a political organization that I could call my own, an organization that would make me a factor in politics. I organized the pushcart peddlers into a Protective Association. In batches of four and five, sometimes as many as ten, I had them sworn in as citizens. My first move was to stop the petty police graft which extorted a quarter a day from each peddler. The peddlers began to hold up their heads. Then I pointed out that too many people were coming in as peddlers. So I had an ordinance passed making it unlawful to peddle without a license, and only citizens with pull could get licenses. All the peddlers flocked into the Protective Association, became citizens, and saw it was good business to limit the number of competitors. The Peddlers' Protective Association voted me a large yearly retainer. My principal service to them was to

stop the constant, annoying and expensive interference
by the police, settling squabbles over profitable spots,
opening up new streets to peddlers' stands, stopping
petty thievery by buying off the leaders of the gangs,
who also gave the peddlers protection from marauding
Irish gangs. The peddlers' vote was mine, solidly,
could be counted as a unit. Big Jim Hallorhan
acknowledged my good services, and I asked him a
favor for the boys. I wanted to keep the good will of
Shimshin and his gang, as well as the unswerving support of Boolkie and his constantly renewed ranks.
There was keen competition for the pickpocket privilege of the Brooklyn Bridge terminal, where swirling,
pushing crowds made pocket-picking easy and lucrative. Detectives were assigned to see that the regularly
designated pickpockets operated without interference
and to keep out poachers from this fine game preserve.
Big Jim awarded the Brooklyn Bridge concession to
my district. I divided it among four pickpockets, two
from Shimshin's gang and two from Boolkie's, which
gave the leaders a good income. A certain percentage
of the pickings went to the guardian detectives and to
the police inspector in charge of the Bridge district.

By this time the tough babies, who were quite grown
up, became the gangsters' meal tickets. They were
sent out on the streets. It was a police privilege for
girls to solicit on certain busy highways. If you were
not in right, your girl was arrested and kept from the
best flesh marts. So I saw to it that my boys' girls
were unmolested, collected the police tribute from them
and gave it to the local inspector of police, who found
it convenient to have me do his collecting. I never
dealt with the girls. I saw to it that Boolkie and Shim-

shin took up the allotted tolls and brought them in promptly.

So it came about that I became the attorney for the flesh brokers, the procurers and resort keepers. To keep up a certain kind of police appearance, to quiet the grumblings of the press and reformers, I arranged with the pimps, procurers, girls, and houses "to stand for a raid," which meant submitting to a spectacular alleged police clean-up, which for a few days filled the newspapers and the courts and was soon forgotten. The court cases were hushed up. And then business continued as usual at the old stands. As Big Jim said, New York is a nine-day town.

I talked over Allen Street with Big Jim and Little Tom, the former's cousin, who was responsible for my district. The reformers were making a fearful stew over Allen Street. It was the crudest of all bawdy-house streets. We decided that Allen Street should shift to other quarters. I knew the sentiments of my congregation and the Peddlers' Association. They did not want brothels so near their homes and children. I thought we could make political capital by making a sensational raid on Allen Street and having it appear that our political party without police aid broke up the vile nuisance. Jim and Tom saw the point. They assigned the nearby district captains to report to me with their strong-arm men. We gave the houses two weeks' time in which to make other arrangements, and advised them of the date of the clean-up. I then went about stirring up the congregation and the Peddlers' Association, telling them how indignant Big Jim and Little Tom were when I laid before them the extent of the abuse. I raised a hue and cry, a battle slogan,

HAUNCH PAUNCH AND JOWL

"Clean up Allen Street; clean up Allen Street." Bool-kie and Shimshin, two big procurers, were my assistants on the day of the clean-up. We marched into Allen Street like virtue incarnate, drove the women from the houses, threw furniture in the street, and in a short hour Allen Street was no more a redlight haunt. The landlords were quite broken-hearted, but everybody else was satisfied, the newspapers playing up and applauding the event. I was the head and center of the publicity, and got the lion's share of credit and esteem. Next election we swept the district as it never was swept before. I named the candidates for the State Assembly and the City Board of Aldermen. They were my straw men, Moritz Krulewitch and Hermann Weisbrod. But ten years ago they were raw immigrants. Having a constitutional dislike for manual labor—back home they were the young sons of the trader class—and having adaptable personalities, they soon got onto the Professional Jew game. They, ostensibly, were insurance brokers and adjusters, notary publics and self-sacrificing executives of the Roumanian and Polish Jewish lodges and societies. So when the election came, their respective compatriots, the Roumanian and Polish Jews, joyfully voted for Krulewitch and Weisbrod, holding it a personal honor in having their lodge members named for official distinction. Krulewitch and Weisbrod knew how to hold their jobs. In all their speeches they unfailingly referred to me as the Shield of Israel in America; they busied themselves doing petty favors for their constituents, protesting against the slightest sign of anti-semitism in schools, parks, public places, newspapers, office-holders and especially in the utterances of their immediate political opponents. They would call upon me, leading sheep-like committees, and ask me as the Leader of My Oppressed People in America to end this or that discrimination. They performed their legislative duties with punctilious attention to the party's orders. In short, their conduct assured them a steady political future in New York, and a rise from poverty to riches. Hymie Rubin, who was developing into an amiable philosophical anarchist with a weakness for puns, called the progress of my office-seeking protegés, "From Wretches to Riches." Hymie could safely joke about everybody, for everybody's wife came to be his patient. Hymie began by having countless maternity cases and no fees, but this unceasing experience made him in time one of America's greatest and best paid obstetricians. When a woman attaches herself to a doctor she makes him her god.

Again we re-elected our nominee for Congress, Joseph Goodman, a high officer of a national Jewish fraternal and protective order. He held tenaciously to the Congressional job by making only one speech at each term of Congress. Goodman made his one speech and then devoted himself to his lodge and other duties. In time this speech became an East Side classic: our best heads had concocted it. It was a hair-raising recital of the horrors of Jewish persecution in Russia that splashed vitriolic denunciations upon the Tsar and his government as being officially responsible for the pogroms, and ended with an hysterical plea to the American government to sever relations with the Tsar's government until the massacres were stopped. His campaign orations gave him no troubles of composition. He simply repeated his Congressional speech. Goodman's Socialist opponent was Avrum Toledo. Avrum made the mistake an honest man always makes, tells the truth as he understands it. He ridiculed Goodman and suggested another cure for pogroms. He was nearly lynched. He must be fearless or foolish to think that he could make the Jews believe, even for a moment, that they themselves, in the slightest degree, may be responsible for pogroms. It was not so much what Avrum had said, but what we had twisted his words into, that made trouble for the Socialist Party, which, we said, was responsible for Avrum's views. . . . Avrum had said that Jewish ways made it easy for the Russian *agents-provocateur* to inflame the peasants against the Jews. That the peasants are naturally irritated and resentful when they find themselves systematically cheated and impoverished by the wily Jewish traders, who seem, in their simple minds, to rob them with the devil's cunning. When fired with vodka and wild reports, and religious fury, the resentment is easily fanned into hatred. He did not say that the Jews as a whole cheated the peasant and deserved his resentment, but accused the trader and moneylender classes.

He said: "Let us look with clear eyes and calm brains at the Russian pogrom question. We know the Government inspires the outrages. We know the Government uses the violence and pillaging as the means of letting off the people's steam, which otherwise might be directed against their rotten government. Is that all that concerns us? How about the people whom it is so easy to incite against our people? Have we wronged them in any way? Where is our fault, in what way do we help along the happening of pogroms! I beg for a little common sense among ourselves, a few home remedies, which will do more than all the impassioned speeches in the Halls of Congress, speeches that are used merely as bait to catch your votes. I say it will not be such a simple matter for the Tsar's government to stir up pogroms when we have won the good-will, trust and affection of our Gentile neighbors. If they have every reason to respect and love us, how then can they be made to hate and destroy us? So it is up to us to stop the abuses of the traders and money-lenders.

"We must tell our people that these traders and money-lenders, the leaders and controllers of our community, this minority of profit-takers, are the root-causes of the pogroms. Let us understand the Russian peasant's mental operations. Is it not easy to be incited against the persons who have been systematically wronging you? Stop the wrong, the first wrong, and you will end the ultimate wrong. Life is reproductive. Wrong begets wrong. Hate begets hate. Love will beget a happy family. . . . In time the Russian government, unable to instigate the peasantry, will have to come out in the open. They will have to use troops to massacre the Jews. The world will ring out in protest against such savagery. Butchery, wearing official garb, attacking a peaceful, unoffending people, will turn the world against Russia. She will be a pariah wherever there is public opinion. It will be savagery without excuse, a savagery stamped with the seal of the Russian bureaucracy, and then we can make a powerful appeal to the world's sympathy and intervention. How different it will be when the Jews come to the world with clean hands and clear consciences!

HAUNCH PAUNCH AND JOWL

No longer will the Russian government shrug its shoulders and say, smugly, 'the pogroms are the anger of the people against the abuses of the Jews.'"

There was the devil to pay. Even the Socialists turned upon Avrum. They said he was a Spanish Jew and did not feel for the Russian Jews, and was like his German ilk in his dislike and contempt for his unfortunate brethren in the Pale. . . . Scratch a Socialist—the espouser of the brotherhood of internationalism—and you will find a rabid nationalist. . . . No man can escape the prejudices and predilections of his blood nor cleanse himself of the pitch of his environment.

Avrum, college graduate, was a garment worker, a plain operator at the machine. And, now, what did it avail him to have sacrificed his personal career to become one in suffering and understanding with the slave to the needle? One indiscretion, one scratch, had angered the nationalistic people. How dare he intimate that the Russ—or Pole—Jews themselves may even in a part be responsible for the pogroms? Why, man, in other words, he was justifying—justifying pogroms!

All the explanations his friends tried to make incensed them more. They hated him for a Spaniard. . . . But Avrum smiled and plodded on in the ranks of the thin, straggly line of unionists. Before long he found it harder and harder to get a job as it became known that he was a labor agitator, a wild-eyed Socialist who could even justify pogroms. Yet Avrum carried on. If he was hurt, he did not let on; if it shook his faith in the people's ability to carry out Socialism, he showed it in an increasing demand upon

[214]

educational programs for the workers. First he wanted to prepare their minds, then he wanted to prepare their hearts, after which he saw the Utopian millennium.

Sometimes he went to the extreme folly of sincerity. He tried to convert the bosses to unionism. He said an improved standard of living and working conditions would make the workers more efficient. He appealed to their interest, then he tried to touch their hearts. There was a twinkle in his eyes and a smile of self-amusement on his face, or he might have been taken for stark crazy, when he said to the bosses:—"You are keeping out the light of a great happiness from your lives. The greatest happiness is to see everyone around you happy. For how can you be happy if even one of your fellowmen is in need and distress?"

And they answered his smile and gave him the sack. . . . After a while only Philip would employ him. Philip said he did not fear his influence in his shop. No one could organize his shop. The minute a man joined the union he fired him. And there were ten greenhorns ready and eager to take his place. Philip enjoyed Avrum's talk, saying it was a fine example of the self-deluded vaporings of the dream-stupefied.

Fancy my surprise when Philip, who never took more than five minutes for lunch, and thereby gave himself a life-time of stomach trouble, called at my office and asked Maxie and me to take lunch with him in a quiet place where we could talk. At lunch Philip announced he wanted our advice on how the unions could completely stop work in all shops and for once really win a strike. . . .

Maxie taunted him, "Getting afraid of the unions?

Worrying if they can win. Want to know when to hop off the fence. . . ." But soon Philip disclosed that he had a deeper purpose. He confused us for a time when he seemed to insist that he wanted the unions to paralyze all the shops for a season.

But we got an inkling when he said, "Except my shop. I want my shop to work in full blast—as a union shop, a union shop while it suits my purpose."

Maxie took him in hand with questions. He brought out that Philip wanted to expand his business, was ready for bigger, better business. He wanted to steal the best accounts in the country from the long-established German-Jewish concerns. If he could stop their production, completely, for one season, he could make an entering wedge that never could be dislodged. He had several things up his sleeve. He had standardized the difficult short stouts, he could fit any man with a ready-made suit better than a custom tailor. He could undersell his competitors. He had stolen the best styles, pippins, sure-sellers. He wanted to spring his lines on the big accounts of the country when they had to listen to him. He needed one season to convince them.

Maxie hit right at the heart of the matter. "How do you manufacturers always manage to beat the unions?"

Philip told him that when the unionized workers quit there were plenty of greenhorns to take their places. Moreover, the workers had so little money that in a few weeks' time hunger drove them back to the benches. "But," added Philip, "our gunmen make picketing impossible. The union might make progress in their strikes if they had a chance to keep the scabs out of the

[216]

shops. We bribe the police and they assist our gunmen guards. They can't talk to the workers, they don't get a chance to win them over to the union."

"Say," remarked Philip scornfully, "doesn't it prove they are worms, these workers? They don't know enough to put up a fight for what they want. Why don't they get gunmen to fight the bosses' gunmen? Gunmen are the cheapest thing in New York. What's the price, Meyer: a black eye, five dollars; a general beating up, ten dollars; a broken arm or leg, twenty-five dollars; an out and out killing, fifty dollars!

"If they won't do their own fighting, too finicky like the respectable manufacturers, why don't they farm out the job to a private detective agency? They don't care who pays them. They'll hire gunmen to fight their own gunmen. That's the cheapest thing they got to sell, human abortions—what am I talking about—monkey abortions. When they're killed nobody'll miss them; good riddance. Beat up the scabs the way we maul the workers. Fight for what you want, and the battle never goes to the finicky."

Uncle Philip's half-joking, half-earnest tirade put a thought in my mind. I was running down a list of union organizers. There were too many pacifists. Life-for-love's-sake fellows. They did not understand life as unending change in conflict. I remembered Michel Cahn. Lately he has been spouting a new creed. . . . "All power to the workers. Seize the industries, workers, and keep them. They are yours, could not exist without you. You created them. To hell with middle class parliamentarism. Act. Direct action." . . . Michel Cahn is my man. I will put my gangs to work for him. Call off the other gangs. I will show the dream-stupefied how to get what you want. Use the simple method of life. Change in conflict.

"When do you want the strike?" I asked. . . . Philip laughed. "Look at him. Mike Hirsch, Shield of Israel. Got everything fixed, already, I bet you." . . . "Pretty near," was my succinct avowal.

My emissary found Michel Cahn taking tea in the Talkers' Café. His answer was, "Let the Honorable Haunch Paunch and Jowl come here if he wants to see me." . . . Haunch Paunch and Jowl—so that's the derisive picture the radicals had drawn of me. The lean, drawn starvelings in their dream-stupefied state were jealous of my well filled out, prosperous form. It had not yet reached the terrible proportions of obesity that years in a swivel chair on the judicial bench had later given me. But I suppose I was beginning to get fat. Well, I knew how to put my pride in my pocket when it served my pocket. Anyway, I was always working for my pocket like the Big Chief of my party. So Haunch Paunch and Jowl meandered over to the Talkers' Café and sought out the ideal-proud starveling, Michel Cahn, word-spewing revolutionist.

I took Cahn by surprise. "Do you mean what you say—the struggle between capital and labor is a class war? If it is war, do you believe in the methods of war? Or, are you just a tea-drinking talker in the Talkers' Café? The union is getting nowhere. You've got an organization. The members are getting tired of paying dues, their payments are not coming in the way they should. They are backsliding, gradually; you'll lose them all unless you give them results."

"Well," he said, measuring me carefully with his eyes, trying to sense my motive, "have you come to tell me something I know, something I am saying all the time?"

"I have come to find out if you know that the unions are in a dangerous fix. What are you doing about it, besides talking? Isn't the time ripe for militant unionism, direct action, fighting the bosses with the bosses' tools?"

"Meyer," he said, slowly, running a finger up and down his glass, "I have watched you grow up. I have watched your dear uncle. I know your breed. What do you want?"

"I want a job. I want to be the union's lawyer. No fee. Just the prestige, just the acquaintances it will get me. I want to run your next strike, but not with your love-mumblers, but with you direct-actionists." . . . I held forth temptation. . . . "Bring the strike to a successful conclusion and you'll become the union's undisputed leader. The men will follow blindly the man who wins for them the long fought and sought points."

"And your uncle?"

"He's frank about it. He put me up to this. I can't and don't want to humbug you on that. He sees Avrum's point. He'll be better off with union conditions. Better conditions will make better workers. Besides it will standardize and regulate production. It will give him more peace, leisure, enable him to plan ahead. But he can't do it unless he has a strong union that will make his competitors toe the mark. A union shop, you know, can't compete against a sweat shop. You've got to unionize the industry. But you can't do it by following namby-pamby methods. There's only one way you can convince pig-headed business men, who as a class think they know better what's best for the world than any other class. They think their business ways are the only ways for the world. Force and strength, and the most convincing proof—getting it done—making them do it, will prove your point to them."

Then we began to talk in whispers.

The following day I met the secret executive committee in the back room of a saloon on Second Avenue. A militant strike was planned. The gangs got their first jobs with the unions to fight the bosses' gunmen. In this way gang warfare became the crux of every New York strike. The battle went to the strongest gangsters reinforced by policemen. Sometimes labor had control, sometimes capital; but it was always a gang fight that decided the vital issues of capital and labor.

Our attacks were concentrated on the shops of the biggest manufacturers, the key men of the industry, whose accounts Philip wanted to nab. They would be taken off their guard because they would not dream of a successful strike. Until now they had found the union easy picking. Their gunmen guards, Irish and Italian guerrillas recruited by private detective agencies, and a strong police guard, were their chief reliance.

I saw the Chieftains of my party, and, thereupon, the police were suddenly needed elsewhere. At this time the garment manufacturers belonged to the silk-stockinged Republican Party, and did not count with us.

Our gangs maneuvered around the shop district in carriages pulled by swift horses. They swooped down upon the guards, who heretofore had received no resistance, and surprised them with assaults in force. Our gangs entered the workrooms with picked union men who spilled vitriol and other corroding acids on the finished and unfinished clothing. The scabs were driven out and the foremen badly beaten up. We established long picket lines, followed scabs to their homes and, if they would not listen to reason and join the union, they were severely mauled. Soon it spread around that it was dangerous to scab. The big shops were successfully tied up, and then we began to harass the smaller men. They quickly signed up with the union. But I advised against letting any shops begin manufacturing. Philip wasn't quite ready yet. Nobody would be allowed to work until he was ready to spring his lines. And he didn't intend offering his sure-sellers until there was a crying need for them.

The big manufacturers had a great deal at stake. The labor turnover was the profit of the day. They increased the number of guards and then set up a virtuous outcry in the newspapers that law and order were being threatened by the violence and destruction of the union's hired marauders. The gangs made feuds over the strike. It showed their lack of intelligence. They invaded each other's home hangouts, fired off pistols at random and occasionally slaughtered an innocent bystander, a pushcart peddler or a child. Rarely was a gangster hurt. Pickets were brutally handled and our men broke the bones and heads of scabs. It became a battle royal, and it began to look as though the superior numbers of the bosses would win the day. I then hit upon the scheme of buying off the bosses' gunmen. I worked it through the ward politicians in the gangs' home districts. I wanted them to lay off for three weeks, by which time the manufacturers' season would be killed. The Irish and Italian guerrillas were under the leadership of Tanner Jones, a young, fearless thug, and Jack the Rock, a Sicilian bravado. Both were amenable to their politicians' request and a handsome piece of change. Frenchie Lavelle also helped. Jack the Rock's girls worked his place, and when he asked the Rock to be a good fellow for a couple of weeks, it clinched the matter.

Meanwhile there was a great hullabaloo in the newspapers. They had an axe to grind. They looked for every chance to hit at Tammany's police administration, and proceeded to make capital out of the reign of lawlessness in the strike. Barney Finn was working for the strikers. His classmate was in charge of the city desk of one of the popular afternoon papers; and Barney interested him in the human interest stories of the hardships of the needle workers, and a sob sister was assigned to accompany Esther through the homes of starving garment workers. The sob sister turned the tide of public opinion. The sordid, semi-starved life of the sweatshop families had a Dickensian flavor and appeal. The vile sanitary conditions and long hours in the shops were described tellingly. The tune of the newspapers changed. Barney Finn emphasized Leader Lewkowitz' point. The immigrant workers were fighting for an American standard of living. The newspapers took up the demand for an American standard of living, just what that was for the average American workman nobody knew. Sociologists were just beginning to stick their noses in the cess-pool of industry. At any rate, our cause became the popular one. In a month's time the manufacturers gave in and patched up a sort of truce with the union.

Philip had gotten the accounts he wanted. He moved his showrooms to a swell Broadway office building, but continued his shop in Madison Street, which now had grown into a place that needed three large floors.

Now I was hailed as the workers' champion. The union began to flourish, and as soon as it showed signs of prosperity and success the grafters and easy-thing-boys began to edge in. They looked for the soft jobs of business agents and walking delegates.

Avrum had protested with unflagging consistency against the methods of warfare and big business in union affairs. He left the union. Cahn, flushed with victory, read him out of the organization. He said Avrum's pacifism was the worst enemy of the union's cause. It would keep the workers supine forever. Force must be met with force. Avrum said there would be no end to wrong if another wrong was used to oppose it. So Avrum said he would now devote himself to educational programs for the workers. He then began a pilgrimage that took him all over the country.

He toiled in coal mines and steel mills, always living in the wretched workmen's colonies; labored with the textile workers at the great looms of New England and the South; joined the migratory pickers and garners of fruits and grains in the East, West, Southwest and the Coast; did loathsome tasks in canneries and fisheries; became a vegetarian after three months' penance in Chicago slaughter houses; felled timber in the trackless forests of the great Northwest; grubbed in the copper and silver mines of the desert regions;

saw the land and the cities, spoke with the peoples in
their jargons, dialects and home-land tongues; returned once in a while to see his family and talk
earnestly with Esther; and then started anew on his
search for the soul and needs and desires of the American worker. Wherever he went he spoke the gospel
of oneness of interests, pleaded for a combining of all
crafts in one common union that would have an overwhelming moral force. He said union money should
be used to found schools and universities for workers.

He was laughed at, but his sincerity in the end won
a hearing. Other migratory workers took up his message, went like wandering missionaries everywhere,
trying to awaken a consciousness in the workers that
they had one cause that should be effectively expressed
in one big union. . . . In the little office of the settlement Avrum told Esther, "I find that *there is no such
thing, as yet, as an American workman.* They are to
each other—Hunks, Wops, Squareheads, Kikes, Micks
and Heinies. They look down upon each other from
the heights of their nationalism. The American will
not associate with the greasy foreigner. The Italian
detests the Hungarian, and so on. Then, there is a
class feeling of crafts. The mechanic holds the meaner
workman as his social inferior. Everyone sees himself
as a potential boss, dreams of amassing big money,
employing others. The class lines are tightly drawn.
But it will be different when the workers of America
become a racial identity. Then they will see each other
as brothers, in sympathy, comradeship and understanding, as Americans all. Meantime, we must keep
at them to learn, to rise above their clannishness, and
mean aspirations; stop the sporadic struggles and

unite as one. When we break down the class lines, the snobbery of nationalism, replace it with a commonality of spirit, then labor in its dignity and knowledge will share equally with capital the good things of the earth.''

IV

I hear amusing stories of Barney Finn's attempts to compete with Boolkie. He is trying to win the boys away from the corner hangout with counter-attractions. What has he to offer? A reading room and a gymnasium. And good precepts. On the other hand, Boolkie purveys adventure, easy money, good times. Dance halls. Joints. Racy tough babies. Jobs as scab-killers, the safe and easy employment of political thuggery and well-paid roughhouse onslaughts in gamblers' wars and disorderly house disputes. His was the life of thrills . . . and something doing all the time. . . . Boolkie's biggest aid is unemployment. There are always more young men than jobs. Then again the jobs paid so poorly and were of such a mean character that it hardly paid to put in ten and twelve hours a day and at the end of the week find yourself without even a margin for a good time. . . . They didn't want to become needle workers; they saw the hell of a life their fathers led. And what of the ambitious fellows who looked for economic salvation in business and professional life? A few rubs of the rough-grained world wore away the idealistic tenderness and left them with a protective skin of callousness. It did not take them long to see that the straight and narrow path was long and tortuous and ended in a blind alley. There was nothing in the conspicuous examples of American life to inspire anything else. Politics stank of corruption and chicanery. Big business set even a worse example. Daily the people were

treated to scandal after scandal in commerce, industry
and government. . . . The order of the day was—
PLAY THE GAME AS YOU SEE IT PLAYED. . . .
It was a sordid generation, a generation creeping out
of the mud into the murk. Avrum was right about one
thing. There was not as yet an American identity.
There was yet to rise up an American standard. . . .
It was the time and process of finding ourselves, a sort
of evolutionary process that began as a creeping thing
in the scum.

Such was my talk, my reasoning. Esther failed to
see the exigencies I cried into the case. I spoke at
length, sincerely. I believed, sincerely, my way was
right. I guess I was arguing more to convince myself.
I was raising up a bulwark of logic against Esther's
plea that I join the so-called forces for good. I had
few intervals of leisure. I was up to my neck in a
swamp of doings. I was a recognized leader. Being
a politician, I had to be responsive to everyone's beck
and call. . . . Sometimes a lull came and then I would
think of Esther. But while my mind and time were
taken up it was easy to fight off the pull of Esther. . . .
Then it began to dawn on me that mine was the fate of
every politician; my life did not belong to me, it belonged to the party and the game. I was in too deep
to draw out. I had taken root in the morass; I didn't
dare try transplantation.

V

We went together to the marriage of Lillie Rosenfeld to Sam Rakowsky, now the Sid Raleigh of song-writing fame. It was a grand affair in an uptown hall. The East Side's Who's Who was there. Sam was a famous son of the Ghetto, who had grown wealthy in the music publishing business. He and Al Wolff were also play producers, mostly musical comedies which were nothing more than glorified burlesque shows. Al said he knows what the public wants; fancy smut and a lot of bare legs.

The jewels and gala gowns of our women vied with the electric lighted chandeliers. Everybody knew everybody. Hearty greetings, hails, shouts, guffaws, shrieks and gales of laughter, screechy children sliding on the dance floor, the zooming of a brass band playing Sam's famous hits—a regular home party without fuss or repression.

Tonight, Hymie Rubin announced his engagement to Sam's sister, May, a school teacher with serious eyes and *café au lait* colored hair. . . . Al Wolff came with his second wife—the first one was some unknown whom he had divorced. Mrs. Al Wolff II. was a famous musical comedy star. . . . Old friends, introducing their wives or husbands, or fiancées. . . . Everybody was married or getting married. . . . Hymen was God. . . .

Esther, dressed in a corn-colored dress, looked so alluring I could not keep my eyes off her. She was such a contrast to the full-blown peonies about her. . . .

HAUNCH PAUNCH AND JOWL

Fat arms, bulging busts, great hips, puffed up faces, double chins. . . . A white flower on a slender stem in a tropical garden. . . . When I found myself alone with her behind an artificial palm in a corner of a little balcony, I lost all control. I saw the luminous white-ness of her shoulders, the smouldering light in her eyes . . . tonight they were not frozen. . . . Love, warmth, sensuousness were aswarm in the hot per-fumed air like bright-hued butterflies. . . . Even Esther thawed, and came out of her sheath as a warm bloom. . . . I had been drinking champagne. I was all aglow, mad, no longer Meyer Hirsch—minus the self I had given myself. I was only the man seeking his mate. . . . Like the summer wind breathing the passion glow into the flower, full-awakening it, so were my words spoken close to Esther's face. . . . I was on my knees before her, entranced by her beauty that diffused over me the odor and charm and promise of a new springtime. I kissed her hands lying in her lap. Then I felt her head lowered near mine and she was whispering. The music played. The whisper was lost, but one word nestled softly in my hearing . . . "boy." . . . And I let my head lay in the caressing folds of her gown and felt the quiver of her limbs. . . . Laughing voices came nearer, her hand pulled at my shoulder and I got up. . . . Love-making couples came seeking our nook. . . . We sat quietly, without talk-ing, like guilty children. . . . A gruff voice . . . like a premonitory grumble of thunder that makes people fly to shelter. . . . Nearer came the gruff voice, and I heard it call—"Mr. Hirsch. Anybody seen Mr. Hirsch?" . . . It was Big Joe, rougher looking for the need of a shave, with baggy clothes and a cap pulled down to his eyes as if to add to his disreputable appearance. His bloodshot eyes seemed like coals with dying gleams of fire. His message was urgent and brief. "Three of the boys pinched. Murder charge. Outside bulls dropped them. Murder charge. Taken right down to Headquarters for the third degree . . . third degree . . . murder charge . . . the Dope, Archie and the Dago." . . . I took leave of Esther hurriedly, told her I hoped I would be back in time to take her home. . . . "Esther, wait until the very last start to go, wait for me," I pleaded. . . . But I did not get back in time.

Boolkie waited outside Police Headquarters. He gave me a quick warning, "Third degree, boss." I hastened in to see the Chief and asked him to lay off the third degree. They were my boys, regular boys. He told me an ominous fact. The railroad bulls had worked up the evidence, and the regular detectives had to join in when the evidence showed up bad. I explained to the Chief that I had to stop the forcible examination of the boys. I knew that Dopie Ikie could not withstand the cajolery of rubber hose, blackjacks and police batons. "Chief," I said, "one of these boys is weak-minded, nothing more than idiot and is bound to cave in." . . . I sent for Big Jim and Little Tom. I got my way. The boys were safely locked up in cells and I saw them long enough to instruct them. . . . "Not a damn word. Don't say a damn word."

The boys were accused of the murder of a ticket seller of the Canal Street station of the Second Avenue elevated. They were also charged with the robbery of over three hundred dollars of the railroad's receipts, the alleged motive of the murder. The crime was now six weeks old. It had caused the usual stir and then seemed to be forgotten. The police did not over-extend themselves in their investigation. General report had it that the boys had a hand in it. But the railroad company did not drop the case. Their detectives planted a stool pigeon in the saloons and other haunts of the gang. Dopie Ikie's beery boast gave the game away. It seemed there would not have been a killing had not the Dope desired to shine as a killer. The boys had held up the ticket seller at the point of pistols, taken the money and were making their get-away when they heard a shot fired. Archie and Dago Jack looked back and saw the Dope grinning, with a smoking revolver in his hand. . . . It was the first notch on the Dope's gun and he was proud of it. He bragged to the stool pigeon, and they were all hauled up to answer the murder charge. . . . The ticket chopper and an old man waiting for a train were positive in their identification of the hold-up men. We tried to reach them via the usual channels of political pressure, money and threats. Boolkie was ready to bump them off himself. But the railroad detectives guarded the witnesses and supported them in grand style. The company wanted to stop the frequent hold-ups of their station agents. . . . The stool pigeon was an ex-convict. The only honest employment at this time open to a jailbird was as spy, informer and instigator. Boolkie wanted to get the stool pigeon. He half killed a barfly who earned drinks by cleaning spittoons in Jarski's saloon, and from him learned the name of the rummy who had been seen chinning with the Dope over glasses of beer in the back room. The rummy was a poor kind of a squealer where taking care of himself was concerned. He started off on a spree with the betrayal money. Boolkie traced him to the saloons and joints in the neighborhood of Jack the Rock's hangout. He put a price of one hundred dollars on the tongue of the squealer. Two days later the hundred was paid. The rummy-amateur-detective was stabbed to death in a bedhouse to which he had been lured by a woman. They cut out his tongue as a warning to other informers.

The case went to trial. Everything was against us. The Dope had blabbed to the railroad bulls the minute after he was taken in custody. The eyewitnesses were clear and convincing. We could not tamper with the jury as the railroad investigated every man that was called and they challenged the doubtful ones. Fortunately, we had one planted juror. He hung up the jury. We got the best we could hope for—a disagreement.

But at the second trial the railroad forces were more vigilant. They had a high-class jury. The boys were convicted and sentenced to die in the electric chair.

The verdict, although expected, came as a shock. For that matter, I labored throughout the trial to get a verdict of guilty in a lesser degree than death. It sounds funny, but is the fact; everybody was fighting and praying for a favorable verdict that would give the boys life imprisonment! Such is the hold life has on us.

In the corridor I found three mournful groups. Dopie Ikie's mother, Mrs. Schneider, her head covered with a knitted woolen shawl, her shrunken face like a stark symbol of the recent death pronouncement, her body swaying as to a rhythm of despair, stood between

HAUNCH PAUNCH AND JOWL

Archie the Cannon's parents, the meek and highly respected Mr. and Mrs. Yonkel Wotin. The Wotins seemed stunned, shrivelled up, as though the tears had been burned out of them. And near them, like a forlorn image, desolate in his Sunday crape suit, waited Dago Jack's father, his furrowed leathern face stiffened with restrained tears. . . . At the head of the wide staircase waited Boolkie, surrounded by bereaved Ludlow Streeters. . . . And yet another group stood watch at the door, a delegation from the social settlement, come like a priestly comforter at the deathbed—Esther Brinn, Barney Finn and Dr. Lionel Crane. . . . Finn's pale blue eyes looked compassionately at the mournful group of parents, and then turned wrathfully upon Boolkie. But Finn could not stay angry for long. Esther spoke to him and they moved over to the mournful parents with assurances that the fight to save the boys would not be given up. . . . I tried to give them hope and cheer, told them there were many chances for a successful appeal, but in my heart I knew there was none. . . . We had one hope left, the Governor's clemency . . . to commute the death sentence to life imprisonment.

The social settlement meant to make a stand against capital punishment. I told them that they would have to move heaven and earth to influence the Governor, a Republican, a hard-boiled believer in the maximum penalty for all offenders.

Dr. Crane said the fight should center around Dopie Ikie Schnieder. His life, he conceded quizzically, was the least worth saving. He saw the execution of Ikie as a piece of barbarism equal only to the legal murder of a child. He said Ikie was sentenced to death because he was legally of age, although mentally he was but a child, and no one is older than his mental years. Society must be very backward in its understanding if it cannot begin to realize that low grade imbeciles like Dopie Ikie are really infants dangerously endowed with the bodies of men. Being infants, they should not be saddled with the responsibilities of normal grown-ups, nor held liable as men of full reason for their acts. . . . Ikie's mentality—or lack of mentality—was one of the issues we fought out in the trial. Legally speaking, no one could testify Ikie was insane. No more than you can say that a boy of seven is insane just because he has a limited, childish comprehension of life and its responsibilities. . . . Dr. Crane, as one of my expert witnesses, contended that Ikie should be treated according to his mental age. It was time that Society took up the question of the relation of the feebleminded to conduct, as we have taken up the insane's relation to and effect upon conduct. They should be isolated like the insane, and kept from reproducing their kind. . . . Kept from reproducing their kind. . . . The judge was a good churchman. He frowned. . . . Man interfering with His Will! . . . The judge ruled Ikie was legally sane and responsible for his acts. . . . Esther knew Ikie, knew him for an irresponsible, foolish baby. Since the murder was due to his act, she reasoned the other two should not be put to death, but punished for their share of the crime. And, again, she did not wholly blame the boys. She felt that Society had neglected these children and now should do something for them. . . . I have observed that Society begins to take an interest in its neglected children as soon as these children take some kind of violent revenge upon Society.

Dr. Harry Wotin came out of the courtroom. He had heard his brother Archie committed to death. He had not talked with his brother in years. But now that he was in trouble, Harry came to help him. . . . Everybody waits, and then gets fearfully busy when it is too late. . . . Harry looks a little better dressed. His coat and pants match; they never did before. Hymie is bringing business to the office. It took Hymie but a few years to become the East Side's most highly valued doctor. But Hymie said Harry was the greater scientist and healer of the two. But that didn't put money in Harry's pocket; Harry didn't know how to play the game. . . . Harry said nothing, took his parents' arms and led them out of the courthouse. . . . And then Esther wept, a silent upstanding grief, a few tears rolling down her cheeks. She wept for Harry. Harry who gave all his time to the settlement babies . . . later I learned the better reason for her tears. She feared the good Wotin father and mother would soon have another loss, another death, another son snatched away. Harry had volunteered to submit to experimental inoculations. . . . The Wotin boys, Harry the doctor, and Archie the Cannon—so different, sprung from the same seed, nurtured in the same soil . . . so different . . . but were they really different? . . . Fearlessness, self-immolation were their common characteristics. . . . I remember . . . early in the trial . . . Archie saw it looked bad for the three of them. He said there was no use in the whole bunch being "croaked." He would be the "fall guy," assume all the blame and exonerate the other two. . . . He made

[235]

up a story that he thought would clear his companions
and implicate him alone. Dago Jack refused the sacrifice—and offered to make a similar one. Even the Dope
would not let Archie take all the blame. . . . And the
Dope . . . he seemed to enjoy the whole mess, had no
conception of what he had done or what was in store
for him. He liked the life in the Tombs prison and
afforded entertainment to his tier prisoners with his
gibberish and silly songs. . . . And how he liked it
when a fellow prisoner rattled his bars and called out,
"Hey, Ikie the Killer, give us a song. Shut up, you
bums, listen to a regular guy sing." . . . Dago Jack
had the blues. He said it was his fault that Ikie came
along. He had a tip that the station agent had a lot
of money on hand, and invited Archie to stick him up.
The Dope, hearing that a job was to be pulled off,
begged to be taken along. The Dago was a good fellow,
didn't want to hurt the Dope's feelings and let him
trail along. . . . They would never have trusted him
with a gun, but Ikie managed to get hold of a gun by
lying to Jarski's bartender, whom he told that Boolkie
had sent him for a pistol. . . . And so it happened. . . .

When I told Esther of Archie's proposal to shoulder
all the blame and die to save his fellows, and how Dago
Jack refused and made a like offer, she recalled Davie's
belief . . . his belief in that something in man's make-
up that was always working, working to exalt human
conduct. . . . She was very bitter at the general
indifference towards the city's children. She felt that
under other conditions these condemned murderers
might have been of some good to themselves and their
community. . . . Yet . . . I tried to point out . . . so

many others, confronted with the same set of circumstances and conditions, had turned out so much different and better. . . . I thought her answer very cold and somehow it rankled in me for a long time . . . "Not so very different, Meyer, not so very different."

A few months later I went up to Sing Sing to tell the boys the bad news. The appeal had gone against them—unanimously. The date of execution was fixed. . . . Archie looked towards the little green door that leads to the fatal chamber, and said, "All right, dust off the electric chair." . . . Dago Jack was equally unmoved. . . . They would live up to their part—their ideal; fearlessness—to the last flicker. . . . And the Dope . . . he paid little attention to our talk and seemed more interested in a new clog dance that one of the death-house inmates had taught him. . . .

We flooded the Governor with letters, petitions, telegrams and appeals. But we could not penetrate his hard-boiled maximalism. Finally, Barney Finn and I went to Albany to plead with the Governor for commutation. He was adamant. He said the crime was heinous and called for dire punishment as an example and warning. . . . Sounded like the railroad's attorney. . . . I had no influence with him. I belonged to the wrong party. He made a slap at me when he declared that the boys' crime could be laid with all propriety at the doors of Tammany Hall. . . . Five years later the Governor and I met again. I recalled his high and mighty condemnation of wrongdoing. I recalled how righteously he asseverated no wrong should be condoned by right-thinking citizenship. . . . When the Governor and I met again I had one of his personal friends in a black pocket. I had him cornered. This friend of the Governor's, a prominent society man, member of an old aristocratic American family, was found out as an unspeakable criminal, a corrupter of children, a poisoner of the spring of womanhood. And this same Governor bought me off, bought me off to suppress the evidence, bought me off with—— Well, that should be told later. . . . Meanwhile, the boys were doomed to die.

I remember the day of the electrocution. Dr. Harry Wotin was on his deathbed in a hospital. I went to see him with a little remembrance from his brother Archie, some little something Archie had fashioned out of horsehair in the death-house. I also brought a horsehair ring for Esther, a gift from the Dope. . . . Harry was surrounded by a clinic of eminent physicians. . . . They were watching his death with keen interest—with deference towards the martyr to science. . . . Up in Sing Sing his brother, too, was being attended by physicians—awaiting the death thrill that would give them the criminal's brain for study. . . . Here in the hospital Harry was proving his important point—by dying. The doctors said he was right; a certain something does cause a certain something which kills. . . . Harry was dying to save others. And Archie was being killed to warn others. . . . Where was Mamma Wotin? She had chosen to go to Sing Sing to be near the boy who was to die in ill-fame's consuming embrace. That boy, in her mother's heart, needed her most. . . . Harry could have the consolation of a great deed done.

Dopie Ikie went to his death doing his clog dance.

He called upon the official witnesses, a solemn statutory gathering, to see how good he could click his heels together. Not a man smiled. They dared not have a sense of humor in the face of death. Ikie was greatly amused when they seated him in the chair and fastened a bandage around his eyes. He laughed outright as if he had been tickled by the copper trappings and straps they attached to his body, and when the juice was turned on, it burned the leer upon his sallow, pimply face and glazed the eyes that never saw life except as a place of playthings. . . . Archie was taciturn. He refused to see both his mother and the Rabbi. He asked for a cigarette, which I gave him. He lighted it, and remarked it brought back a certain taste to him. . . .

"I taste it now," he said, as though chewing, "the potatoes we used to bake in our street bonfires. Do you remember how good they tasted, Meyer; do you remember?" . . . And they escorted him through the little green door. . . . Dago Jack marched to his death in all the glory of Catholic repentance and forgiveness. . . . He made a strange request. . . . They had taken the Dope first, as they thought he would be least able to stand the ordeal of waiting. As the Dope passed the Dago's cell, the Dago whispered, "Wait a minute, kid. C'm here an' let me kiss you." . . . He kissed Ikie's cheek. . . . "Forgive me, kid, will you forgive me? I should ha' never let you come. You're only a baby. I should ha' never let you come . . . poor kid . . . you're only a baby." . . . And so they died. . . .

VI

Now comes gossip to torment me. . . . And it drifts
in to me, the talk in the bazaars—the jostled world of
pushcarts and stands, stalls and trays and baskets, the
talk of the lullful moments, when hucksters and bar-
gainers forget fish, and apples, and underwear and
pillows, for more toothsome fare. . . .

"Did you hear——"

"What are you talking . . . tchk . . . a shame, as I
live, a shame for Jewish people."

"You didn't hear. . . . Thou knoweth Brinn—a fine
man and learned, and what is more, a good Jew . . . his
daughter . . . thou remembereth little Estherril—a dark
one——"

"Yeh—yeh—I remember——"

"*Nu,* they say . . . they say she's going to marry
that long *goy* (Gentile)." . . . Meaning Finn. . . .

"For sure . . . you know for sure, *landsfrau* (lands-
woman)?"

"So I should know of my troubles. . . . Who am I
to be the confidant of Americanskies, hah? . . . They
say . . . and so I say—if you'll let me have the potatoes a penny cheaper I'll take ten pounds——"

"I can't, believe me, we should both so live, the way
I can't—— They say, you say . . . utt . . . if they
say, it must be something already, if they say."

"And that means called America . . . such a calam-
ity to parents . . . to marry a *goy* . . . Tchk. A mad
shame, such a year and luck on me, *nach* what a

shame! . . . I go . . . can you let me have it a little cheaper . . . or I go. . . .''

Esther and Finn were seen so much together as to bring out a great clucking of ''they say''—— But suppose. . . . What a hateful blow to my ego were Esther even to consider another one when I, I—Meyer Hirsch—wanted her.

Shadchans (marriage brokers) are after me. . . . They bring alluring offers of dowries. They keep the marriage idea in my mind, an idea to summon up one image—Esther's. And now gossip buzzes disturbing warnings in my ears. . . . Esther. . . . Your Esther . . . she who fills the secret places of your being . . . the places you never look into, don't want to look into. . . . Esther of the secret places . . . look out, you'll lose her. . . .

But wouldn't I be a fool . . . just when things are shaping my way. . . . Marriage might be the biggest stepping stone of all, the big boost up to the High Places. . . . Consider. . . . Why are you looking for trouble! . . . Think. . . . You're so well off for the biding period; you have nothing to complain of; bide your time. . . . There is Gretel, a divan of delight for your tired head. . . . A comfortable, unannoying, storm-free arrangement. . . . Why, why look for trouble . . . you're fair on your way to the biggest career in New York . . . how you are sizing up! . . . Time . . . just more time. . . . The cynosure of all eyes; looked up to; catered to; they'll run after you. . . . And power! Power. Money. Position. . . . Beautiful cultured damsels with tempting fortunes . . . of high-up families . . . anointed and arrayed for you . . . paraded before you as before a king . . .

yours to choose . . . to pick the queenliest of all to grace your kingly court. . . . Bah . . . and that other . . . that nobody . . . well, what if her grandfather was the *Vilna Gaan* (Chief Rabbi of Vilna) . . . look at her father, what a father-in-law, a father-in-law who sells penny-a-glass soda water . . . puh!

These are the thoughts filtering into my mind like hot ashes. . . . I am getting ready for bed. . . . It is the beginning of another summer. . . . I stand by the window . . . a young moon rides the heavens, trailing the gauziest of nebulae . . . like a bridal veil . . . a bridal veil. . . . Gretel calls me . . . is she apprehensive . . . does she sense that I am seeing a heavenly virgin bedecked in nuptial lace? . . . "Come away, Meyer. . . . How long! . . . you have been staring at the moon! They say it is not good to look at the moon. Do not look at the moon . . . come, Meyer, my heart, come now to bed." . . .

Gretel murmurs over me in the way of her nightly wooing . . . "My tired one, rest here. May my arm be your pillow, beloved. . . . King among men, so, my tired one . . . so."

In the brooding quiet the bothersome thoughts return. The moon's glow invades my closed lids. I turn from the moon, turn and fidget. . . . "Rest, my heart, rest . . . Meyerelle . . . you are uneasy . . . I will whisper you to sleep. . . . You looked at the moon and stars, my pretty, my Meyerelle. . . . But I, your Gretel, I look at you. . . . Sleep then, my prettiness, sleep. . . . You are my shining moon and stars, my shining moon and stars . . . and the world . . . you are Gretelle's world, heart mine. . . . Here you rest upon my heart. . . . I ask nothing more . . . rest upon my heart . . . the world is mine." . . . Her hot lips press upon my eyes, searing into them, as if to burn out all other images and visions. . . . Divan of delight, diva . . . drooping, lulled, soothed . . . asleep.

I rouse up in terror. A red glare seems to have burst before my eyes . . . but the room is yawningly black. . . . Had not a bell clanged insistently, clanged . . . and was there not a rushing, blood-curdling outcry? . . . And the moon has gone, left me in a terrifying darkness. . . . Maybe Gretel cried out in her sleep. I bend over her face and feel her breath upon my cheek. She sleeps calmly. . . . I wait and listen, straining my senses. . . . What waked me? . . . The glare. The bell. The wind of anguished voices. . . . All is quiet, the dead stillness of a tomb. The blackness expands. I am dropping in an abyss—a speck in the deeps. . . . I clutch the coverlet. . . . The blackness contracts. . . . Now it is pushing upon me . . . the walls are drawing together, the ceiling sinks down upon me. . . . I gasp for breath, I am stifling. . . . I thrust out my hands to stay the crushing walls. . . . I strike Gretel. She awakes, grasps me in her strong comforting arms, holds me to her breast like a slipping, fainting child and pours beseeching endearments upon my face. . . . Slowly, I come to and sink my face in her dress, glad to shut out the nightmare like a boy covering his head with a sheet. . . . "Tell me, now, you are quiet. What is it, my life, what is it? Tell me. You were tossing and tearing. . . . Your brow is cold and wet . . . so rest, here by my heart . . . so." . . . Shaken, spent, I snuggle to her side and hold her tight.

"Nothing, Gretel. I'll sleep now. Just a bad dream."

I shake off the childish dread. . . . I must dismiss the bothersome thoughts and then I can sleep. I had taken them to sleep with me. . . . Quietly, I consider, clear-brained. . . . I know now. . . . There is no other way. It is settled. I know. . . . Push on. Push on, Meyer Hirsch. Now, the momentum is carrying you. . . . push on. . . . Ambition is the undying desire . . . push on. . . . Ambition is the un——

SIXTH PERIOD

> . . . *And sit we upon the highest throne in the world, yet sit we upon our own tail. . . .*
>
> MONTAIGNE.

SIXTH PERIOD

I

"The time has come to throw Gretel overboard."
Little sparks eddied and then were swooped up the
chimney. A log adjusted itself with a painful crunch,
spurting new flames and sparks. Philip and I sat
alone in the unlighted library, ensconced in deep
leather armchairs, basking in the fitful glow of the open
fireplace. . . . Philip waited, waited for his words to
burn in. Flicking a little cloud of ashes from his cigar
into the tumult of flames, he sat forward, bringing his
steady inquiring gaze upon my immobile face.
"Get rid of her, Meyer. Your ship's putting into
port . . . don't need ballast any more . . . get ready
for a rich cargo." . . .
He watched my face. I did not so much as flicker an
eyelash. But he seems to read my thoughts. . . .
"She's becoming a fixture in your life. What's worse;
don't let her become an unbreakable habit. . . . Mark
you, Meyer . . . your prescience of old has not become
dimmed, I hope. See through . . . and ahead. . . .
Since we moved uptown we had to give the lovely
Gretel a new status; we invented a pretty fiction—
she's a companion for your aging mother—lives in
your mother's apartment—but in *your* apartment,
too—on the top floor . . . we think, away from the
servants' prying eyes . . . we think we are fooling
the world. . . . But Gretel is too much the buxom
beauty, a beauty that is seen too much as your mother's
[247]

companion . . . good clothes, handsome carriage . . . a suggestive picture. . . . What then shall we expect but that the world in its private little whispers should say it suspects? . . . And so a pretty tale spreads.''

An anguished hiss; the living sap is scorched as in a flame of hate. Change in conflict. Hiss, sizzle, hiss. Moaning, dying, expiring in a simmer. Gretel. Overboard. The sacrificial logs crackle in answer: overboard with her, overboard; we're burning up for you; let her drown for you. The cold hearth—the end, the grave. But Philip throws on more logs. A merry sparkle. Gayety—Glamour. The song of life in death; death feeding, giving life. Change in conflict. Everything dies for you, for you—Meyer Hirsch.

Philip falls back, lost in contemplation of the gloom over the mantelpiece, speckling with gleams, like fireflies in an overcast night.

Thoughts pile on me. I daresay it's a fleeting moment that Philip has kept the silence. Like a flash of the myriads of the heavens, thoughts, images, happenings and talk spun out in this mere breath of time. The world's agony is told in a sigh. . . . Gretel . . . get rid of her. Esther; don't think of her, don't, don't. Esther. . . . Last night Dr. Hymie Rubin came to see mother. Suppose she dies. Then something will *have* to be done about Gretel. . . . His knock-knees are funny. How he waddled around the room. Picked up books and threw them down. With a bang, down went the books. ''What's the use?'' he squeaked, recalling Hi Rube of Lavelle's . . . Lavelle's. Gaslit glories. . . . ''Damn books. What's the use?'' . . . Philip snorted. He knew what Hymie meant. . . . ''Uptown; the animal on top. Uptown, a new world of get-onjohnnies living off downtown stay-where-you-are-mutts." . . . His knock-knees were funny, and his beard. He said there's nothing the matter with mother; she's just homesick, lonesome for the Ghetto; her world. He did not even say good night; banged down the stairs, sounded as if his knees were banging together. . . . Uptown. The apex of prosperity. Fitted snugly in the smug brownstone West Eighties overlooking Central Park. Uptown. On the crest. Uptown. But downtown, there I maintain a voting residence, the mouth of my tentacle. Politically, I am still an East Sider, politically only. I am still feudal lord, but as a sort of political absentee landlord. New style in politics for political bosses. Convenient. Absentee feudal lord. Somebody said that. Barney Finn. The hell with him. The hell with him. . . . Hirsch & Freund, going bigger than ever, still draws its great practice from the East Side, but it's spreading around that we are a firm for results. Results. Doesn't matter the who or the how; get the results. Results; and they flock to us. . . . What a grand suite of offices, ours, Hirsch & Freund's—an entire floor of a skyscraper. Last word in skyscrapers, rugs, desks, clerks, files, pretty stenographers, partitions, water-marked stationery, tricks——and results. . . . And Philip is getting results. A smart array of showrooms and offices in a Broadway loft edifice. Edifice; not just a building. An edifice—to results. But Philip manu-factures in the good old way . . . hiss, swelter and seethe . . . the Good Old Way—sweating on a grand scale. In barracks, that's where he manufactures the sure sellers, The New World Brand for Men Who Know Clothes for Men. . . . In dingy barracks, asoak

[249]

with sweat. . . . But they get the results. The shekels.
And Philip is rich; how rich no one knows. Everybody
says he is a millionaire; which is nearly as good as
being one. . . . Five years. The last five years of our
great Coming Up in the world. . . . Turned down the
nomination for the Superior Criminal Court bench.
Good judgment—Meyer Hirsch's! Saw it was an off
year for my party. Won't do to be tagged as a de-
feated candidate. No black mark of defeat on the
record of M. H. My party just went down to defeat.
Didn't hurt my prestige; my district rolled up a big
vote for Tammany. Even defeat made me shine—by
contrast. . . . So, I'll wait and run in a sure year.
New York's reform spurts are shortlived. Took all
the Good Elements to lick us. A fusion ticket; sour,
left-out-in-the-cold Tammanyites, disgusted Jeffer-
sonian Democrats, and clever Republican politicians
aching for a whack at the public crib. They raised a
tremendous fuss. A storm of old stuff; abuses, scandals, graft, redlight, waste, inefficiency; old stuff. A
virtuous fuss and pother that even got the people to
vote who usually were too respectable and superior
to bother going to the polls. Just the same my district
showed up fine in the count. Privileged class' plural
voting; repeaters, floaters, stuffers. Control. Organization. Cash. Showed I kept my district in my vest
pocket. Funny; the reformer Barney Finn ran on the
Fusion ticket for alderman. Snowed him under.
Damn him; he raked me over the coals. He called my
number. Called me out of my name. He and the
Socialists may think they've got my number. Can't
harm me if they have my number, so long as the bulk
of my voters don't know how to figure. But I get a

sick feeling thinking of those damned Socialists. How
they attack me; describe me as Colossus of the Fleshpots astraddle the East Side. One foot on its belly
and the other foot on its neck. *Haunch Paunch and
Jowl.* And they print caricatures of me in their scur-
rilous daily. *Haunch Paunch and Jowl.* The Socialists
are gaining votes. I'm keeping the regulars, the good
old standbys, the favor-seekers. But the Socialists are
gathering the new crop of voters; the untested generation. The younglings. The Russian newcomers taught
in the school of revolutionary thought. Bah! the
Socialist of today is the bourgeoisie of tomorrow.
Wait until they bunk against realities. Wait until they
get a little worldly goods. They'll change. They'll
come around. When a radical grows up he is a con-
servative. . . . Everything is fuel. . . .

"Did you speak, Meyer?"

I'm not going to talk about Gretel. I'll shift the
subject.

"Just thinking, Phil; are the unions bothering you
much?"

"We're gunning for them. Organized my manufacturers' union. Slip of the tongue; not a union. An
association of manufacturers; an association. . . ."
A sardonic laugh. . . . "A vast deal is in a name. A
union is un-American. An association fights for American principles. Get me, Meyer. . . ." Hiss. Sputter.
Angry snaps and bites. . . . "Unions are opposed to
the grand American institution—Personal Liberty.
They deny workmen the right to work. None of the
unions' business to tell free American workmen for
whom, what and where and how to work. They can't
tell us how to run our business. We're American, the

association; and the union, a foreign invasion. . . .''
Overboard with Gretel. Phil is consistent. After the
union served his purpose he threw it overboard. . . .
''Can't say. . . . In a way, yes, Meyer, in a way, the
unions have done the industry a certain amount of
good. Improved the workers' standard of living and
with it the standard of the industry. But can't let the
unions grow too strong, learn too much. Always
the danger of their getting wise unto themselves and
taking over the industry. And where would *we* get off
at? . . . Slowly, imperceptibly, let the unions whole-
somely regulate the industry. Good for the bosses and
workers to end the body-destroying and nerve-racking
seasonal rush. . . .''

But Philip doesn't want to talk about business. He
lapses into cigar-puffing, a sort of let's-drop-it hint.
After leaving his offices Philip had made it an inflexible, self-defense rule never to talk shop. In the beginning he found business an exacting mistress. Madame
Business said, if you want to keep me, and if you
want me to keep you, you must give yourself wholly
to me. . . . Now Philip is rich enough to relax, to
seek other interests. He didn't want to belong body
and soul to his business. All around him he saw the
awful bores it was making of nine out of ten business men. They could see, hear, talk and read only
business.

Philip finished his coffee, rang for the butler, who
gave him a light for a fresh cigar. . . . Once more he
swings my thoughts to Gretel. . . . True, she had
taken on a new status uptown. She calls herself Gertrude; only lets me call her Gretel when we are alone.
Bit by bit she has picked up a fair English, though

HAUNCH PAUNCH AND JOWL

I prefer her musical Yiddish with its poetic flexibility. As mother's companion she gets around everywhere in the automobile, shopping and visiting. . . . Private whispers. . . . Sizzle. Her full figure with pleasing roundness shows off the good clothes she wears, and I see with pride that men's eyes follow her. . . . Will the fiction be found out, the whisper flare into a burning scandal? . . . Get rid of her? . . . I had never thought of that. . . . Everything is so cozy and comfortable and well-ordered. . . . The last five years had really seen me grow fat—*Haunch Paunch and Jowl*. My chin seemed to start at my cheek bones. Hogshead belly and cabbage head. . . . Did Henri Fabre ask, why does the white butterfly seek the cabbage? . . . Gretel. Surely, now I was getting to be like most fat people, willing to let well enough alone, to stay put. . . . On the other hand, look at Uncle Philip who has kept himself slim and erect, remained a vital fighter. He is stirring my hulk, prodding the fat upon my sensibilities, urging me out of the lethargy. I know what's in his mind. Another big step forward. The old Philip; never satisfied. In fact he's getting ready, himself, for such a step—marriage.

"Don't wait until she is an embarrassment. . . ."

"Gretel will never stand in my way. . . ."

"You can't count on a woman. You never know a woman even after you've lived a lifetime with her. You don't know her because she don't know herself."

Someone came into the room, a gliding, nigh soundless presence. The Japanese butler with a tray. . . . I mused over the coffee. Philip threw away the half-burnt cigar for the luxury of a fresh smoke. "Only the first two inches, no more," he says with epicurean, millionairish diffidence. He bent over the match, brought his face nearer the firelight, and I studied his heavy shock of black hair, clustering into little groups of tiny curls, with its strange wide swath of gray. He has the tight mouth of a dyspeptic. Little hollows have been clawed out of his cheeks. Yet a handsome, rather distinguished face, for its spareness. Is it the deepening firelight . . . his eyes . . . a jest . . . eyes of a dreamer, a poet . . . but his cheek bones and chin bone and forehead bones . . . the steel skeleton of a skyscraper. . . . Indeed, a skyscraper, steel, stone and iron-flanged concrete, personality. . . . Once he remarked it is a wonder he had survived at all the mad fury of the early struggle. His business had indeed been his mistress; a passion greater than the passion of blood, the passion for power wealth would bring. An eighteen-hour day was the usual thing, hardly even pausing to eat. A snatch, gobble and guzzle—lunch. Late in the evening, as he worked, hunger would claw, remindingly. Dinner—supper. Open a can of salmon, soak it in briny artificial vinegar and spoon it up with a hunk of bread; with a large raw onion for a condiment. On. Drive on. And his had been a seven-day week. . . . And now Philip had a stomach to remind him. The stomach reminded him that there was life. The stomach made him repent. . . . At last, almost at the brink of stomachic demoralization he saw there was life—life to be lived. Like all the commerce-cursed, he said he would live—live the way he wanted to *live*—big, grand, wonderful, when he had made his pile. But nearly always, they get buried under that pile. . . . At last life was there to live, but he had lost the habit of living, had not the capacity, mental, physical or spiritual, to live. Everything in him was almost sapped out by the vampire. Toil was a habit. Sometimes it seemed he could not live without the pressure. . . . But he was Philip and took himself in hand. He tried to win back the habits of interests, reading and living. It came hard. He had to teach himself over again. He had to wean himself of the business man's contempt for culture. And the stomach needed the tenderest ministrations of a great dietitian. He heard the verdict, die or diet. . . . But the great thrust of the incentive to live came when Phil decided to attack the citadel of the Jewish Four Hundred, the exclusive social aristocracy of the German Jews. He tried and was rebuffed. They wanted not a Russian Jew in their midst. So he decided to hold aloof a while. He would find a way to sneak into the holy city and stay in.

Phil became a princely entertainer. A host of sycophants flocked round his lavish purse, and became the town-criers of his greatness. He started first-night parties at the theatres, followed by memorable suppers to the chief actors of the play. He financed shows with Al Wolff, became an angel of support and success to would-be prima donnas and tragediennes. His company was graced by beauteous women. He was the high patron of charity benefits. He became the man about town. He had his box at the opera, hob-nobbed with the famed persons of the stage and opera. In his business district he created a luncheon club, censored its membership list and made it fastidiously exclusive. In truth, he was a prince among business men. Downtown he was sought out by everyone. But, somehow the unwritten law kept him from being asked into the charmed inner circle of the Jewish Four Hundred. He had not pedigree. He was a *nouveau riche* Russian Jew. And the élite had a definite rule against Russian or Polish Jews, just as the real Four Hundred had a hard and fast rule against Jews entering their intimate circle. How then may a society remain exclusive unless it is exclusive? . . . And it came to pass in Philip's mind that he would marry himself into the elect. Not for a second was he thinking of marrying a wife. He would take unto himself—a pedigree, a social license. . . . And he was nearing the stage of negotiations with his prospective father-in-law, which accounts for Phil's pressing of the subject of Gretel tonight. For tonight Philip expected Herman Solomon Munsterkase—his potential father-in-law—to call with a rich banker to play pinochle in Philip's famous bachelor quarters. . . . And this Munsterkase had an unmarried daughter on his hands, a leftover in the social shuffle for husbands. More to the point was Miss Josephine Rauch Munsterkase's most apparent age. She was old enough to worry her parents, who belonged to a world that regarded old maidenhood in one of their daughters as a personal, insufferable reflection. . . . I met the lady on the steps of the Fifth Avenue Temple, a temple which Philip joined as a maneuver in his siege of the Four Hundred. She was a dried-up specimen, without even the saving grace of personality. But Phil minded only one thing—the pedigree. And the Munsterkases had a flock of cousinships in the social aviary atop the upper crust where inbreeding of social self-sufficiency had made them like royalty—one family. So their pedigree was the prize he was after—a life pass into the sacred precincts. . . .

HAUNCH PAUNCH AND JOWL

It is laughable, ironic. What have you got, now that you've got it! That is what Philip exclaimed when at last he had reached the peak. And what did he find? The rare people of the high altitudes were like all landlocked mountaineers, dull, gloomy, backward and painstakingly provincial. . . . The tragedy of Phil's life is that he always got what he wanted. . . . How longingly he looked at that social High Place of the Jewish Four Hundred. . . . As soon as a Russian Jew, the crass and despised herring-eater, makes a heap of money, he is obsessed with a consuming yearn to mingle with high-up German Jewish society. And, I suppose, his longing is intensified by the latter's unabiding contempt. . . . In my own case, though, I was more like the new-born American Jew, holding myself as a part of a new aristocracy—the American aristocracy of success, hall-marked with the dollar sign . . . dollar land . . . dollar land. . . .

"If you'll take my advice, Meyer, you won't lose any time. Don't wait for——"

"Mr. Munsterkase and Mr. Mortimer." . . . The announcement came with the click that turned on the electric lights. . . . Munsterkase was a man of about sixty, short, stoop-shouldered and potbellied; his yellowish complexion was relieved by a Van Dyke beard of reddish white; and his narrow thin face seemed smaller because of a great curved nose. You remembered Munsterkase by his nose. He crossed the room with a slight swaying motion, and presented Adolf Mortimer, his cousin. . . . Mortimer of the banking family of that name: the great Mortimers! The room seemed to light up with their august presence. . . . Again I was struck by Munsterkase's heavy Teutonic accent, and was more surprised since I learned he had been in America over forty years. . . . It was the accent of his shut-in clan. . . . Mortimer was different. Tall, broad-shouldered, with an outdoor complexion and easy physical bearing, he looked the American developed on a university campus. His enunciation reminded me of Dr. Lionel Crane, whom I was expecting this evening. The Harvard Tone. . . . Munster-kase had a lineal hold in a department store, and Mortimer had inherited a vice-presidency in a banking house founded four generations ago in the free city of Hamburg and now was financing copper mines and railroads in Western America. . . . Here are people to kotow to . . . chief seat holders of the Fifth Avenue Temple. . . . For a certainty we are getting there . . . but there is a sour taste in my mouth . . . Gretel. . . . Well, I suppose, what else . . . overboard. . . . I am incoherent tonight—small talk—Phil is telling a story—did I hear him say overboard . . . no, board of directors. . . . Now Esther jumbles up my mind. . . . Gretel. . . . Esther. . . . Why does her image come to worry me tonight . . . it's so long now that I have even talked with her. I thought she had quite faded away . . . but tonight. . . .

A committee from the temple files into the room headed by young Rabbi Drucker. They have come to confer with me. I have been sticking my oar into the temple affairs. I have been busy raising an issue. A successful politician knows how to make capital out of his opponents' material. Finn is getting too much influence in the East Side. What is worse, he is singling me out for attack. I have suggested to the temple that our congregation start a social settlement in the

HAUNCH PAUNCH AND JOWL

Ghetto to salvage the drifting spiritual life of the new generation, who are falling too much under the un-Jewish influence of persons like Finn. . . . I invited Munsterkase and Mortimer to advise with the committee. My mind is again clear and keenly alert. I am mindful to make a good impression on Phil's intended papa-in-law. . . . "We won't be long," I console them; "and then we can play pinochle with a good conscience;" which makes everyone laugh. . . . Soon we are settled comfortably before the fire; and our gliding Japanese servants offered smoking things. . . . Drucker was assistant Rabbi to the venerable Joseph Roseman, for many years Rabbi of the Fifth Avenue Temple. The young Rabbi was an ambitious fellow and knew all the wiles of the climber. His sure method was to praise and puff up influential members. . . . He mentioned the topic of the committee meeting, using it as an opening to flatter me. He spoke the readily understood sanctimonious phrases . . . Judaism . . . Judaism. . . . Again he sees a chance to flatter me. . . . "Mr. Hirsch . . . long known as untiring defender of Jewry and its enduring-through-the-ages ideals and culture. . . . Now with great insight Mr. Hirsch sees a situation that develops, menacingly. . . . Among ourselves, we must really keep it among ourselves, for no good purpose may be accomplished by advertising our shame . . . therefore among ourselves we must see as Mr. Hirsch has wisely seen, the young Jews of the new generation are being weaned away from Judaism." . . . Munsterkase shook his head in solemn distress. Mortimer suppressed a yawn. . . . The Rabbi at best was a dull fellow, outside of knowing how to play his particular game well. I feared he

[259]

would drag out the meeting and deny Munsterkase his coveted pinochle game. Fortunately, Dr. Lionel Crane arrived at this juncture. . . . I had asked Crane to give us the benefit of his expert advice. I was playing a little game with Crane, seducing my enemy after the infallible Turkish fashion of demoralizing a dangerous man with a pashaship and a seraglio. I had a sneaking feeling that giving Crane a good job and a chance to mix with the higher-ups, he would play the game, and forget his crusade against the Professional Jew and his theory of intermarriage as the saving tonic for the Jewish race. And I wasn't far from right, for Crane sought eagerly the job of establishing a social settlement under the patronage of the exclusive Fifth Avenue Temple. Besides Crane now had a wife and baby to support. . . . Crane stood in the center with his back to the fire. He was getting a little bald now, and carried a respectable corporation. His manner was suave. In the past his talk used to bite into you. Tonight he brushed you gently. . . . Yet, he had his old way of scaring off contradiction; he knew too well anything he talked about. . . . Said Crane, "Are you aware that Christian Science, New Thought, Theosophical, Ethical Culture and Unitarian churches are attracting Jewish membership, particularly among the younger Jews?" . . . Munsterkase literally pricked up his ears. . . . Can it be! . . . "Yes, they are attracting the spiritually hungry who are repelled by the crudities and absurdities of our own orthodox religion. Your temple is a reformed synagogue, it expresses your departure from orthodoxy. But you have kept to yourselves. How are the young Jews to find out that a Jew may worship and live in a sane, dignified

[260]

and American fashion and yet remain a Jew! You have got to bring them the message of your ways in the same way that the social settlements founded by the Gentiles bring them the appeal of their ways. And yet when you get down to it, your ways are no different from the refined Gentile's. . . . Really what we are concerned with is to gain respect for Judaism, and to gain respect for Judaism we will have to dignify it. Our next task is to tone down our high-pitched personalities. . . . In order to win over the minds that have become emancipated from the dread and superstition of orthodoxy you will have to show them that our religion is reasonable and purposeful. Purposeful; a religion that does something besides praying. Then there are others whom we will have to attract from the social side. The propertied middle classes like the business of going to church on Sunday morning; it's something nice to do on Sunday morning when there's nothing else to do. . . . So the old world synagogues in this new world are inadequate, unsatisfying, socially and spiritually. . . . But there is yet another serious phase of a growing Jewish population that is religionless. A great number are finding their spiritual craving gratified in Socialism and philosophical anarchism. I hold radicalism is an expression of spiritual need. . . . Do you think it will improve our position in America when our people become known for radicals, enemies of existing institutions? It will be another cause for dislike and distrust . . . a people always swinging between extremes. . . . It is time that the Jew in everything he does should cease to make himself a marked man. . . ."

Voices spring up in agreement. . . . An elderly

man, "Who could believe it would come to this? Alas! A little liberty and our young abandon the religion their fathers died for. . . . What persecution could not do, a little liberty does. . . ." . . . Drucker, "Mr. Hirsch has the right idea. . . ." Munsterkase, "The wurst is thot Socialism . . . owfull . . . and anarch-ismus— that is terrible." . . . A committeman on the fringe: "Save them from the proselytes. . . ." Whereupon Drucker dilates upon our duty to our people. He has a steady flow of stereotyped phrases and bromidioms, and it is getting a little drawn out. After all, a problem is only a problem, but pinochle is a fascinating game. Deftly I take the lead from Drucker and bring the meeting to practical considerations. As usual, the job of getting something done is delegated to a sub-committee of three, in this case, Crane, Drucker and myself. A safe social settlement guided by the Fifth Avenue Temple is practically assured. Philip has watched the meeting with interest. He is pleased because Munsterkase has been impressed favorably. . . . The committee began the confusing business of shaking hands and taking leave, sprinkling their farewells with solemn asides at the seriousness of the problem. Drucker shook hands with me in his sleek way, and asked casually if I had read the evening papers. . . . No. . . . "The nasty headlines you missed them, Mr. Hirsch. Imagine my feelings as I read, 'Poor Jewish Girl Marries Millionaire Sociologist'—a *goy* . . . what's his name—the man who started the settlement; yes, Finn. Seems an aunt or two died and left him a few millions, so he is a subject for publicity. Look at the headlines—poor Jewish girl. . . . Who is the girl? . . . the paper named someone, I think her name

sounds something like his . . . yes, yes, now that you
mention it—Esther Brinn . . . scandalous. . . . They
say she married him for money . . . see the implica-
tion . . . everything against the Jew . . . she married
a *goy* for his money. . . ."

Crane confirmed the astounding news—"Yes, took
Finn years to win her. Something seemed to stand in
the way. Perhaps the difference in religion. Or,
maybe another man . . . who knows. . . . They were
married quietly a few weeks ago. Ethical Culture ceremony . . . But now that Finn has inherited millions
the marriage has become a newspaper sensation. . . ."

I slipped upstairs to my room. All was still. Mother
nodded in her rocking chair, and I could hear the slightest kind of a hum, almost like a faraway river murmur,
probably Gretel busy in another room. . . . I was very
calm; a terrible quietness had settled on me. I took
my hat and coat. . . . Again, the trick of rapid incoherent thoughts flipping about my mind. . . . I looked
at mother. She always wanted to sit in a corner, just
as she did in Ludlow Street after father's death. . . . I
slipped past her into the hallway. I have put on my
hat and coat without an idea of going anywhere. It
seems I just had to go. Where, did not matter. . . .
Go. . . . In the library the pinochle game has begun. . . . I make an excuse, just called away by an
important case. . . .
Esther married! The December wind seemed to
howl it through the side street I paced on my way
towards the river. Esther . . . your Esther—married . . . to Finn . . . your enemy. . . . I came to the

granite parapet and looked on the dark river. . . .
Overboard with Gretel. . . . I turned my back to the
river. . . . Esther. . . . An electric arc light over the
roadway shone upon a bit of white paper, shone
whitely and reminiscently, and then was swept up
and away on the black wing of the screaming wind. . . .
Esther married. . . . Do you remember . . . the whiteness of that bit of paper . . . do you remember, Meyer
Hirsch, once, when you went for the second time to
look into Esther's window? How you pulled yourself
up to the sill, and with your head moved the shutter
aside, and the moon shone in for a moment. . . . Esther
asleep on the bed . . . a moonbeam upon her shoulders, and she moved . . . the coverlet turned down
and you saw the whiteness of a marble bust, a Grecian
bust . . . and a cat rankled over the cans in the backyard and you fled. . . . Oh, the sheer beauty of the
Grecian bust. . . . Meyer Hirsch, you will never forget. . . . The wind screeched in my ears . . . you
thought you would forget . . . but you will never forget Esther . . . her eyes . . . her hands . . . her
quick smile . . . and her voice . . . you will never forget. . . . Everything is rushing on, swiftly. The wind
is sweeping the world away from me. . . . I am left
alone clinging to the granite block . . . the trees rush
past, the houses swoop away, the river rages on its
flight from me; below me I feel a rumble; now comes
a gaseous snort . . . a freight train flees after the
wind-borne trees, houses, river, and swirling roads. . . .
The wine of her lips—one kiss . . . limbs quivering
beneath silk . . . a whisper . . . dust off the electric
chair . . . charred potatoes but sweet . . . a whisper . . . hands tingling under my hot lips. . . .

"What the hell is the matter with you? You made your choice. What're you bellyachin' for?..."

The wind is stilled for a brooding moment. Two men have passed. Their pungent talk is like an answer to the flipping images in my mind. Be quiet. You made your choice. So I face the river and I hear the rhythmic wash, and it seems to be querying, "What the hell is the matter with you? Go home, go home to your Gretel. She waits and longs for you. Go home to your Gretel."...

"You're givin' me the go-by. Please, Jack, don't give me the go-by...."

The wind whips up the dust and dead leaves.

"It's good-by for good, Margot, good-by and good luck."

A girl stands beside me. First she sobs, and then she snickers. "Where did you come from, fat daddy?"

I stand stolidly watching the river lashing its white little children hither and thither—they are like my ghost-thoughts tumbling and dashing and getting nowhere.

"Hey, are you ossified, fat daddy?"... She poked me in the ribs. I looked around as a hand came up to my shoulder.

"Say, fat daddy, sweet daddy, I wisht somebody would take me off on a drunk. I want to get stinkin', paralyzin', forgettin'-drunk . . . forgettin' . . . forgettin' . . . drunk. . . . Did you see him gi'me me the go-by? He's through. That's all—through. Said I was a fast filly but no thoroughbred. Said when I got a few drinks in me the streak showed. . . . Why didn't I take Madame Mina's advice? She's the wise old owl. . . . A girl like me should stick to fat guys and

old blokes, safe, nice fat daddies like you . . . shouldn't
get tangled and twisted with a young fellow . . . they
gives you the go-by" . . . .

She took her hand away. She began drumming
her fingers on the stone. . . . "Say, fat daddy, warm
my hands, won't you? Warm my hands, they're dead
cold. . . . That's me all over. I always ha' got to
have someone. . . . I can't be alone. . . . I can't stand
bein' cold . . . I can't stand the gaff of just bein'. . . .
I got to be doin'. . . . I got to keep goin'. . . . I got to
have lovin'. . . . That's the way, sweet daddy, I'll
stand clost and keep my blue fingers inside your nice
fur coat . . . ain't that nice fur! . . . I'll bet this
benny cost a nice piece of change. . . . You got a nice
friendly fat face . . . hey, but you, too, ha' got cold
college eyes . . . what's a matter with you educated
guys . . . what do they do to your eyes? . . . I'm
gonna put my face on your nice soft lamb's collar . . .
that's what I need—soft lamb . . . not killin', draggin'
muscles. . . . Sweet daddy, take me home, take me
home." . . .

"Move along, now, keep movin', can't loiter here all
night; come on now, get a move on." . . . Peremptory,
cold, cutting words hurtled at us as though out of a
gust of the wind. The policeman swung his baton as
he waited to see how quickly his order would be
heeded. . . . The girl pulled my arm, saying, "Come
on now, daddy—" now whispering, "see, the cops
are gettin' fresh now, gettin' ready for next month
when the new reform mayor comes in. Come along
now, and have a good time while the goin' is good.
Next month the lid goes down tight." . . . We moved

along the path of the little strip of parkway, and the heavy-footed policeman passed us.

"Daddy, seems like you was drunk. But I don't smell nothin' on ye. . . . You ain't been hittin' the dope, fat boy?"

Pitying me . . . she is pitying me . . . this little creature of the crossways . . . pitying Meyer Hirsch, fat, ungainly, phlegmatic . . . a safe man for the little chit; no other woman would steal him from her. . . . Say, where is that remote yesterday of conquests? . . .

The hall door shut behind us. . . . Walking up the stairs she tells me little confidences in my ear, "My name's Margot. You're a Jewish lookin' gent and so I'm gonna introjuce you for—let's see—Mr. Cohen, that's a Jewish name like Jones is one of our names. This place is Madame Mina's. She likes Jews. They was good to her. There was three old fellows what owned shares in her like in a stock corporation. They couldn't afford each one to keep his own woman, and they wasn't the kind to knock aroun', so they took shares-like in Mina. Now she's old and she keeps a nice respectable call flat. No joint." . . .

. . . Margot settled me in an armchair, and perched herself with ingenue childishness upon my knee.

"Now then, have them fetch a couple quarts of champagne," I suggested.

"Say, you're a regular sport," said Margot, admiringly, "I figured you for a white sport. . . . Champagne . . . for a giddy drunk . . . first the world am dark and dreary . . . but wealthy water brings the rosy dawn . . . champagne." . . .

The colored maid brought a cooler with champagne. Margot put a little screen around the armchair which

gave us a little air of privacy, but only an air. . . .
But it is pleasant here. . . . Margot is so engaging,
winsome and disingenuous that she charms away disturbing thoughts and memories. Margot does not live
in life, she plays at living. She is casual, gracious;
and life just happens to her. She follows naturally
the trend of the next happening, and so goes on; one
moment broken-hearted, and again blithe and gay . . .
she adorns the idling hour. . . Her eyes are deeply
blue, and her nose a bit of a turned up thing; she has
boyishly rounded cheeks, a small living mouth, good
teeth, and a tiny perfect chin. Her throat arches
slenderly, and her chest and waist are like a supple
lad's. . . . She tilts the glass against my lips and bids
me quaff long and deep, promising a rosy awakening
from "your dumps." . . . "You don't have to tell me
your real name," says she, "but it's more chummy-
like to call you by your pet name, you know, somethin'
the boys call you . . ." . . . Involuntarily, I utter,
"Haunch—" and catch myself . . . "Hunch," she repeated as the word of her understanding; "hunch,
that's a good handle. You must be lucky. You get
the hunch of what to pull off. Good hunch. Hunch.
Hunch, that's what I'll monicker you. Hunchy-
boy. . . . Say ain't this grand stuff . . . hits you in
the right spot." . . .

. . . .

    I am quite drunk . . . my own self . . . my past . . .
everything up to this hour seems to have detached itself from my consciousness and flown away. . . . I am
happy. . . . I have taken myself out of the cellar of
my hulk . . . and I quit holding back—I let myself
sail in life—I am a little fuddled and uncertain on my

feet. . . . Someone has come to help with Margot on the other side. . . . They take me into a half-dark room . . . a bed sways before me . . . but they manage to let me slide onto the bed . . . then I remember that at home they will fret and worry. . . . Gretel will . . . and I grunt, "Margot—good girl—telephone —gotta telephone home—waiting—worrying—" She staggers a bit, pulls herself together, speaking thickly: "Damn right—can't have 'em waitin' and worryin'. . . . Mikeen, hel-lup him up wi'ye, take him over the phone . . . got to call up . . . wife or sumpin' . . . sumpin' . . . waitin' . . . worritin' . . . he's a white guy . . . hel-lup him to—" They sat me on the floor and put the telephone in my hand. With a great effort I concentrated on the number. . . . Quickly came the anxious voice of Gretel's, as from another world, another existence. . . . I managed to speak and conveyed to her. . . . "Case . . . would take all night . . . would call in the morning again" . . . and I heard her speak anxiously in Yiddish, something or other about being careful of myself and I slumped over. . . . Forgettin'—drunk——

II

A voice kept at me, began to percolate in as a vague whisper, and then worked clearly into my mind. . . . "When *do* you have to get up . . . when *do* you have to get up?" . . .

I opened my eyes and for a moment or two was puzzled by the unfamiliar face peering at me. . . .

"Are you pretty groggy, sweet daddy? I'm doin' time with a hang-over myself . . . but it's a beaut. . . . Wait now, sit pretty, and I'm gonna fetch a pitcher of ice water, and then I'm gonna hand you your breakfast —a large pot of demi-tasse." . . .

Oh, my head. Little sharp things are picking at my head in a million places. . . .

"Hey there, Hunchy, don't guzzle that ice water so fast, want to give yourself a chill and heartburn? . . . Thataway . . . easy." . . . And she rested my head on her breast. . . . "No go to the well again . . . slow, now." . . . She put my head back on the pillow, tucked the sheets under my chin, and then kissed me on the tip of the nose, the last being a trick seemingly peculiar to Margot. . . . "Listen, Hunchy-boy, have you got a job to go to or sumpin'? Thatawhy I've been razzin' you like a puppy at the shoulder of a Saint Bernard. . . . Now tell your little sweetie, what time you got to make it. It's clost to nine now." . . .

"Thanks little girl, I'll have to get up pretty

soon. . . . I'll rest a few minutes . . . get myself together." . . .

"All right, you look kinda shot to pieces. . . . Now
I'll go and make the coffee." . . . I looked after her,
and saw she staggered a little. . . . I called out, "Say
you ought to be lying down yourself—" . . . And she
answered cheerily, "I'll say so—but I'm a little sticker,
another name for sucker, that's the way I'm made. . . .
I want you to know, Hunchy," she stopped to say at
the doorway, "this ain't no panel joint, no shake
down crowd. I've done a little rough work in my
time . . . just for fun . . . but Mina don't stand for
nothin' rough. . . . I checked your bankroll with
Mina. . . . But boy, oh boy, you need that bankroll for
the check you gonna get. Wait till you see the bad
news for all that champin you slewed . . . but it was
a gran' little party . . . and I don't care . . . Daddy
is rich, ain't you?" . . . and she skipped away.

Madame Mina came into the room with Margot. She
had my pocketbook in her hand and gave it to me with
a little memorandum for the drinks. Madame Mina
had something on her mind and she came to the point
with German abruptness. . . . Said she, "I looked in
your pocketbook. You understand that. I went over
with Margot to make sure how much was in it. I see
you are a lawyer, and I got a case for a lawyer." . . .
Wherewith Margot, pipingly, broke in, "Look alive
now Hunch, we're gonna throw you some good business." . . . Madame Mina continued, "Downstairs is
the janitor woman, a widow, she's got one girl, only
sixteen. She's been away for four days. She was
away with the iceman's girl. All evening the mother
was after her Jenny to tell where she's been and what's

she been doing. . . . A millionaire . . . you know the
reformer . . . yes, that's the name, an old fellow——"

When I heard the details I got up with alacrity.
Here was the prospect of a big killing. I told Madame
Mina that I would have a man work on the case immediately. In the meantime she must see that the
girl does not leave the house. . . .

Margot helped me gather my scattered things and
put myself together, presentably, meantime, carrying
on a one-sided racy conversation.

Later I watched her as she stood by the window,
marvelling at her boyish form now draped in a diapha-
nous pale green kimono tied with a girdle around the
hips. Her bright hair fell in ripples about her face
and shoulders. . . . She appeared to be lost in a little
reverie, a sort of child's absentmindedness. . . . But
when it came time to say good-bye, she again put her
face upon the Persian lamb collar of my overcoat, and
spoke in a wistful though detached way, "Wonder,
Hunchy, if I'm gonna see you again." . . . And I remembered that she was my chit of the crossways and
that I owed her an earnest. . . . "A fur coat for
Margot, how would that hit you?" . . . "A home run,
Hunchy." . . . And I told her where to go and select
a coat after her own heart. . . . She just looked at me.
Then she got up on her toes and kissed me on the tip
of the nose. . . . "You mean it, you ain't kiddin'
me. . . . I said you was white . . . shake, Hunchy, and
thanks . . . but lookahere, daddy . . . you don't think
you're buyin' me . . . you ain't buyin' me. . . . I'm
promisin' nothin'. I am myself—Margot . . . got to
keep doin' . . . and goin' . . . and if that Jack with

hunky white teeth should come aroun' . . . well I ain't promisin' nothin'." . . .

There in the queerly lighted room, where sputtered a low gas jet, and, a black blind, three quarters drawn, was at odds with the pushing, strong morning sunlight, Margot, in the changing shadows and glare as of a wood, seemed elfin, indeed a will-o'-the-wisp love sprite. . . .

III

The office staff looked nervous and fidgety when I came in late in the morning. Maxie flew into my private chamber the minute he heard I had come in. . . . Gretel had been making frantic inquiries concerning me; apparently my muffled abrupt message at an eerie hour of the night had mystified and worried her. . . .

"On a bat . . . or on a case, Mike?" . . .

"Both, Max."

He smiled as he regarded my pasty face and bloodshot eyes. . . . I called for our expert runner, Lurie the Rat, a labor spy and an expert blackmailer. . . . I outlined the case to Maxie and the Rat. . . . With staccato clearness Maxie instructed the Rat. . . . "Get both girls. Stick with them. Let them tell their stories to each other. See that they agree with each other. Don't open your trap till they have talked themselves out. Then line up their stories over and over again until they never can forget that *that's the story*. Then write it down—in their own language—you're a notary, —swear them—but don't dare use legal phraseology. Don't stultify and paralyze your witnesses with legal words. Be careful, Lurie, you amateur lawyers love legal *shmooserie* . . . avoid it like a plague . . . always have your affidavits in your witnesses' own language . . . slang . . . filth . . . everything . . . then you can't go wrong. A witness can't go back on his own pet terms."

Maxie never interviews witnesses, especially in cases where blackmail may be charged. None could accuse

[274]

him first-hand. But he knew how to instruct his wit-
ness-handlers. Our rats knew how to whip witnesses
into shape. . . .

Lurie was despatched with a second runner who was
to bring the girls' sworn statements back to the office
while Lurie stuck to the girls. . . .

The runner in good time returned with the girls'
own stories. . . . In a few minutes two plainclothes
shakedown specialists from Police Headquarters reported and asked to hear the town's latest dirt. . . .
They smiled in anticipation of the nice fat drippings of
a millionaire on the spit. . . . They were instructed to
go to the accused's home, ask for him, and of course
they would be referred to his lawyers. The detectives
were then to go to his lawyers and intimate that the
charges had been made but that a certain law firm had
the accusers' depositions . . . and then leave the rest
to Hirsch & Freund . . . big lawyers are our meat. . . .
The news came in that Judge Martin Hussing of the
Superior Criminal Court had died last night. Maxie
regretted that the Governor was a Republican; otherwise I might get the appointment. . . . And he put a
thought in my mind. . . . The millionaire was a prominent reformer and high in the national councils of the
Republican Party. . . .
I waited alone in my office. A fur dealer called up—
"is it all right"—"what's that"—"a fur coat for a
young lady"—for a moment I could not understand—
my mind was filled with the vacant judgeship which
could not be filled by an election now but by the Gov-

ernor's designation—"what did you say"—"name—
Margot"—"Yes . . . yes . . . give her a good coat . . .
no bill. . . . I'll be up and give you the cash . . . yes,
Mortie . . . that's right." . . .

Now I considered the judgeship . . . seemed to stick
in my crop. Now I know . . . the judgeship is the
price for squashing the case. . . .

An august name is announced—the former governor,
who had refused clemency for my boys. . . . I guess
he has come about the millionaire's case. . . . He beats
around the bush in an elegant fashion, but I remember
his brusque treatment of me and I call him to time and
tell him to come down to brass tacks. . . . He hems . . .
"would be unfortunate . . . a really great man . . .
philanthropist . . . humanitarian . . . no good served
by prosecution and publicity . . . no good at all . . .
some matters best if quieted . . . for good of public
morals . . . of course, girls and their people properly
compensated . . . and the lawyers . . . and detectives . . . the same good accomplished . . . terrible
warning to man . . . a mistake." . . .

"Good citizenship should not condone wrong-doing."
I have repeated his memorable bromidiom, but he is too
wrapped up in his worry over his client and personal
friend to detect ironic shading. . . . He takes me seriously and starts over again his lame extenuations. . . .
So I come to the point.

"Listen here, Mr. Ex-governor, it isn't going to cost
your friend one cent to squash this case, not a cent. . . .
He'll get a retraction and exoneration in the girls' own
handwriting. . . . I will pay the hush money to their
parents and the detectives . . . but I expect a piece
of writing in return . . . a Christmas present from

your Governor—a certificate of appointment naming Meyer Hirsch to fill the unexpired term of Judge Hussing. . . . Meyer Hirsch, Judge of the Superior Criminal Court.''

He was so taken aback that he half rose from his chair.

''Make the next train to Albany and you ought to be back the first thing in the morning with the—appointment. It will give your governor a chance to show what a sweet believer he is in one of your pet planks in your platform—a non-partisan judiciary. A Republican governor appoints a regular Democrat, Meyer Hirsch, whose knowledge, experience and sterling character so well fit him for the Superior Criminal Court. Where the judiciary is concerned the Governor shows a fine non-partisanship. It will be something in his favor besides doing a favor to big Republican contributors.''

He tried to talk me out of my idea, tactfully mentioning a neat sum, a staggering sum, but I said curtly, ''Take it or leave it, I'll wait until eleven tomorrow morning.'' . . . I opened the door for him as an unmistakable cue that the interview was concluded. . . . He shook hands pleasantly and said he was leaving for Albany on the next train. . . .

IV

Philip is still an early riser. . . . The next morning I was awakened by loud rapping on my door, and then Philip rushed in with a newspaper in his hand. He cried, "You scamp, why didn't you tell me before? Don't you think my future father-in-law would be delighted to know he is marrying his daughter into a judge's family?" . . . I demanded to know what he was talking about. . . . Philip waved the paper, exclaiming, "Here it is on the front page. . . . Governor Appoints Hirsch to Superior Court. . . . Republican Executive Designates Democrat. . . . Victory for Non-Partisan Judiciary—Hirsch A Well Known Practitioner—A Leader of National Jewish Societies" . . . I grabbed the paper eagerly and saw it was a midnight despatch from Albany. A certain man must have been so importunate that he had had the anouncement made at once to reassure both himself and me. . . .

By the time I got to the office the place was jammed with people come to congratulate me. Big Jim came in to find out what the hell it was all about and was I a turncoat and was I going to double-cross him after all he done. . . . I took him into Maxie's office, explained my strategy and received his congratulations on my quick thinking. Judge Hussing was a Democrat and to have had his place taken by a severe Republican would have hurt our popular prestige. . . . The ex-governor was in my private office. . . . He was my warmest congratulator and well wisher. . . . Now I

was a judge . . . he kotowed . . . the whole world
seemed to be kotowing. . . . Maxie came in grinning
and hugged me. . . . The world never heard of a certain case. I saw to it that everybody concerned was
amply satisfied . . . and in this wise I became Honorable Meyer Hirsch, Justice, Superior Criminal Court.

V

A formula of polite nothings has given me a stupid fifteen minutes. . . . I try my best to make conversation. . . . Once more begins the tiresome formula: "Really . . . how kind . . . thank you . . . very good of you . . . do come again." . . . An awkward hiatus. . . . An early spring breeze stirs the curtains. I take in the rich-looking room of Philip's Riverside Drive residence. He has just returned from his honeymoon, and is now established in a modern duplex apartment which he has furnished with distinguished taste and elegance. . . . The former Miss Munsterkase, now my Aunt Josephine, received me with set graciousness, which, I soon observed, was a drilled-in, learned-by-rote system of saying something. . . . I daresay had pert Margot been present she would have sized up the situation succinctly—"nobody home." It came to me as I watched the expression of her face that Mrs. Philip Gold was like Dopie Ikie Schneider, but she had the advantage of thorough drilling in how to keep up a semblance of talk. No wonder she was let go to a Russian Jew. . . . After all, I consoled myself, it wasn't a wife that Phil wanted . . . hardly mattered that she was mentally below par . . . she was a means . . . a stepping stone. . . .

At last Phil comes to my relief. After Josephine left the room I could almost hear the irrepressible Margot exclaim, "Some sap, but—some sap." . . . That little red-head with her zestful charm sticks in my mind. . . . I'll have to contrive to see her without

reflecting on my judicial dignity. . . . A zestful little
thing spicing the cup of life. . . .

Phil makes a wry face at his wife's retreating back.
He draws near, and says with a twisted smile—"Well,
Judge, give the verdict. Speak up. You and I never
deceive each other. Say it, Philip Gold's wife is nothing to look at and no one to talk to. . . . A wife . . .
an admission ticket . . . everybody's cousin. . . . I've
picked the prize moron . . . hasn't she got a lovely
moronish profile——"

I grinned. Philip made another wry face. . . .
"Oh—that honeymoon. . . . One thing is certain . . .
After all, honeymoons serve their purpose. . . . One
thing is certain—my wife never travels with me
again. . . . The bargain is made: that's done with.
She has a husband and I have an admission ticket.
Henceforth, our lives go their separate ways. . . .
Remember, Meyer, sometime they may bring a wife
poisoner before you. Be easy with him, poor
fellow."

Philip took me to sit in the window embrasure. The
river was opaque in the April twilight. Shining motor
cars sped by. The lawns glistened greenly sleek, and
the trees lifted their clean limbs to show their new
little leaves. I watched the boats floating their pen-
nants of smoke and steam, and saw the river turn a
gleaming blue under the changing sky. Philip, too,
looked on in silence and then remarked, "A little different from the view on Ludlow Street, eh, Meyer? . . .
By the way, Meyer, your uncle has an ambition, and
you will have to help along. . . . What would you think
of Philip Gold as ambassador to Turkey—seeing that's
the only ambassadorship open to a Jew? . . . Picture

it, will you—His Excellency, Philip Gold, Plenipotentiary to Islam. . . . A great world opens up before me, a new world, greater interests, world problems. . . . But I won't get there by belonging to your high-binder party. You fellows have a good system for local elections, but you don't stand a show to win the presidency again. We manufacturers and industrialists know what butters our bread. . . . I am a high tariff Republican, and with an eye to what I want I shall become a large contributor to the national campaign fund. Emulating your excellent example, I am organizing the Garment Manufacturers' Republican Club. Papa-in-law knows what I am after, and he and the royal family are eminently delighted. Banking and department store influences will count a great deal. Fancy my surprise when I found that father-in-law had presented me with a handsome dowry, which dowry I shall drop into the political pot. . . . Now, your honor, this is where you come into the plot. Your distinguished conduct on the bench will be an aid to me. If you are going to be a typical Tammany judge you'll smell up all the works. The royal family will be distressed. Here's your chance: you have been selected as a non-partisan jurist. Play the part to perfection. Avoid anything that may turn into a scandal. An outstanding record will compel the party to name you for higher office.''

''We have considered that already, dear uncle—ambassador,'' I told him. ''In fact I have won over Big Jim and the other Big Guns in Fourteenth Street to leave me off dirty work. It is easy. The district attorney simply does not assign such cases to me where political favoritism is necessary. I am beginning to shine out as a judge that deals severely with criminals.

HAUNCH PAUNCH AND JOWL

Tomorrow I am going to impose a record sentence on a burglar. The game is to make the poor slobs pay for the leniency we show the politically favored. If you have no friends in our court you are given a long ride in the black maria. Also I am becoming a learned advocate of the probation system—a cloak for leniency where the bosses need it. Besides, Maxie analyzes cases in advance, and tells me when it is safe to throw a case. In short, I am grooming myself for the mayoralty candidacy. Our party needs a man with a good public record to minimize the reformers' hullabaloo. . . . Behold, Your Excellency, Meyer Hirsch, Mayor of New York.''

We both laughed. Philip's face soon turned serious. And he asked, abruptly, ''And Gretel—what are you doing about her?''

''Well, Phil, I really—well——''

''I can see you've done nothing, and don't know what to do. I think it's a case where someone will have to do it for you. . . . Don't you see how an advantageous marriage will help along your plan?'' . . .

Suddenly it was night. All the colors and shapes, with their shadows and contrasts, were swallowed up.

''The time has come to settle that matter. Go away to the country club for the week end. I'll see Gretel. Financially, she'll have nothing to worry about. I'll satisfy her on that score. Then I shall point out to her how decently you've treated her all these years and where her duty lies. I think I'll make her see the light, and save you an unpleasant scene.'' . . . I pulled the bar and shut the window. The wind was blowing up cold. I thought the cold air made me shiver. . . . Philip pushed the point, mercilessly,—''What do you

[283]

say, there's only one way—decide and do it."... I
sat still for a moment or two; then I heard someone
walk into the room. Aunt Josephine's screechy voice
asked, "Really, why sit in the dark?"... I touched
Philip's arm and said, "All right, do it."...

SEVENTH PERIOD

Cæsar once, seeing some wealthy strangers at Rome, carrying up and down with them in their arms and bosoms young puppy-dogs and monkeys, embracing and making much of them, took occasion not unnaturally to ask whether the women in their country were not used to bear children.

PLUTARCH.

SEVENTH PERIOD

I

Philip is dead . . . dead and buried.

Gretel . . . better say Gertrude . . . she who used to be Gretel . . . now that she is my wife won't even let me call her Gretel . . . was never a hypocrite. Ever since a memorable day seven years ago, she has hated Uncle Philip. . . . Today she went to the funeral as my wife, not as a mourner; nor did she as much as once dab her eyes with a stuffy handkerchief for appearance's sake. I think she enjoyed the dull knell of spadeful after spadeful of earth and pebbles beating upon the coffin. She heard the Rabbi's touching eulogy with composed features. Under her arm she held mother, supporting her to her side. As for mother, I believe Philip's death opened up the wells of grief for father. . . . On our way home in the automobile Gretel said pointblank that a just retribution had overtaken the ruthless Philip. . . . Primitive, natural in all her emotions and reactions. . . . And mother murmured, "God overlooks no one . . . no one." . . . They agree in everything. Never did a mother-in-law and daughter-in-law live in such perfect accord as did mother and Gretel. . . . Strange . . . strange indeed . . . mother hadn't talked with Gretel in all the years until the crucial day when Philip had me sneak off to the country. He tried to buy off Gretel. . . .

. . . . . .

We have just come home from the funeral. . . . It has been a trying day on my nerves: better to say a

trying day on my avoirdupois. Seven sedentary years
in the upholstered judicial swivel chair and rich living
have made me nigh massive. The first *Haunch Paunch
and Jowl* cartoon was prophetic. . . . So I sank into
the armchair facing the window to rest myself, watching the placid river. The afternoon is on the wane.
I study the oversize busses crowding aside the puny
motor cars. . . . Children romp . . . but there are so
few children. . . . I see plenty of dogs dawdling slack
leashes. . . . Sickening: I wish Gretel wouldn't make
such an ado over that miserable mutt. . . . There is
one thing I thought of at Philip's grave. . . . Long
ago . . . that dim time of dreaming and striving . . .
he had said we would make ourselves notable ancestors
to be looked back to . . . ancestors . . . to whom . . .
lap dogs . . . lap dogs who whined if they were made
to walk across the floor. . . . Here's Gretel. And
Josephine, dear Aunt Josephine of the thirty-two quarters escutcheon, adores a Chinese chow which she carries upon her flat bosom, and deifies a great Persian
cat which sits on a shrine of soft silken cushions. . . .

Cancer of the stomach—that is what did for
Philip. . . . Social climbing, fortune building, political scheming for an ambassadorship were all thrown
in the discard and he began a new deal in life, a stub-
born combat with the malignant, pitiless disease.

Philip lost with a smile. . . . The last days in the
sickroom: Philip lying like a spent monarch in a high
four-poster, a mediæval bed he had picked up in an
auction in London; the Persian cat with a becalmed
Buddah expression at the foot of the bed; and the chow
snivelled on a silk rug under a chair. I suppose Aunt
Josephine didn't quite make it all out: that is why she

was all over the sickroom with her little gods. The
nurses wanted to put them out, but Philip's sense of
humor had it that he would die mocked by the crowning
symbols of his success. . . . Towards the end he was
attended by Dr. Hymie Rubin. The great specialists
with their fabulous bills had cut and radiumed to the
tune of tumbling doubloons. Philip did not cavil at
stupendous fees; for that matter he declared he would
gladly give his storehouse of gold—with his moronish
wife and the worshipped dog and cat for good measure.
But the priceless surgeons said—too late: they could
not repair the digestive engine after it had been
knocked to pieces by years of neglect and abuse. . . .
So he sent for Hymie—for conversation. He wanted
to be taunted, taunted, to die fighting. More, he asked
for Avrum Toledo. He wanted to have it out with
him for the last time. But Avrum was somewhere in
the lumber camps of the Northwest. . . . "Let me
die . . . let me die lulled by the anodynes of the dream-
stupefied." . . . A satyr's head: Philip's; his bone-
gray hair rumpled into puffs like horns; a carved face
with pointed nose and sharp chin. . . .

Maxie came to draw the will.

"Have you any particular bequests you wish to
make?" asked Max in a businesslike voice.

The satyr grinned . . . mayhap he winced, but he
intended it to be a grin. His voice asked banteringly
of Hymie Rubin, "Little doctor, you say what shall be
done with the filthy lucre . . . you know, the blood
money——"

Hymie sat down on the bed. Musingly he stroked
his beard and his features relaxed in a smile to meet
the laughing mask before him. His nasal tones hung

lazily in the still air. The chow uttered a tiny squeal and the royal cat majestically scratched an ear.

"I believe you capable of anything, my superman," said Hymie; "anything: even to the extent of taking my advice. May I ask you to be consistent with the capitalists who have been your models? . . . You capitalists are unconscious scientists. You are vivisectionists. You experiment on humans. You spend your life keeping creatures on the rack. Then when you die you devote your money for research—cures for the devils you have half-killed. So I ask you to be consistent. Leave your money to found a sanitarium in the Adirondacks for those suffering from the shop sickness—a sanitarium for consumptive garment workers."

"A merry jest, Dr. Hymie, a merry jest. You want me to die like all weaklings—afraid, contrite, kneeling to the confessor. You misjudge me, Hymie. Do you think I'd die knowing the worms would gloat over my cadaver? You think I'd give them a chance to say that Philip Gold became conscience-stricken in the fear of death and sought to make amends for the wrongs he had done? I have done no wrong. I have been life. I lived after the plan of life. . . . No, no charity will keep the worms, worms. Let them evolve through suffering." . . .

He left everything to me, saying that I was the only one for whom he had ever had any affection. But he remembered to rebuke me for having let myself get in so deep with Gretel. . . .

I drowsed a bit, but was annoyed by the dog come snuffling at my shins. . . . Yes, I should tell how Gretel came to be my wife; Gretel, the last person in the world I thought I would marry. . . . I went to the country club . . . a shadow seemed to linger near me, a fore-boding. . . . The next day Philip telephoned . . . a snag . . . better come back. . . . Gretel was in a chair, crying. Mother stood at her side, comforting her. It looked so queer. Philip stood looking out of the window. When I came into the room Gretel rose and looked at me searchingly. Philip came forward with his hands stuffed in his pockets. For several seconds no one spoke: it seemed the longest time. Finally Philip said, smartingly—

"A fine thanks you're getting for being decent. Treat them like dogs and then they'll expect nothing better. Do you know what she's done? She's black-mailing you, holding you up! Threatens a breach of promise suit . . . some kind of legal entangle-ment . . . going to claim you're her common law husband. . . . After I spoke to her she rushed out of here. Where do you think she went? Went where everybody with a kick goes—to that Finn and his settlement. Told him everything. And he said he would take her case. . . . We could beat that . . . but what more has she done? She has won over your mother. Your mother is your worst enemy. She backs up this woman. Says she will go into court and tell that you and Gretel have been living as man and wife all these years. Whew! What a fine scandal—— Go ahead, Meyer. I warned you. Now go ahead and see if at this stage of the game you can talk them out of their madness. I have offered twenty-five thousand dollars——"

"I don't want money," said Gretel, like a flash from flint.

Finn . . . Esther came into my mind. . . . Esther

. . . she knows all. . . . Finn, my enemy, has been given this weapon against me. . . . Mother . . . backing up Gretel . . . mother . . .

"I don't want money." Her voice was tired.

"Is it true—Gretel, tell me, is it true——"

"Yes."

I felt exhausted and dropped into a chair. Gretel made a quick move towards me, but held back when she saw my frowning face. But mother came and touched my arm, saying, "You hear, you have not been as a child to me. Now in my old age, show me that you will obey me as a child. Show me in my ending days that you can do a fineness for me. Marry Gretel. She has been as a wife to you. You told me yourself that you found her a good girl. Who knows better than I how good and true she has been to you these many years? It is right that you should marry her. I will not see a sin done to a good girl. Do not heed that Philip. Let him rage, let him storm, let him tear down the walls, and bring the roof upon my head. I will stand by her. I will tell the truth. It is the right——"

"There she goes with that damned respectableness," Philip snarled.

"I would talk with you, Meyer, but let Philip go out. I would talk to you alone," Gretel pleaded.

I looked at Philip and he withdrew.

"You look tired," Gretel ventured to say.

My voice was husky. "Why did you go down there— down to that place?" I asked.

"I was afraid of everyone. How Philip tore at my heart. I needed someone. You were not here. He said you would not come back until I was gone and had signed the papers your partner made out. I was in terror. Did you think those years were as nothing to me—to me? Did you not think I loved you? . . . Oh, he went at me so. I was insane. I used to hear the people say that Finn kept a secret and was a friend of people in distress. I have no one here. Mother said Philip wanted you to marry someone else. The right was that I should be the one to marry you. Your own mother says so. . . . Oh, Meyer, and does not your heart say——''

She choked and cried. Then came a wild burst of passion.

"Nothing will stop me, nothing. That Philip has made me so afraid. . . . What is money! All those years burned into my heart. . . . I am not to be considered. . . . My life . . . my feelings . . . my bursting heart. . . . What is money! . . . There is nothing in life but you; I live in you, Meyer, in you. . . . What is money. . . . I better go and kill myself. . . . I will, I will. . . . Meyer, will you think of our love life these years? . . . Marry me, Meyer. . . . I am afraid . . . afraid . . . oh, he made me so afraid. . . . It was like trying to tear everything away from me . . . to be left with nothing to live for. . . . Marry me——"

Her words rang out in the room, clanged in my head.

But mother was the hardest of the two. She stood like a stone wall against Philip's importunities . . . and mine she silenced. . . .

What was to be done? An open scandal would be terrible. It is unthinkable. . . .

So, I married Gretel.

How the world talked! There was no open comment. It was a still scandal, a gaseous undercurrent poisoning

the roots of my political tree. I was done, politically.
But I clung to the judgeship. . . . I was addicted to
power and honor. . . . I clung to the judgeship. . . .
When my appointed term was over and I came up for
election, my party made a deal with the Republicans,
securing their endorsement, thus avoiding the mud-
slinging of an open campaign. . . . The still scandal
went through the city . . . a judge of a high court
married his servant girl . . . had been living with
her all these years. Garnishings made the tale a
prettier one.

Society was out of the question. Gretel was rather
crude. She spoke a self-learned English of many
peculiarities. A former servant girl and mistress
could not pass muster in the strict society of the German Jews. Besides, Philip and Gretel could not so
much as bear the sight of each other.

II

So here we live in *Allrightniks* Row, Riverside Drive. The newly rich Russian, Galician, Polish and Roumanian Jews have squeezed out the German Jews and their Gentile neighbors. Great elevator apartment structures are being put up to house the clamoring *Allrightniks*. The Ghetto called anyone who was well off—one who is *all right in this world,* that is well fixed, an *Allrightnik.* We moved in the world of *Allrightniks.*

Allrightniks: plump and fat women who blandished the extremes of the latest styles in clothes, trying to outvie one another; and were never seen without a blinding array of diamonds on ears, breasts, fingers and arms . . . the men were always business men—business was their cult, hobby, pastime—their life. Did they collect in little groups of a social evening, then they discussed the fascinating details of some speculation or enterprise. They interpreted life in the terms of moneymaking. Their faces were puffed and sleekly pale; their bellies stuck out as the show windows of their prosperity. Invariably you found them chewing fat cigars; their middle fingers ablaze with many-karated solitaires: eye-openers. . . . The women played poker in the afternoon and in the evening came together to gossip and flaunt clothes and diamonds, mentioned significantly what they paid for this and that, complained of their servants, to whom they left the care of their children, and told risque stories: their talk was a hysteric din, and their laughter un-

[295]

restrained . . . while, in the adjoining room, their husbands, loud-mouthed and coarse-humored, gathered to play stud poker or pinochle for high stakes. The game was not the thing: they were charmed by the gamble. Their craze for speculation expressed itself in steep gambling. Once the play began their faces set in grim lines, and they attended passionately to the fluctuations of chance with such skill and craft and bluff as they could command. . . . High-priced, vivid-hued automobiles with liveried chauffeurs helped to blazon their success. . . . Having given themselves over wholly to wealth, then show was the only sign of their existence. . . . Show. Show. . . . Even in their charity. Charity was another outlet for display. Pompous, righteous beneficing. . . . Show. . . . Even to the marrying off of their children. Spectacular matches, big money in alliances with big money, money the standard of this special aristocracy. . . . Dollar-land. . . . Gretel, after living a shutaway, dubious rôle, now revelled in the extravaganza-life of this *Allrightnik* society. . . . And *Allrightnik* religion was a bumptious holding forth in swell temples and synagogues. . . . And they took to their bosoms canines and griffins, aping the so-called swell society of the *goyim*.

I am bitter and sore this evening. . . . The gang, who came in as impoverished immigrants unused to wealth, were made dizzy and giddy by sudden riches. . . . But I wondered about the East Side. . . . It was not the same place I knew as a boy, a young man. . . . I had lost contact with that world. . . . Crane said we were always swinging between extremes; a pendulum of emotion. . . . In the East Side the radicals were making headway. Were they bringing spiritual fare for the spiritually hungry? . . . Who would believe fifteen years ago that the Socialists would carry one of my assembly strongholds as they did last election? . . . Money chasers and dream chasers. . . . In the Ghetto there was a large, growing, fanatic cult of intellectualism . . . a fine-frenzied idealism . . . art, literature, music, social science and politics in the pure meaning of the word—calling the new generation . . . to me a strange generation, so different, so alien to my understanding. . . . The new generation, this queer stranger, seemed to be creeping upon me . . . what is their meaning . . . what do they want . . . where will they end . . . will the money craze get them and dazzle them? . . .

I drowsed again, and opened my eyes because someone was looking at me. It was Mr. Bernard Lowe, my neighbor, come to condole with me. . . . Bernard Lowe, a sweet-faced, aging man, gazing upon me with kindly blinking eyes . . . Bernard Lowe . . . do you remember Berel of yesteryear, Berel Lotvin, the harness fixer in the Ludlow Street cellar . . . Berel——

"Sleep . . . rest . . . don't let me disturb you, my friend." His voice is gentle and pleasing.

"Just a little catnap, a fat man's drowse," I told him, clasping his hand. "And, how do you feel, Berel?" I asked. He responded with his ready good humor: "What a question to ask of a Christian Scientist!"

And we both laughed. Funny: Berel is a Christian Scientist and a sincere one: always ready to give his personal testimony of its healing, pacifying wonders. . . . Once he told me his story in his unaffected

way. He was a man of considerable means. But Berel
attributed his wealth to mere chance. Someone told
him the automobiles were come to stay and multiply.
He gave up the harness-fixing hole and opened a little
tire repair shop in upper Broadway. It was a new
industry: the firstcomer got the pioneer's big chance.
But what was more to the point, Berel's good humor
and dependable word won him respect and friends
among the Gentiles. . . . In time he grew to be the
largest distributor of tires and accessories. . . . In the
heyday of his prosperity he was laid low with diabetes,
commonly called the Jewish sickness. He tried every
famous doctor and cure. He was given up. . . . In her
despair Berel's wife called in a Christian Science
healer. . . . And Berel said faith and love healed him
and made him whole and well; best of all, it brought
him equanimity and peace: being took on meaning.
His simple exposition was very touching.

We talked of his two boys, big young men, putting
in their last years in Yale. Berel did not want them
to go into business. He said business soils . . . he was
encouraging his lads to give themselves to art and
science . . . life was something more than mere com-
peting for money. . . .

"Life speeds on . . . just think . . . soon you'll be
thinking of marrying off the boys," I said.

"I don't have to think about it at all . . . they're
thinking of it themselves. . . . They used to go to
church with me Sunday mornings when home . . . but
now I notice they're going to Rabbi Drucker's New
Temple. There's a reason. . . . You know the beautiful daughters of Sid Raleigh . . . you know our old
boy friend, Sam Rakowsky . . . he has two golden

beauties . . . like their mother . . . two clever girls, musicians, who detest their father's songs. . . . Funny, he doesn't mind what they think of his music. He's sending them abroad to study under the masters. Well, my boys are after the golden beauties with the golden voices. . . . Now, just to please me, they join me to church Wednesday nights. . . . Well, there's one thing I owe the lads, the right to choose their own wives and own beliefs. . . . Good evening, Meyer, mamma will be looking for me for dinner. Good evening——"

I'll not stay home tonight; I am too depressed. . . . I'll slip out and telephone Margot . . . Margot, my consolatrice. . . . I interested Al Wolff in her. He put her in a show, a show I financed. She was an excellent investment. She was to the theatregoers the pert personification of the New York pleasure girl. The critics praised her vim and originality. All the artists wanted to paint her exquisite hands and feet. Her legs were a stage classic, having the shapeliness of a Greek vase. Al starred her in a big revue called "The Chicken of the Crossways"—the crossways being Forty-second Street and Broadway. Then came the movies to tempt her with a big contract. Always she consulted her sweet daddy. She never forgot to be grateful, although she was occasionally unfaithful. The public adored her as their whimsical Margot of the Movies. . . . Margot lived in a bizarre apartment chaperoned by an ancient duenna, an aunt created for my protection. . . . I can't complain of Margot. She was always honest. She tried her best to keep her little affairs a secret from me. . . . But I knew she had love affairs lurking around the corner, and I tried not to think of this unpleasantness. . . . Sometimes when I stood over her I felt like a hulking pachyderm, gross, flesh-odorous, snorting over a white gazelle, a white gazelle with a burnished head. . . .

Again I drowsed, and I seemed to have a pleasant dream that Margot was on my knee gently pinching my ear. But it was that confounded dog who had been placed on a cushion on a table near me. His little paw had been touching my ear. . . . Gretel is humming Sid Raleigh's latest hit, a topical song he wrote for Margot. It is a hodgepodge of sentiment, mixing sunshine and rain, love and jealousy, joy and grief, laughter and tears, commonplaces for the masses, easy thoughts for the sluggish multitude. Margot had made its refrain famous, something about . . . "tell me, life, tell me, what's it all about; tell me, life, what's it all about?" . . .

Gretel calls, "Come, Meyer, come and eat. I got something you like. *Gedamfte brust und patate lahtkes.*" (Potted breast and potato pancakes.) . . . I heave my great bulk and waddle towards the dining room. . . . Again Gretel sings . . . "Tell me, life, tell me, what's it all about; tell me, life, what's it all about?" . . .

What——

It smells good.

Gedamfte brust und patate lahtkes——

THE END